Faith stories

Manchester University Press

Faith stories

Sustaining meaning and community in troubling times

Anna Hickey-Moody

MANCHESTER UNIVERSITY PRESS

Copyright © Anna Hickey-Moody 2023

The right of Anna Hickey-Moody to be identified as the author of this work has been asserted in accordance with the Copyright, Designs and Patents Act 1988.

An electronic version of this book is also available under a Creative Commons (CC-BY-NC-ND) licence, thanks to the support of the Australian Research Council, which permits non-commercial use, distribution and reproduction provided the author(s) and Manchester University Press are fully cited and no modifications or adaptations are made. Details of the licence can be viewed at https://creativecommons.org/licenses/by-nc-nd/4.0/.

Published by Manchester University Press
Oxford Road, Manchester M13 9PL

www.manchesteruniversitypress.co.uk

British Library Cataloguing-in-Publication Data
A catalogue record for this book is available from the British Library

ISBN 978 1 5261 6524 4 hardback

First published 2023

The publisher has no responsibility for the persistence or accuracy of URLs for any external or third-party internet websites referred to in this book, and does not guarantee that any content on such websites is, or will remain, accurate or appropriate.

Typeset
by Deanta Global Publishing Services, Chennai, India

For my dear friend Aislinn O'Donnell, and for those of us who find the shape of our faith difficult to explain.

Contents

List of figures   *page* viii
Acknowledgements   x

1. Contexts / *Comhthéacs*   1
2. Faith: a new materialist approach / *Creideamh*   24
3. Mapping and making / *Ag déanamh*   49
4. Affect and joy / *Áthas*   77
5. Belonging / *Muintearas*   95
6. Connections / *Naisc*   119
7. Incapacity / *Neamhábaltacht*   141
8. Other worlds / *Neamhshaolta*   171

Conclusion / *Conclúid*   187

References   195
Index   212

Figures

Note: Unless otherwise stated, all images are the author's own photographs.

3.1	'Refuge' tent built by children in London, 2018	*page* 71
3.2	The first patchwork made in Sydney, 2017	72
5.1	Street photos from Claremont, 2019	103
6.1	'Our home', blue fluorescent light art on Caleb and Abul's housing block, inner-north Melbourne, 2019	124
6.2	Children in north-west Manchester draw their streets filled with names of football players, mixed media on canvas, 2018	125
6.3	Three girls wearing hijabs and playing soccer, mixed media on paper, Melbourne, 2018	128
6.4	'Flying soccer ice-cream factory', pencil and felt-tip pen on paper, Melbourne, 2019	129
6.5	'Future City', acrylic paint on board, Manchester, 2017	131
6.6	'I love ice cream', screenshot of digital animation, south-west Adelaide, 2018	132
6.7	'Legendary pickaxe', mixed media on paper, inner-north Melbourne, 2019	135
6.8	Screen capture from an animation of Burj Khalifa and friendship, south-east London, 2019	139
7.1	The Manchester Bee 1, drawn by children in Manchester as a symbol of 'what really matters' directly after the Manchester Arena bombing in 2017	149

7.2	The Manchester Bee 2, drawn by children in Manchester as a symbol of 'what really matters' directly after the Manchester Arena bombing in 2017	150
8.1	'All the streets are rivers', Manchester, 2017	175
8.2	'Future City', in the centre of which is a tree of life, inner-north Melbourne, 2019	177
8.3	A city where 'everyone has a home', acrylic paint and felt-tip pen on canvas, south-east London, 2017	178
8.4	A housing estate where the children live, a soccer pitch, and Frankie's imaginary house, inner-north Melbourne, 2019	180
8.5	High-rise housing with a Tesco on top, mixed media on canvas, Manchester, 2018	181
8.6	Frankie and his uncle in a canoe, mixed media on fabric, Melbourne, 2018	182
8.7	Frankie's self-portrait, mixed media on paper, Melbourne, 2018	183
8.8	Two of the boys drew themselves into the future city, mixed media on canvas, Melbourne, 2019	185

Acknowledgements

This book has been a long time in preparation and is the result of the kindness of many friends and scholars. I am incredibly lucky to be funded for this work by the Australian Research Council Future Fellowship FT160100293 and an RMIT Vice-Chancellor's Senior Research Fellowship. Genuine thanks to Lisa French and Robert Crawford for supporting my work in the School of Media and Communication at RMIT. Work on this project was also undertaken by a number of fantastic individuals, some of whom did research assistance for parts of the book and many who helped with fieldwork. Thanks to: Kate Lonie, Mia Harrison, Thu Le, Beverly Irving, Joanna Dennis, Zoe Walshe, Marissa Willcox, Lucian Marine, Angelica Harris-Faull, Lutifye Ali, Eloise Florence, Kate Johnson, Tia Roko, Robina Akhter Uller, Katerina Eleftheriadou, Shabana Baig, Ann-Marie Atkinson, Christine Horn and Tilly Johnson. Thanks to Louise Merrington and Alisa Dodge for editorial advice and Eloise Florence for formatting the manuscript. In some parts of the manuscript I have re-worked sections of previous publications. These are A. Hickey-Moody, 2020, 'Faith', *Philosophy Today*, 63(4), pp. 927–41; A. Hickey-Moody, C. Horn, M. Willcox and E. Florence, 2021, *Arts-Based Methods for Research with Children*, Palgrave Macmillan, New York; and A. Hickey-Moody, 2010, *Unimaginable Bodies: Intellectual Disability, Performance and Becomings*, Sense, Netherlands.

Tom Dark, my commissioning editor, has given this book the opportunity to be shared with the world. I have been fortunate enough to have been given a number of visiting positions to support my fieldwork while abroad and for this I am very grateful to Harry

Torrence, Maggie McLure and Kate Pahl at ESRI, Manchester Metropolitan University, and to Joanna Hodge for inviting me to MMU in the first instance. Thanks to Les Back and the Centre for Urban and Community Research at Goldsmiths, London and Tess Lea at the Department for Gender and Cultural Studies at the University of Sydney. Thanks also to Nancy Lesko for hosting me at Columbia University, New York City. Useful feedback on various parts of the book came from Beckie Coleman, Greg Seigworth, Carolyn Pedwell and Kath Browne. My most sincere thanks to each and every one of you.

1

Contexts / *Comhthéacs*

Introduction

As a child, I grew up with languages from two places: Ireland and Australia. The word *comhthéacs* is an Irish masculine word for contexts: places, histories and experiences that fold together to make contexts. The chapters in this book each have a title written in English and an Irish word expressing the focus of the chapter, to bring the two worlds that make up my context to the fore. My research participants also inhabit multiple worlds, and this book is made up of resonances between vastly different people's experiences and their many different worlds. These shared voices, which have come together and been torn apart across countries, places, religions and cultures, have also become part of me as I have been immersed in them over the last five years.

In writing this book, I am reminded of the fact that I am attached to structures of feeling that are associated with Irish Catholicism in ways that are complex, largely involuntary and marked by conflict. I was born in 1977 to a politically left-wing father from the north of Dublin, of Catholic upbringing, and a mother from London who was raised in the Church of England. My mother was not religious when she married my father, who, in his younger years, fancied himself quite a rebel and devoted his life to performing political protest songs. My parents spent their honeymoon in an Irish Republican Army (IRA) safe house in Derry after marrying in Cambridge, where they lived for the first years of their marriage. They moved to Australia in 1974 and later my mother converted to Catholicism – and, to my father's fury, I was raised a Catholic. These constellations are just the very beginning of a complex emotional attachment I experience to religious icons, an attachment that has oriented my research methods.

When I was eight years old, I visited St Gabriel's Church in Clontarf, Dublin, while staying with my grandparents in Ireland. I had travelled from Australia with my friend Emily and her father, Ciarán, who was also my father's childhood friend. There, I discovered what I would come to call 'the Virgin Mary section' that miraculously inhabits all Catholic churches. The stained-glass windows arching around the plaster of Paris statue painted eggshell blue framed the sea of tea light candles at her feet beautifully, and the image resonated with me in a way that has stayed.

This first encounter with the Virgin Mary has to be understood in the context of wanting to recuperate my father's social and emotional displacement, which has affectively shaped my life. My father's displacement was also informed by his furious disavowal of the religion in which he was raised. This disavowal seemed symbolic of trying too hard to move away from Ireland. Or had the Church committed injustices against him, about which I will never know? Such questions will never be answered, but I suspect not, as on his deathbed my father asked for his last rites and to be taken back into the Church. In *Six Days to Shake an Empire* (1966), Charles Duff sketches the psyche of the distressed Irishman by saying that there is a particular kind of dark, angry man who is also ferociously divorced from his religion, and that turn of phrase rings true to me when thinking of my father.

Regardless, there I was, an eight-year-old girl in my best dress, staring at a plaster of Paris statue in a church and thinking that perhaps it was actually quite magical to be a girl. If I wore a blue-and-white dress with a veil, perhaps people would also light candles at my feet one day and make statues that looked like me. Indeed, as trips to the family farm in Charleville (County Cork) taught me, women wearing the white dress and blue veil are displayed with candles even in totally destitute surroundings, next to sickbeds, in dark corners of shabby rooms and in unruly, cold gardens. In fact, most places that might need brightening are quite brought to life by a plaster of Paris woman, a set of tea lights and some rosary beads – or a bottle of holy water, if the organising purpose behind the shrine is illness.

Contexts / Comhthéacs

Three doors down the road from my grandparents' house in Dublin, my friend Emily's father became very ill. She looked sad and pale. Everyone spoke in hushed tones. Feeling lonely without her to play with on the street, I asked if I could sit with her at her dad's bedside. She took me through their red front door and as we went upstairs the air got heavy. When Emily opened the door to her dad's room, thick incense smoke poured out. Her grandmother, a priest and several aunts stood around her father Ciarán's bed, holding plastic Virgin Mary bottles filled with holy water that was hopefully going to save his life. They prayed in Latin and shook water all over him. Clearly this Virgin Mary has many uses, I thought.

I returned to Australia, equipped with rosary beads chosen by Ma (my grandmother), determined to become a better Catholic. This wasn't because I thought Catholics were correct, or better than others; rather, it was because they were where I belonged, and where my family was from – I was one of the people who gave women their own statues surrounded by tea lights. I hate to admit that the organising power of the plaster of Paris statue may actually have been top of my list of reasons.

My father read children's stories to me in Irish and I learnt a few turns of phrase. I was told about the injustices of the English from a young age, but, more specifically, I witnessed some affective recounting of the issues played out between my mother's English parents and my dad, which, as a grown woman, I have to say my father did nothing to appease. Suffice it to say, the emotional geography of my attachment to icons, sounds, smells and places was established, and this mapped across complex feelings of diaspora, class and nation. I am no more Irish than English. But I was raised Irish and not English and, by the age of eighteen, I had chosen my passport to match. My identification with Mary has never left me, although in what I would now characterise as the decolonial feminist consciousness of my late teens and early twenties, I developed a critical reading of the brightly lit shrines that had populated my childhood. In an aesthetic and symbolic reconfiguration of this attachment, I became increasingly interested in Our Lady of Guadalupe, who is not only non-white, but has clearly been through puberty, and in some representations has a natural moustache. She looks like she has not only given birth but also masturbates. At age twenty-one, I decided to mark this attachment to Mary with a tattoo on my back.

There are much more complicated histories of domestic violence, alcoholism, abuse and chronic illness that resulted in my father's death, and which are woven through my experience of growing up. But these aspects only matter so much as to say that I have a complicated, critical, yet enduring attachment to Catholicism. It is not 'religious' in the sense that I am not a practising Catholic, nor do I believe in the orthodox teachings of Catholicism, but I am attached to aspects of affective landscapes of Catholicism, which are partly constituted through 'the unchosen complexities of religious experience' (Kitching, 2020: 6). This attunement to religious culture in everyday life has remained with me and informs my approach to fieldwork.

Subjective experience is a result of socialisation. Raymond Williams (1977) identified the imagined 'distance' placed between our feelings and society as a strategy of governance. Imagined distance between feelings and society is a way of suggesting to us that it is not society's fault that we feel depressed or unsatisfied. On the contrary; those bad feelings are our own fault for not being more-successful people – or so says society, anyway. Feelings, in other words, are as much products of institutions, formations and positions as biographies – and, of course, they in turn shape biographies. The 'Virgin Mary section' of St Gabriel's Church is very special to me, but St Gabriel's is also not so different from any other Catholic church, all of which have their own version of a 'Virgin Mary section' featuring a statue, candles and other adornments signifying cultural value. The economy of the Virgin Mary, and of her precursor, the Muslim figure Maryam, runs worldwide.

These connections between religion, culture and everyday life are at the heart of my research. In the Australian Research Council (ARC) grant application that funded this research, I argued that counter-radicalisation initiatives are not working because they too often focus on, and misrepresent, the Islamic religion and, therefore, are divisive. If the Australian Government actually wants to address concerns about religious intolerance and violence, it needs to change popular, inaccurate attachments between religion and radicalisation. More than this, popular media and mediatised discourses of religion need to be informed by everyday religious or faith experiences.

The strategy I put forward for this was to conduct arts workshops with children, exploring their attachments to religion, social values and 'what really matters', alongside focus groups and interviews with parents examining themes of identity, religion and belonging. This qualitative work was followed by a quantitative survey that established whether the qualitative data generated was reflective of broader community sentiments. This methodology has been refined in process, but the key components of the method were established in the initial bid and the qualitative findings are the substance of my discussion in this book. The quantitative findings are discussed elsewhere (Hickey-Moody, Horn and Garg, 2023).

My empirical research for this book began in 2016 with funding from the University of Sydney's Faculty of Arts and Social Sciences. This faculty grant supported an experimental pilot of my methods and ways of recording them, which formed the basis for the methods that feature in this book. This early work was undertaken at a community service provider in west Sydney. This organisation became an ongoing partner in the research, hosting three series of week-long workshops for children and follow-up focus groups and interviews with parents and carers. I was able to examine experiences of community, belonging, attachment, faith, belief and 'what really matters' in contexts as diverse as Manchester and London in the UK, and west Sydney, Melbourne, Canberra and Adelaide in Australia. Each of these sites is geographically and culturally specific in ways that shape residents' experiences of community and belonging. The methods I developed for working with children and communities were employed consistently across all sites, with variations depending on available materials, environment and weather (see Hickey-Moody et al., 2021). At the time of writing, the project has 628 research participants, adults and children combined. I have run thirty arts-based research workshops (each taking three to four days) in Australia and the UK, and I have undertaken twenty-two in-depth interviews with parents or carers and twenty-four focus groups. Artworks made in the project have been exhibited in four exhibitions to date, with more planned.

As I have suggested, during my fieldwork I try to be as consistent as I can about the ways I invite children to make art, and the materials I give them. I have developed a set of nine workshop or lesson plans for encouraging collaboration through making, which scaffold and build on children's skills. These lesson plans are designed to be implemented in sequential order and are discussed in my methods chapter. The workshop structure I have developed supports debate and collaboration exploring values, beliefs, history and culture (Barker-Perez and Robbie, 2021; Vertovec, 2007; Vertovec and Wessendorf, 2010) – the big stuff of life. After a round of failed papier-mâché and some pilot research questions that were too direct to elicit interesting or complex answers, I developed methods that have proven effective and enjoyable for children aged five to twelve, and which can also be modified to be used with different age groups. The artwork produced as a result of these collaborative making processes offers engaging windows into children's experiential and imaginary worlds, and illustrates their values and experiences of daily life. Such windows into experiential and embodied worlds provide a unique base from which to build relationships with parents, carers and members of the community. Parents have usually heard about me through their children's stories about their art-making before they actually meet me in person.

In this chapter, I introduce research locations and some key themes, while the following chapters explore my theoretical framework and then my methodology and methods, unpacking arts-based research and multi-sited ethnography in detail. I will begin by introducing the themes of faith and object attachment, as seen through the eyes of my research participant Philomena, who is describing her sacred wall at home:

> There's a saint everywhere, wherever you look. And … so I knew – I always knew I wanted a place like that in my own home. When we first moved in, I made it. The Muslim plaque is from a Turkish friend of mine. We used to live in a unit and she was our neighbour and even at the unit I always had a religious spot, so that was a gift from her and so I very proudly put that up on my wall. I didn't even give it a second thought – it was, 'Wow, what an amazing gift, I'm going to put it up with the cross', and I've had that cross since I was fourteen years old. So … what else is up there? Oh, then there's another plaque there, which I picked up, I remember which shop and everything and, that meant a lot to me, so I put that up on the wall as well. And these ones here, I went searching for a picture and I ended up finding these … which I loved and I got my husband to put the shelf up, no questions asked. He didn't say, 'No, that's not Muslim' or whatever, just – yeah, it's just a given, just 'I want this, put it up'.
> (Philomena, west Sydney, interview, 2019)

Contexts / Comhthéacs

Like Philomena's wall of saints, symbols and memories, adults' worlds are made up of complex ways of beliefs, images and experiences. Of living and dead people, icons and places. Children's worlds are also shaped by such images and memories, and by their very visual imaginations. Flying soccer balls that are ice-cream factories inside, cars with wings, mobile recycling plants, streets that are rivers: these are just some of the many inventions that children have offered up to me as examples of 'what really matters to them', their childhood version of Philomena's special wall featuring 'a saint everywhere, wherever you look'.

There are religious saints, social ideals and icons throughout the stories in this book. The social and cultural contexts in which my research takes place are united by complex, postcolonial circumstances and policy agendas that are racist strategies used to transmit cultural fear. These historical, sociocultural and political colonial contexts are the 'big picture' within which my research sites are located, but each site has a distinct demographic, atmosphere and sense of identity.

Places

West Sydney

My first site for the project was Auburn, in west Sydney, New South Wales. My trousers would stick to the train seat on the ride out west. Wollongong (my home when I started this work in 2016) to Auburn (where I was researching) is a minimum two-and-a-half-hour commute by train. Finally escaping the train, I would buy coffee at a hole-in-the-wall cafe and walk along the side of the station, taking in the wall-length mural featuring faces of people from different backgrounds and symbols of hope such as two large white doves, multi-coloured handprints and the words 'peace' and 'love'. I'd stop and look at the fruit-and-veggie shops, wondering whether I would ever be inspired enough to cook again, and more than once I enthusiastically bought a mezze plate so big I couldn't fit it all in. I really like Auburn. It has a feeling like you can be whoever you want and no one cares, a multicultural demographic and atmosphere, with streetscapes peppered with Lebanese, Ethiopian,

Vietnamese, Chinese and Greek grocery shops, cafes and eateries and various types of doctors and fortune tellers. Auburn is well known in Sydney as a multicultural area.[1]

My research sites in Auburn were a settlement services association and a mosque. The settlement services association became a significant and enduring research site for the project. The service provider in Auburn and the mosque invited their communities to be involved in my research.

Auburn was always hot and busy and had a life of its own that carried me away. I was always exhausted, as there were significant numbers of children and families involved in my project. Parents brought me food, and I made friends with some English-speaking families and became acquainted with those who didn't speak English. I had the most delicious Lebanese lunches and planned the details of workshops on train station platforms, while my 'car next door' rent-a-car was stuck in traffic, or while enjoying a respite from the heat on the Bankstown-line train. Chinese medicine clinics, migrant support centres, churches, halal cafes and money lenders are offset by the silhouette of the gorgeous Turkish mosque. It is a place where all kinds of people are making a life for themselves in all kinds of ways, which is freeing and interesting. I ran three three-and-a-half-day workshops, three focus groups and numerous follow-up interviews in a range of locations across the suburb over two-and-a-half years. It was enlivening, exhausting, rewarding and eye-opening to be welcomed into such a complex community.

Manchester

Blue and yellow 'magic' buses with free Wi-Fi and cartoon wizards painted on them, colourful corner shops selling everything from twine to tahini to halal meat, long walks along Chorlton Brook, and multiple visits to art-supply shops in the Arndale shopping centre: my second research location was Manchester. I had three research sites there: Levenshulme, Hulme and Moss Side. In terms of community life and liveability, Manchester is an interesting, engaging and very human place to undertake ethnography. The local shop owners in Levenshulme, where I was staying, got to know me; my colleagues at Manchester Metropolitan University (MMU) listened eagerly to stories from the field on days when I felt like my head was

Contexts / Comhthéacs 9

exploding; and I felt grounded within the community. Levenshulme is the most gentrified area of Manchester I worked in. A former working-class neighbourhood, 'Levy' is rapidly developing a large middle-class resident base.[2] Levenshulme is economically much more well-to-do than some of my other research sites, including the neighbouring sites of Moss Side and Hulme. My research sites in Levenshulme were in a primary school and a 'kids' club' daycare facility. I recruited children and their families through these sites.

Not far from Levenshulme, but noticeably bleaker, Moss Side has a reputation for its history of gang violence, which came about in the 1980s as a result of the large council investment in social housing in the 1970s. A lack of accompanying education, training and development opportunities led to a lot of people with little money and little to do. Moss Side is much less dangerous now than it was in the 1980s, but it is still economically deprived and, broadly speaking, felt like a desolate place in which to work and live.[3] My research site in Moss Side was a local primary school. The school was notably different from the other research sites in terms of its very strict attitude to discipline and an associated broader atmosphere of anxiety. The data from this school is quite different from the data from other sites, which are clearly connected thematically. Consequently, my work in this school is not a focus of the analysis in this book, but it does form the subject of my ongoing analysis elsewhere (Hickey-Moody, Horn and Willcox, 2023).

My third research location in Manchester was a fabulous primary school in Hulme.[4] Floor to ceiling, the walls of the school corridors were covered in children's artwork telling popular stories from British history (the Wars of the Roses, the Great Fire of London) and the narratives of famous Shakespeare plays (*Hamlet*, *Macbeth*). Soon after my first visit, the brightly coloured canvases that the children had made in my workshop took pride of place on the walls of the upper-primary reading room. The school had well-kept grounds and a genuinely inclusive culture. The communities in which I worked in Manchester are majority-white communities but significantly ethnically diverse (see footnotes for specific breakdowns). Despite this fact, my research participants in Manchester were mainly non-white; they were largely migrant families and not English speakers at home. They came from Somalia, Pakistan (often via Italy), Nigeria, Kenya, Syria, Yemen and China, and there was also one white Canadian and one white English-born mother who took part in the work. The other research site in England was London, and two primary schools formed the location of my research in south-east London.

London

Grey streets with blue skies, street markets that sell vegetables by the coloured plastic bucketload alongside ladies' underwear, the gentle sway of the Light Railway ambling over the river: my fieldwork in London was embedded in south-east London, not far from areas in which I had lived and worked previously. I have a familiar feeling for that part of the city and the kinds of communities that constitute it. My research sites were primary schools in Charlton and the Isle of Dogs. The primary school where I worked in Charlton shares the name of the neighbouring housing estate. The families whose children attend primary school are mainly the white working-class residents of the housing estate, who, in most instances, have lived on the housing estate for a couple of generations. Gentrification has transformed London, and although Charlton[5] has a working-class history, and the estate and school in which my work was located are very clearly working-class, the area is gentrifying.

The Isle of Dogs is in the Tower Hamlets borough. Tower Hamlets is renowned for being one of the most multicultural areas of London. Some of the suburbs in Tower Hamlets include Blackwall and Cubitt Town, Millwall, Limehouse, Stepney, Old Ford, Poplar, Bromley-by-Bow and Bethnal Green. Tower Hamlets is huge and includes the shiny business district of Canary Wharf, as well as the residential areas named above. Within this broad and famously 'multicultural' borough profile, the primary school where I undertook ethnography for three years is part of the Millwall ward in the Isle of Dogs.[6] Both London sites showed signs of gentrification and poverty mixed together. The next place in which I began my research was Adelaide, South Australia.

Adelaide

I grew up in Adelaide. For six years, between the ages of sixteen and twenty-two, I waited for my chronically ill father to die, so that I felt able to leave. Adelaide is a city of 1.306 million people, and it operates at half the speed of most urban centres. Its highlights for young people include two shining mirror balls in the central shopping area, Rundle Mall, popularly known as 'the Mall's Balls', and a green water fountain in the middle of the same shopping strip.

Our past is a place that lives on in all of us. I try to avoid Adelaide as much as I can. It reminds me of a childhood marked by violence, disability and conflict, a place that moves so slowly that one feels escape is impossible. Most of my high-school teachers were pathetically surprised when I was accepted into my university degree of first choice, and sitting in classes at the University of Adelaide, I remember looking at my female peers and wondering, 'Are you filling in time until you get married and have kids?' At the age of nineteen, I knew these were not my goals, but exactly how I was going to get out of Adelaide was not clear. I thought that maybe I would suffocate with grief and never escape. Whenever I go back there, I think maybe I still will.

Most of my research sites were chosen because they have a notably diverse population. This is only the case for one of the two research sites in Adelaide: the mosque. The first site I discuss here is a church that approached me. After hearing about my research, they invited me to come and work in their community. Although I was aware that their congregation was more white and middle-class than my other fieldwork sites, their views towards faith and religion added new perspectives to my research. My experience with churches in west Sydney was very difficult. All the churches I approached refused to be involved, and I was left crying in a hot street by a church administrator who told me I was 'going to hell' because I believed all people are equal. I had coffee with a pastor who asked about the 'gay and lesbian radicalisation' of children being undertaken in contemporary culture, and he wanted to know: was I able to fix this? I encountered suspicion layered upon suspicion. The Sydney mosque in which I worked welcomed me with open arms, as did the multiple mosques I visited on field trips to Manchester (fifteen in total and more shared meals than I care to count. I remember the imam at Manchester Central Mosque chasing after me with a bag filled with rice and curries for my dinner). Yet churches proved a completely different story. I not only hit a series of brick walls when trying to approach Anglican churches in Sydney, I found the brick walls attacked me. Consequently, I felt that I could not refuse the offer of coming to work with a church in Adelaide, even if I risked accidentally drowning in a sea of grief with each return visit. The open and reflexive nature of this church community is most likely due to its liberal nature, which is embedded in its constitution; the many church stories that run throughout this book are from this wonderful community.

My second fieldwork site in Adelaide was a mosque and, in the third round of workshops, the church and the mosque came together and the communities collaborated across three days of art-making. The church that invited me is in Norwood, Adelaide.[7] The church members with whom I worked were welcoming, and their church has a lovely outdoor garden and a well-equipped children's Sunday School room. The second Adelaide suburb I worked in is not that much more ethnically diverse but of lower socioeconomic standing.[8] The mosque is a huge hub for the Islamic community in Adelaide, with fantastic facilities and a warm and welcoming atmosphere. The mosque congregation is very multicultural, far more than the demographic of the area suggests, and the imam delivers all services in Urdu. Though the church site is less diverse than most of the other communities with which I work, by bringing the church group together with the mosque community, a rich community backdrop was formed that allowed for imagining the possibilities of how to create future cross-cultural collaboration.

Melbourne

I am based in Melbourne and my fieldwork sites here are ongoing. The first of these is in Noble Park.[9] Driving through the sprawling suburb, houses look similar: new builds sold off the plan that quite suddenly appear out of nowhere. The local shops remind me of growing up in the suburbs of Adelaide. Things feel far away from Melbourne's city centre here, with large houses and little to do within walking distance of the school. I wonder what the young people do for fun. I sip my coffee on a crisp August morning and get ready to meet the children. It's cold in the community room, so I turn up the heating and unfold the making tables.

My site in Noble Park[10] is an accelerated arts-based learning program for artistically talented children, which is also a skills and

Contexts / Comhthéacs 13

mentoring training session for children that may need support outside the classroom for working on their creative talents. The program recruits from different local primary schools, so the children involved in my research are from a selection of local schools. The incredibly diverse nature of the participants in my focus groups, and their eagerness to respond to my questions about interfaith and intergenerational experiences, speaks to the complex nature of the program. It supports children in developing artistic talents, but it also offers a service that provides childcare on weekends and a space for mentoring and skills training for those who may not get this at home. It is hard to describe in words how engaging this fieldwork site is, which I go on to analyse further in a later chapter.

My second fieldwork site in Melbourne is in a gentrified inner-city area; a bilingual primary school that services the residents of a large council housing estate built on the same road as the school. Fitzroy is a suburb of contrasts.[11] As I jump off the tram and walk around the corner to the school, the smell of old beer wafts from the cellar of the local bar. Workers are unloading kegs through the basement door. A tree-lined street features a mixture of well-to-do terrace homes, dilapidated share houses with couches and beer bottles littering front lawns, and the high-rise Atherton Gardens council housing estate, which stands imposingly out of the hustle ipm. The people that pass me on the road vary from hospitality workers stumbling home at 7 am after their Tuesday nights out ('hospo' nights in Melbourne offer cheap drinks for service workers), a group of mothers in orange-and-pink headscarves dropping their kids off at school and a man in a suit getting into his BMW. This area is made up of differences. New immigrant populations occupy many of the council housing estates, while hospitality workers, students and professionals take up the area in different ways. The area is alive – thrumming with artists, murals, food and cultures. This primary school remains an ongoing research partner. The two Melbourne sites could not be more different in terms of the areas in which they are located, although both have mainly non-white communities who are non-English-speaking.

The final research site is in a suburb of Canberra in the Australian Capital Territory (ACT). This Islamic school was also an originally unplanned research site that invited me to come and work with them.

14 *Faith stories*

Canberra

A sea of moving blue. As the research team drives up to the school, the sea of moving blue parts and groups of girls in light-blue hijabs stare while we lug our suitcase full of quilt materials onto the steps of the school office. The surrounding grounds are brown, and the school, likewise, had a greyish-brown appearance. In summer, Canberra has a monotone brown nature: dry grass, brown rolling hills. The houses near the school are clean and neat, alike in appearance. The brown school disappears amongst a sea of blue hijabs. The school doesn't currently have an art program, so the children and teachers are eager to partake. It is worth noting that, due to the fact this is an Islamic private school, a lot of the students do not live in the local area of Weston[12] but travel in. Consequently, the statistical profile of the area does not reflect the multicultural make-up of the school and my participants. The children in this research site were unusually focused and well-behaved. Excitingly, ABC Canberra, the local branch of the Australian Broadcasting Corporation, the national public broadcaster, featured the arts workshops on their television news and morning radio show during the 2019 fieldwork, bringing the Islamic school's efforts to create intercultural community collaboration into Canberra's media headlines.

As you can see, the Australian research sites span incredibly varied socioeconomic areas in west Sydney, Adelaide, Melbourne and Canberra. There are three notably middle-class areas: Norwood in Adelaide (South Australia), Fitzroy in Melbourne (Victoria) and Weston in Canberra (ACT). The differences between these sites and the lower-socioeconomic sites of the project, such as Noble Park, Moss Side and Auburn are stark, not just in statistical terms but in terms of the aesthetics of place, the values expressed, the children's energy and modes of engagement. The Australian fieldwork sites are two primary schools, a charity, a settlement services provider, two mosques and a church. Some outreach has been undertaken with the Islamic Museum of Australia and art gallery exhibitions in Adelaide and Melbourne, with further engagement workshops and exhibitions scheduled. As noted, the fieldwork in the UK across Manchester and London was undertaken in three schools in deprived (Moss Side, Hulme) or working-class (Levenshulme) areas in Manchester and two schools in traditionally working-class areas in London. Some outreach work in galleries also occurred in the UK, at P21 Gallery (London) and the Whitworth Gallery (Manchester) and several mosques across Manchester. As a result, the sensory scapes of the places in which the research was undertaken vary quite significantly, as do my experiences of working in and with these places.

Orientations

My research sites feature a broad selection of orientations to faith and religion, which range from engaging children and parents who belong to religious or spiritual communities as a recreational and/or devotional practice, to working with those who identify as secular, humanist or searching. For example, one research participant in Manchester stated she hated being called a 'non-believer'; she said, 'Look up at the stars – something's got to be there'. While she isn't religious, she clearly wants to believe in the possibility of other worlds or higher powers. I have developed a unified approach to thinking about the orientation of my research participants as a result of working with, and across, this range of different orientations to religion. The people involved in my research are all united by the fact that they have faith. Whether it is faith in the secular nature of society, faith in family, faith in God, faith in the promises of capitalism or faith in the belief that life is worth living, everyone maintains, and is maintained by, faith. In Chapter 2, I draw on Braidotti's suggestion that 'all beliefs are acts of faith' (2008: 11) to argue that faith is an ontological state, an orientation and a capacity to act. I develop an affective notion of faith as a set of practices, an embedded emotional geography that choreographs subjectivities and communities.

Philosophies of religion often account for transcendental frameworks, as a religion is a belief structure; however, like Ammerman (2013, 2014), I argue that as much as it can be seen as being transcendental, faith is material – it is a capacity to act that is characterised by belief in the world that brings together those who identify as being religious or spiritual and those who do not. Faith in the truth of a secular perspective remains a form of faith.

To put this another way, I am working to open up, rather than close down, the plurality of ways we can think about faith attachment to include thinking about aspects of involuntary experience, non-verbal attachments, material and geographic actants, embodied and inherited memory and trauma. To use Raymond Williams's (1977) famous phrase, I am interested in the 'structures of feeling' that make up faith.[13]

For now, I want to situate my approach to faith as one that builds on this cultural studies tradition of understanding everyday life, and the structures of feeling that shape everyday lives. As I introduced above, my approach is aligned with Karl Kitching's work, and Kitching draws on Saba Mahmood in advocating approaches to religion, and, I would say, faith, that are grounded in cohabitation with icons, images and symbols (Mahmood in Kitching, 2020: 6). It seems to me that neither Kitching, Mahmood nor I is for a moment wanting to objectify or essentialise experiences of faith and religion. Quite the opposite: I want to examine intersections *between* religion and culture, between class, race and faith, between material cultures and attachment. For example, a mother in one of my ethnographic sites in Melbourne is a newly arrived Australian who speaks Arabic. She wears a hijab and identifies as Muslim, yet does not identify as either Sunni or Shiite, and neither she nor her husband attends a mosque. Rather, they pray at home and have a designated prayer space in their house. I read this story as illustrating the broad range of ways people practise religion. Once, after I joined in with Sunday evening prayer, a mother at the Adelaide mosque asked me how I distinguished between 'culture' and 'religion'. The nature of this question suggested to me that I was involved in questions of culture and not attentive enough to questions of religion. My answer to the mother at the time still stands: there is no universal dividing line between religion and culture; this distinction is different for everyone. As much as some people can clearly identify religion, other research participants say they are religious but may not have much knowledge about their religion. Everyone involved in this project defines distinctions between religion and culture differently, and the most consistent thing this project has taught me about religion is that everyone who identifies as 'religious' in some way does 'religion' very differently. Like the instance of the Melbourne mother above, not all Muslims attend mosques or, like the Manchester mother, not all 'believers' believe in God – some might believe in a higher power that is evidenced by the stars. Across this broad spectrum of ways of knowing and believing, people are sustained by various forms of their faith.

Five years of conversations on this matter have left me with the conviction there can never be a right or wrong way, or even *one definitive way*, of categorising faith experiences. One person's belief in a clear divide between culture and religion is completely disproven by another person's unorthodox religious identity, which they nevertheless experience as being religious.

Conclusion

I have designed this book as an investigation of faith and belief systems in ways that respond to empirical experiences rather than theoretical framings. I hope this has resulted in an explanation of the systems of cultural value that articulate through faith. This book will provide a set of resources for those who wish to explore similar themes in complex social circumstances, either as 'research' or as 'community engagement'. In such increasingly divided times, work like this is needed now more than ever.

In this chapter, I have attempted to show how places live on in people, even when they leave them. The contexts of my ethnography are pasts and presents brought together in themes, experiences, colours, symbols, sounds, smells, the earth and the stars. Entangled with the places in which we live are complex histories and belief systems. Whether it was the harsh refusal of Sydney churches to accept my work, or the open arms of the mosques in Sydney, Manchester and Adelaide, affective moments have changed both the ways I conduct the research and also the ways I see faith unfold through everyday life, through people and place. I hope this chapter has given a glimpse into the richness and complexity of the diverse places and people with whom I conducted this research. May the saints that bless Philomena's mantelpiece be a marker for the everyday lived experiences that faith has in making life worth living. Faith can, if you let it, mean that 'there's a saint everywhere, wherever you look' (Philomena, west Sydney, 2018). Faith sustains people, and it is the most unifying aspect I have found across diverse populations. Because we all have faith in something.

Notes

1 Auburn's population is 37,366 (Australian Bureau of Statistics, 2016), and the average household size is 3.5 persons. It is rapidly gentrifying, with most of my research participants travelling 'in' to Auburn from further out west. Median monthly mortgage repayments are $1,733 and the median weekly household income is $1,240. (Please note all uses of the $ sign refer to Australian dollars unless otherwise specified.) The most common ancestries are Chinese (18.2 per cent), Turkish (8.0 per cent), Lebanese (7.3 per cent), Nepalese (6.1 per cent) and Indian (5.7 per cent). This was reflected in the constitution of my research group in Auburn, which had participants from China, Sri Lanka, India, Pakistan, Afghanistan, Iran, Iraq and Syria. No participants were white Australian. 29.5 per cent of Auburn residents were born in Australia, and the most common other countries of birth are China (12.7 per cent), Nepal (6.5 per cent), Afghanistan (6.1 per cent), Pakistan (5.5 per cent) and India (5.0 per cent). The Auburn area is a migrant community, with 84.6 per cent of residents having both parents born overseas. This is reflected in my research, with only one family out of sixty having parents born in Australia. The most common religions are Muslim (43.0 per cent), no religion (15.5 per cent), Catholic (9.7 per cent) and Hindu (8.8 per cent). This diversity is also expressed through language, food and religion. Everyone speaks multiple languages, and many residents have very little English. Just 12.9 per cent of people speak only English at home. Other languages spoken at home include Arabic (13.3 per cent), Mandarin (12.0 per cent), Turkish (8.4 per cent), Cantonese (6.8 per cent) and Nepali (6.7 per cent). The community is broadly known as working-class, and this is statistically supported, with the most common occupations being technicians and trades workers (19.1 per cent) and labourers (18.0 per cent).

2 The 2011 UK census (UK Office for National Statistics, 2011a) states the neighbourhood currently has a population of 15,430 and its most common ancestries/ethnic groups are white (58.9 per cent), Asian/Asian British (27.8 per cent) and Black/African/Caribbean/Black British (5.1 per cent). The most common passports held are United Kingdom (73 per cent), no passport (10.8 per cent) and Middle East and Asia (7.9 per cent). In contrast to the low English-speaking population of Auburn, in Levenshulme 75.5 per cent of people speak English as their main language at home. This whiteness is expressed in artisan craft markets and 'open garden' days. 10.3 per cent of people have at least one person over the age of sixteen in their household who speaks English as a main language, and just 11.9 per cent have no one in their

household who speaks English as a main language. The most common religions in Levenshulme are Christian (38 per cent), Muslim (28.4 per cent), no religion (24.6 per cent), religion not stated (6.5 per cent) and Hindu (0.9 per cent). A large proportion of my research participants here were either no religion, Muslim or Christian, which is reflected in the census data.

3 The population is 18,902. The most common ancestries/ethnic groups are white (32.8 per cent), mixed or multiple ethnic groups (7.3 per cent) and Asian/Asian British (18.5 per cent). While 65.2 per cent of people speak English as a main language at home, 19.5 per cent of people aged sixteen and over have no one in their household who speaks English as a main language. This shaped my focus group discussions, as we needed interpreters for a large amount of the discussion. The most common religions in Moss Side are Christian (36.2 per cent), Muslim (34.0 per cent), no religion (19.1 per cent), religion not stated (7 per cent) and Hindu (1.8 per cent). Household tenure in Moss Side consists of 44.2 per cent social renting (11.1 per cent of this group rents from the council or local authority), 32.2 per cent privately rented and 20.7 per cent owned home. The most common occupations in Moss Side are elementary occupations (22.6 per cent), professional occupations (13.8 per cent) and sales and customer-service occupations (13.6 per cent) (UK Office for National Statistics, 2011a; UK Office for National Statistics, 2011b). As this occupational profile suggests, Moss Side is still very much a working-class area.

4 The population of Hulme is 16,907. The most common ancestries/ethnic groups in this area are white (56.8 per cent), mixed/multiple ethnic groups (6.7 per cent), Asian/Asian British (16.9 per cent), Black/African/Caribbean/Black British (14.8 per cent) and other ethnic groups (4.8 per cent) The most common passports held are United Kingdom (65 per cent), Middle East and Asia (12.3 per cent) and no passport (9.4 per cent). Household languages in Hulme are reflected by the fact that 74 per cent of people aged sixteen and over speak English as a main language. 17.6 per cent have no people in their household who speak English as a main language, while 7.2 per cent of people have at least one English speaker in their household, but not all people over sixteen in their household speak English as a main language. Most of the participants in my project did not speak English at home. The most common religions are Christian (38.8 per cent), no religion (36.3 per cent), Muslim (13.1 per cent), religion not stated (7 per cent) and Buddhist (1.8 per cent). The household tenure in Hulme is 41.3 per cent privately rented, 38.1 per cent social renting (11.7 per cent of this group rents from the council) and 18.7 per cent owned home. The most common

occupations in Hulme are professional occupations (23.6 per cent), associate professional and technical occupations (17.8 per cent) and elementary occupations (13.4 per cent).

5 The population of Charlton is 14,385. The most common ethnicities/ancestries are white (63.8 per cent), mixed/multiple ethnic groups (5.5 per cent), Asian/Asian British (13.6 per cent) and Black/African/Caribbean/Black British (15.5 per cent). Places of birth were United Kingdom (69 per cent), other countries (23.2 per cent), EU countries (6.5 per cent) and the Republic of Ireland (1.4 per cent). Passports held are United Kingdom (68.1 per cent), no passport (12.7 per cent), other Europe (7.2 per cent), Africa (4.4 per cent), Middle East and Asia (5.3 per cent), Republic of Ireland (1.7 per cent) and North America and the Caribbean (1.2 per cent). 79.4 per cent of people aged sixteen or over speak English as a main household language and only 9.4 per cent of people have no others in their household that speak English as a main language. The most common religions are Christian (47.2 per cent), no religion (29.4 per cent), religion not stated (8.4 per cent), Muslim (6.8 per cent) and Hindu (4.0 per cent). Household tenure is 41.1 per cent social renting (19.2 per cent of this of this group rents through the council), 15.9 per cent privately rented and 41.7 per cent owned home. 71 per cent of people are economically active and 60.2 per cent are employed, 5.8 per cent are unemployed and 5.0 per cent are full-time students. The most common occupations are professional occupations (22.8 per cent), associate professional and technical occupations (15.9 per cent) and elementary occupations (11.5 per cent). My second research site in south-east London was not far away, in Harbinger Primary School in the Isle of Dogs, which has a more multicultural make-up than Charlton.

6 The population of Millwall is 23,084 and the most common ethnicities are white (52.4 per cent), Asian/Asian British (34.7 per cent), Black/African/Caribbean/Black British (5.6 per cent) and mixed/multiple ethnic groups (4.4 per cent). The most common countries of birth are the United Kingdom (47.9 per cent), other countries (38.5 per cent), other EU (12.6 per cent) and Republic of Ireland (1.1 per cent). The most common passports held are United Kingdom (57.8 per cent), other Europe (14.1 per cent), Middle East and Asia (13.8 per cent) and no passport (4.3 per cent). Household languages are broken down as follows: 62.2 per cent of people aged sixteen and over have English as a main language in their household, 23.4 per cent have no people in their household with English as a main language and 12.3 per cent of people have at least one but not all people aged sixteen or over in their household who speak English as a main language. The most common religions

are Christian (32.1 per cent), no religion (22.4 per cent), religion not stated (19.6 per cent), Muslim (18.0 per cent) and Hindu (4.9 per cent). Household tenure is 48.1 per cent of people rent privately, 27.5 per cent own their home, 20.6 per cent rent through social housing, 2.3 per cent have shared ownership (part-owned and part-rented). The most common occupations are professional occupations (32.2 per cent), associate professional and technical occupations (22.7 per cent) and managers, directors and senior officials (17.0 per cent) (UK Office for National Statistics, 2011a and b).

7 According to the Australian Bureau of Statistics, Norwood has a population of 3,322 and the average number of people per household is two. The median weekly household income is $1,485 and the median monthly mortgage repayment is $1,829. The most common ancestries are English (26.3 per cent), Australian (17.0 per cent), Irish (8.2 per cent), Scottish (7.2 per cent) and Italian (6.3 per cent). Over half the population of Norwood are people who were born in Australia (64.4 per cent). The broadly white nature of the area can be understood from the popular suggestion that there are 'a lot of Italian people' in Norwood – indeed, a whole 6.3 per cent of people with Italian heritage, which is obviously noticeable against a backdrop of white privilege. The most common countries of birth outside Australia are England (4.9 per cent), China (3.2 per cent), India (2.1 per cent) and Italy (2.1 per cent). Nearly half (43.2 per cent) of people have parents both born in Australia and slightly over one-third (36.3 per cent) of people have both parents born overseas. The most common responses for religion in Norwood are no religion (40.8 per cent), Catholic (18.7 per cent), not stated (11.2 per cent), Anglican (9.3 per cent) and Orthodox (4.1 per cent). Christianity is the largest religious group reported overall (46.8 per cent; this figure excludes not stated responses). Two-thirds (71.7 per cent) of people speak only English at home. Other languages spoken at home include Mandarin (3.6 per cent), Italian (3.2 per cent), Greek (2.8 per cent), Cantonese (1.1 per cent) and Hindi (0.9 per cent). The most common occupations are professionals (41.3 per cent), managers (14.9 per cent) and clerical and administrative workers (11.5 per cent) (Australian Bureau of Statistics, 2016).

8 Marion is 10 km south-west of the Adelaide city centre. It has a population of 3,902 (Australian Bureau of Statistics, 2016). The average number of people per household is 2.2, the median weekly household income $1,129 and the median monthly mortgage repayment is $1,517. The most common ancestries are English (28.0 per cent), Australian (25.2 per cent), Scottish (6.2 per cent) and Irish (6.2 per cent). In Marion, 68.6 per cent of people were born in Australia. The most common

countries of birth for residents born abroad are England (5.6 per cent), China (3.5 per cent), India (2.8 per cent) and the Philippines (1.5 per cent). Slightly more than half (52.1 per cent) of people have both parents born in Australia and just over one-third (33.5 per cent) of people have both parents born overseas. The most common responses for religion in Marion are no religion (31.5 per cent), Catholic (18.8 per cent), Anglican (10.3 per cent), Uniting Church (10.2 per cent) and not stated (8.4 per cent). Christianity is the largest religious group reported overall (56.8 per cent; this figure excludes not stated responses). A majority of people (75.7 per cent) speak only English at home. Other languages spoken at home include Mandarin (3.3 per cent), Greek (1.3 per cent), Italian (1.2 per cent), Punjabi (1.1 per cent) and Cantonese (1.0 per cent). The most common occupations include professionals (23.2 per cent), clerical and administrative workers (15.7 per cent) and community and personal service workers (15.2 per cent) (Australian Bureau of Statistics, 2016).

9. Noble Park has a population of 30,998. According to the 2016 Australian census, the average number of people per household in Noble Park is 2.7, the median weekly household income is $1,108, and median monthly mortgage repayment is $1,500. The most common ancestries are English (10.6 per cent), Vietnamese (10.0 per cent), Australian (8.7 per cent) and Indian (8.3 per cent). Slightly over one-third (34.7 per cent) of the population was born in Australia. The most common other countries of birth are India (10.9 per cent), Vietnam (9.0 per cent), Cambodia (5.3 per cent) and Sri Lanka (4.4 per cent). In Noble Park, 76.5 per cent of people have both parents born overseas, while just 12.1 per cent of people have both parents born in Australia.

10. The most common religions in Noble Park are Catholicism (20.3 per cent), no religion, (17.0 per cent), Buddhism (16.4 per cent) and Islam (9.8 per cent). Nearly one-third (31.0 per cent) of people speak only English at home. Other languages spoken at home include Vietnamese (12.1 per cent), Khmer (6.8 per cent), Punjabi (6.4 per cent), Sinhalese (2.9 per cent) and Mandarin (2.4 per cent). The most common occupations in Noble Park are: labourers (18.5 per cent), technicians and trades workers (14.4 per cent) and professionals (12.9 per cent) (Australian Bureau of Statistics, 2016).

11. Fitzroy has a population of 10,445. The average number of people per household is 2.1, the median weekly household income is $1,715 and the median monthly mortgage repayment is $2,286. The most common ancestries are English (20.4 per cent), Australian (15.6 per cent), Irish (9.5 per cent), Scottish (7.0 per cent) and Chinese (4.8 per cent). Just over half (53.3 per cent) of people were born in Australia. The other

most common countries of birth are England (3.9 per cent), Vietnam (3.3 per cent), New Zealand (2.9 per cent) and China (2.7 per cent). One-third (33.0 per cent) of people had both parents born in Australia and 40.7 per cent of people had both parents born overseas. The most common responses for religion are no religion (48.2 per cent), not stated (16.8 per cent), Catholic (13.1 per cent), Muslim (5.5 per cent) and Buddhist (4.1 per cent). No religion, so described, constitutes the main belief group reported overall (58.0 per cent). Well over half (61.0 per cent) of people speak only English at home. Other languages spoken at home include Vietnamese (4.1 per cent), Mandarin (2.5 per cent), Cantonese (2.1 per cent), Arabic (2.0 per cent) and Greek (1.6 per cent). The most common occupations include professionals (44.6 per cent), managers (16.6 per cent) and community and personal service workers (9.7 per cent).

12 Weston, Canberra has a population of 3,576 and is the best-resourced area in the research project. The average number of people per household in Weston is 2.5 and the median weekly household income is a generous $2,096. The median amount for a monthly mortgage repayment is $2,167. The most common ancestries are English (24.4 per cent), Australian (22.3 per cent), Irish (10.7 per cent) and Scottish (8.5 per cent). Over half (68.3 per cent) of people were born in Australia. The most common other countries of birth are England (3.9 per cent), India (1.4 per cent), New Zealand (0.9 per cent), China (0.9 per cent) and Pakistan (0.8 per cent). Slightly less than half (49.3 per cent) of people had both parents born in Australia and 27.6 per cent of people had both parents born overseas. The most common responses for religion in Weston are no religion (35.8 per cent), Catholic (22.4 per cent), Anglican (11.3 per cent), not stated (9.9 per cent) and Uniting Church (3.4 per cent). As a result, Christianity is the largest religious group reported overall (52.2 per cent). 76.1 per cent of people speak only English at home. Other languages spoken at home include Arabic (1.0 per cent), Mandarin (1.0 per cent), Urdu (0.9 per cent), German (0.7 per cent) and Italian (0.7 per cent). The most common occupations include professionals (35.4 per cent), managers (18.7 per cent) and clerical and administrative workers (16.5 per cent).

13 Williams developed the notion of 'structures of feeling' (1977: 128) in the 1970s to facilitate an historical understanding of what he called 'affective elements of consciousness and relationships' (1977: 132). Since then, the need to understand emotions, moods and atmospheres as both historical and social phenomena has become more acute in an era of social networking, and indeed this has become a key focus of the field of affect studies (see Coleman, 2018, 2020).

2

Faith: a new materialist approach / *Creideamh*

In this chapter, I develop a new materialist philosophy of faith. Through mobilising affect theory and writing from the new materialisms, I demonstrate how faith operates as both a form of what Spinoza (1996) calls 'joy' and, alternatively, what Lauren Berlant (2011) calls 'cruel optimism'. I show that a change in the capacity to act (affect), such as that which is created through belief, is an experience that unites both secular and religious people. For example, belief in the superiority of secular culture over religious culture, and vice versa, are two affectively similar corporeal orientations that, to quote Braidotti, show how we are 'all too human' (2019: 1–5) and all 'in-this-together-but-not-one-and-the-same' (2019: 157). I outline the three scales across which faith entanglements and resulting unconscious orientations articulate: macro, meso and micro. On a macro level, global material economies, worldviews, geographies and networks of faith impact substantively upon an individual's capacity to act, as these assemblages are both political and world-making. On a meso level, the individual and community geographies of belonging that constitute people's everyday lives demonstrate the complex entanglements of matter and belief that make up lived faith worlds. At a micro level, 'joy' is the feeling that is brought about by an increase in our capacity to act and, alternatively, 'cruel optimism'[1] is deferring pleasure (for example, sexual pleasure) in the hope that the act of deferral will lead to reward. We are all consciously or unconsciously enmeshed in various systems of faith relations, both formal and informal, religious and secular. This chapter puts forward a unified approach to thinking about the social and individual politics of orientation as expressions of different forms of faith.

Faith is an ontological state, an orientation and a capacity to act. It is a set of practices, an embedded emotional geography that choreographs subjectivities and communities. Philosophies of religion often account for transcendental frameworks, as a religion is a belief structure; however, religious belief structures interpolate objects and in so doing, give them meaning. As an affect, faith is material; it presents as a capacity to act characterised by belief in the world. My new materialist theory of faith presents it as a cosmological, ontological condition, drawing on resources from the field of new materialist scholarship (Meyer, 2015, 2019; Braidotti, 2019; Coleman, 2020) to think about what it means to have faith. For some, faith begins with a faith in a god, or *gods*, although for many others it doesn't; for them, faith is about connectedness to community, family, values, places and rituals. Faith is a way of being a person and belonging to a community. It is a capacity to act, or a set of embodied orientations that limit capacity to act.

My contributions in this book extend existing work in new materialist writing which focuses on religion (Arab, 2019; Bräunlein, 2019; Burchardt, 2019; Hazard, 2019; Meyer, 2015, 2019), but I offer a very different contribution to these. Faith brings religious and secular communities together; it is expressed as systems of cultural value rather than abstract beliefs. Drawing on Iris van der Tuin's analysis of diffraction, as a practice designed to 'provoke change ... [through paying attention to] cracks in the academic canon' (2015: 100), I offer a diffractive engagement with philosophies of religion as examples of some ideas that motivate bodies who have faith. Yet often, philosophies of religion have very little to do with people's faith practices, which are usually performances of commitment to community, values and belonging rather than an investment in existential ideology. As one of my research participants explains, she is drawn to community rather than abstract belief:

> *Growing up white Anglican ... there wasn't that huge amount, you know, that really convivial, come to my bosom and let's all have a big casserole and all that kind of stuff. It was really quite austere and quite straighty-one-eighty. When I married Simon, who was at the time Baha'i religion, something that I found really, absolutely delightful about that was all these Persian people who bring you into*

the house, and feed you and cuddle you and just I absolutely adore that. (Nancy, Norwood focus group, 2018)

For Nancy, her faith community provides emotional sustenance. While acknowledging that philosophies of religion have limited impacts on the lives of many people who have faith, thinking about philosophies of religion is a way of mapping some of the many thought constellations that are reflected in faith-based patterns of feelings. Often these constellations are points that those who have faith define themselves against, or as being different from.

In his 2014 book *Reinventing Philosophy of Religion: An Opinionated Introduction*, Graham Oppy draws his readers' attention to the impossibility of a consistent definition of religion – since, although over half the world has faith in a religion, it is always a context-specific task to define exactly what a religion is. Oppy explains:

> Perhaps the very first question that arises for philosophy of religion is whether there is any such thing as *religion* [original emphasis]. This question seems straight-forward. We are all familiar with Hinduism, Buddhism, Confucianism, Jainism, Sikhism, Shintoism, Taoism, Judaism, Christianity, and Islam. What are these, if not religions? Of course, recognizing that the major world religions are religions does not guarantee that we can decide harder cases, nor does it guarantee that we will not go seriously wrong if we try to give a definition of 'religion'. On the one hand, you might well be unsure whether Scientology – or Discordianism, or the Church of MOO – is a religion; on the other hand, you might think that we simply misunderstand ancestor worship if we think of it as being a kind of religion. (2014: 3)

My in-depth conversations about faith with people who belong to religious communities have taught me that people's faith and attachments often come about as a result of lived experiences, habits and values more than abstract beliefs. Faith is largely an embodied practice, not an abstract idea. While Oppy's inquiry is shaped by a liberal understanding of what religion is, he develops a new idea of philosophy through his study of religion:

> On any account of religion, it is clear that there are many ways that one might choose to study it. History, anthropology, geography, sociology, demography, and psychology all promise to yield significant information about religion. Perhaps the study of literature, music, painting, sculpture, and architecture will do so as well. However, while

philosophy of religion ought not to proceed in ignorance of the information that is yielded by other approaches to the study of religion, the questions that are taken up by philosophers of religion will not be straightforwardly answered by that information. (Oppy, 2014: 6)

To put this another way, there are multiple knowledge systems produced through religious practice and belief. In some cases, these systems could nearly be seen as mutually exclusive (for example, the philosophy of a religion versus the sociology of how it might be practised). Further, a contemporary philosophical perspective on faith must be informed by, or at least developed in relation to, religions that inspire so many people's faith. This requires a diffractive reading of religion that takes 'off elsewhere' from a strictly religious reading and has 'differing effects' (van der Tuin, 2018: 100) from canonical engagements with philosophies of religion. Indeed, as I have suggested (Hickey-Moody, 2019), in thinking through faith as an embodied experience we can see that people who belong to different religions have more in common than they have separating them.

A Deleuzo–Spinozist reading of faith as increasing (joy) or decreasing (sad affect) capacity to act shows us that belonging to a religion is not so much about having one worldview, but rather about feeling belonging and being connected to communities, or being prevented from connecting to communities. While, for Oppy, religion as a philosophical approach is cognitive rather than embodied, drawing on Spinoza (1996) we can understand that cognitive constellations need to be understood as images of things around which beliefs and capacities to act are organised.

Other significant works in the interdisciplinary space of new materialist studies of religion include Birgit Meyer's formative and enduringly useful 2003 piece 'Material Mediations and Religious Practices of World-Making'. This essay offers resources that are in line with the contemporary philosophy of faith I develop here, although it is focused on religion rather than a broader experience of faith. Meyer argues that:

> [s]ecularization theory with its inbuilt teleology gave way to an understanding of religion as being in constant transformation into multiple directions. The question of how (and why) religion transforms is at the core of much current research, yielding a strong emphasis on detailed case studies that place religion in broader social-cultural settings. (2003: 1–2)

As Meyer attests, the experience of having faith makes religion; it is a located, historically situated, embodied imagining of what the future might be (Braidotti, 2008: 18) and how the present is constituted. Meyer argues that the fact religion is a located and embodied practice has rightly shaped religious studies and should continue to do so:

> Scholars signalled the need to pay urgent attention to actual religious practices of engaging with things, words, pictures, and other religious forms. Materiality became a key term. Far from designating simply the empirical study of religious material culture from a practice perspective, the point is to 're-materialize' our conceptual approaches to religion. (2003: 2)

Meyer is asking us to think about the role that materiality plays in religion. I cannot agree more with her proposition, and I would extend such considerations of religion to include all forms of faith. A 're-materialisation' of often abstracted belief structures requires a critical engagement with the post-Enlightenment, romanticist Protestant bias that Meyer (2010) argues still haunts the modern study of religion, as well as openness toward the spheres of the everyday level of 'lived religion', asking how religion becomes tangible in 'the world' (Meyer, 2003: 2). I try to do both these things in writing about faith as a vernacular, lived aspect of everyone's everyday life. Faith is bigger than religion and, while it is often inspired by religion, or is developed in response to religion, it is experienced rather than thought, felt rather than written, and happens rather than is planned.

In *Religions, Reasons and Gods: Essays in Cross-Cultural Philosophy of Religion*, Clayton, Blackburn and Carroll (2006) argue that cross-cultural philosophies of religion are much more about the ways religious beliefs orient a body than about abstract ideas. Religious beliefs thus provide frameworks in and through which a body becomes:

> Theistic arguments as forms of conceptual analysis might help us better understand the place and nature of gods in religious traditions, thereby leading to a clearer sense of the comparative grammar of religion: the rules of discourse about the gods. Such rules of discourse would show what would count as gods, the kinds of properties such beings possess and their place in different religious forms of life – for we cannot assume that the gods play the same role in all traditions any more than we can assume, e.g., that constitutions play the same

role in all countries. Identification of the rules of discourse about the gods might also serve specifically philosophical ends ... From this point of view, religious contexts would provide particularly interesting examples of some of the most difficult philosophical puzzles, and could contribute to their clarification or even solution. (Clayton, Blackburn, and Carroll, 2006: 306)

The contexts in which philosophy is generated, appreciated, and given life are the pathway to understanding it. Context makes religion over again and again; it makes faith over again and again. I think about 'a thousand tiny faiths', after Deleuze and Guattari's 'thousand tiny sexes'. Everyone's faith is uniquely their own, just like everyone's sex. Clayton, Blackburn and Carroll continue, explaining that:

[c]ontrary to dominant post-Enlightenment emphasis upon consensus, examining the actual contexts in which theistic proofs are used leads to a greater appreciation of the differences, not the sameness of humankind's understanding of divinity. The craving for all rationally achieved consensus is in part an indirect reaction to the competing claims of religious traditions and more directly a protest against the sectarian bitterness that had arisen during and in the century or so of conflict after the Reformation. A Utopian dream it may have been, but its achievement should not be underestimated. In any case, in a pluralist world it that is increasingly becoming, substantive consensus about means of goals is unlikely; the only consensus for which one can hope is a framework in which differences can be protected as well as commonalities identified. (2006: 307)

The differences and commonalities to which the authors refer are enacted on and carried through the body, through faith and through (in)capacities to act that shape cultures and perform life worlds.

I propose a reading of faith as an embodied experience that is shaped by material cultures of religion and by the 'post-secular' state. Here, I take my cue from Rosi Braidotti, who astutely observes that:

[t]he legacy of psychoanalysis allows us to challenge received ideas about the rationality of political subjectivity. Let us take a simple notion, such as faith in social progress and the self-correcting powers of democratic governance. In a psychoanalytic perspective, the operational concept here is faith itself. Psychoanalysis is a sober

reminder of our historically cumulated contradictions: we are confronting today a post secular realization that all beliefs are acts of faith, regardless of their propositional content – even – or especially, when they involve the superiority of reason, science and technology. All belief systems contain a hard core of spiritual hope – as Lacan put it: if you believe in grammar, you believe in God. (2008: 11)

Here, Braidotti show us the necessity of faith. She alerts us to the fact that various forms of faith are what animate all human actions. There is no purely transcendental faith. For those who are religious, even when they subscribe to transcendental beliefs, the modulations of faith they experience are embodied affects. These affects are co-created through visual and material cultures of religion, as John Cort shows:

> A look at the material culture of a religious tradition indicates that texts alone are insufficient. Texts at best provide only a limited perspective on a religion. Two centuries of textual studies have led to an academic understanding of Jainism as an ascetic, world-renouncing, unaesthetic religious tradition … Looking only at texts has blinded scholars to the extent that Jains for centuries have built temples, sculpted and adorned images, painted, embroidered textiles, and created a myriad of other objects – in short, have created a full material culture. (1996: 630–1)

Touching and feeling, objects and places, are too quickly left out of the philosophy of religion. Material cultures are at the heart of faith practices; they are just not always at the heart of *academic methods* for understanding faith and religion. This argument is further developed by Matthews-Jones and Jones who explain:

> On the one hand, objects are shaped by people and cultures and become expressive of their beliefs and values. On the other hand, objects have the potential to shape and condition people. An appreciation of these twin processes is essential to understanding religious faith and spirituality. (2015: 2)

Here, we see that visual and material cultures of religion are key in constituting how faith is experienced, especially by those who are involved in religions:

> Rather than perceiving them as the end product, or as a reflection, of social and cultural systems, material-culture scholars prefer to see

objects as playing an active, constitutive role in the construction and maintenance of these very systems. (2015: 2)

Objects co-create systems of cultural value. There is an alignment here with Braidotti's argument that the contemporary political and cultural globalised world generates faith experiences through material, embedded engagements with worldviews. Indeed, Matthews-Jones and Jones continue and extend this point, stating that:

> [r]eligiosity is not simply an internal belief that comes to find codified form in the written texts of religious institutions. Religion is also constructed in the day-to-day, through people's engagement with material things. Thus belief is not static, but negotiated through contact with everyday objects. *Belief is highly dependent on the sensory experiences that enable people to make meaning out of their faith.* (2015: 3, emphasis added)

Through a Deleuzo–Guattarian lens, faith is not dependent on sensory experience, but rather is a *product* of sensory experiences. Such sensory experiences are both responses to transcendental knowledge that is taught as religion and participation in the everyday events and cultural experiences that shape religion. Everyday experiences of being involved in visual, material and sensory cultures of religion produce our embodied imagination. Experiences create ideas of things, beliefs and faith in beliefs. From such a perspective, we can see that *religion is created as a response to faith*, which in turn is created by visual and material cultures.

Visual and material cultures are both located and globalised; for example, while Christianity's colonising project is echoed in its continued quantitative popularity (there are currently around 2.1 billion Christians worldwide), links between Christianity and colonisation have long been muddied by exceptions. For example, the Republic of Ireland, the first country to decolonise, has a substantial Catholic population; another example can be found in the contemporary majority of non-white Christian believers across the globe. After Christianity, Islam is the most practised religion, with around 1.3 billion followers, while Hinduism has 900 million. Of course, this list goes on. Religions always have been, and are now more than ever, global and globalising. This has implications for the continued and varied ways in which the colonial project is carried on through religions. Further, as Richard Mann (2014) shows, the colonial imperative was originally translated into scholarship in the form of disdain for the material:

> For many archaeologists and art historians during the colonial period such as Henry Cole, Alexander Cunningham and John Marshall ... the historical appearance of material culture in India was interpreted as a sign of religious decay. In the case of Buddhism, the tradition was perceived of as having degenerated from its 'original' rational and ethical heights to a corrupt, superstitious and idolatrous tradition. Indeed, for many, the sign of this degeneration was the emergence of Buddhist iconography, ritual and material culture. Similar narratives of decline and debasement were used to characterize Hinduism as well. The materiality of Hinduism and Buddhism was perceived as an indication of a society that had de-evolved from sophistication to superstition; a slide the British argued they would correct with their own notions of high religious culture. (2014: 267–8)

In order to avoid recolonising culture through scholarly paradigms that perform conceptual abstraction, we need to heed Braidotti's call for Europeans to develop a critical perspective on their imagination of themselves as 'moral guardians of the world' (2008: 8). We need to refuse to exchange transcendental thought for immanent thought which is mobilised in similarly problematic ways. This appeal is restated in different terms in Matthews-Jones and Jones's later work:

> The intellectual tradition that has privileged religion-as-thought over religion-as-material is part of that highly problematic modernist tradition in which all sorts of binaries – mind/body, male/female, modern/pre-modern, civilized/uncivilized, and so on – have taken on the appearance of universal truth rather than ideological construct. Just as we have come to question these binaries in relation to histories of gender and sexuality, for example, so too we should question assumptions made about practices of belief in modern societies. (2015: 4)

Materiality is as, if not more, constitutive of faith than thought. Belief is experienced as faith, because all faith needs to be understood as felt and embodied; it is a response to objects, ideas, places and practices. In *Material Christianity: Religion and Popular Culture in America*, Colleen McDannell (1995) offers a located perspective on the material organisation of feelings by explaining that:

> [t]he symbol systems of a particular religious language are not merely handed down, they must be learned through doing, seeing, and touching. Christian material culture does not simply reflect an existing reality. Experiencing the physical dimension of religion helps *bring about* religious values, norms, behaviors, and attitudes. Practising religion sets into play ways of thinking. It is the continual interaction with objects and images that makes one religious in a particular manner. (1995: 2)

As McDannell, Matthews-Jones and Jones, Cort and others show, material cultures shape patterns of feeling. Indeed, this is the case for those who have faith in the power of science and whose faith experiences are choreographed in relation to science laboratories and periodic tables, but also for those who have faith in religious deities or God.

A contemporary approach to thinking about faith, then, needs to be informed by both human and non-human intra-actions (Bräunlein, 2019). Visual and material cultures of religion need to be one of many key resources, along with philosophies of immanence that locate the body as core to knowledge production. This is a moment where philosophy needs to look outside itself and fold in otherness. Indeed, we can take Deleuze's (1992a) Spinozist dividual, the idea of the body as one part of a larger whole, filled with immanent knowledge; Gatens and Lloyd's (1999) bodies that share collective imaginings; or collaborative social fictions in Braidotti's (1994) nomadic subject as philosophical models that show us how the body intra-acts with the otherness of material cultures in ways that are constitutive of meaning. People draw on each other, their surroundings and lived as well as religious philosophy and science in determining their approach to faith. Philosophy becomes the 'subject looking for the ways in which otherness prompts, mobilizes and allows for the affirmation of what is not contained in the present conditions' (Braidotti, 2008: 19). To put this another way, philosophy and religious belief structures become ways people can think outside their immediate context: portals into other worlds, not the defining matter of faith.

This move to draw on material and visual cultural artefacts in developing our understanding of religion is carried on by the work of many. For example, in 'Integrating Texts and Material Culture: Methodological Approaches to the Study of Premodern Religions', Abhishek Amar (2012) suggests that 'the privileging of textual sources over archaeological ones has been a major problem in the historiography of premodern South Asian religions' (2012: 528). Amar's call for a reconsideration of the material echoes the earlier work of Jerome Levi (1998) who, in 'The Bow and the Blanket: Religion, Identity and Resistance in Rarámuri Material Culture', argues that 'renewed consideration of the material markers of internal differentiation is a complementary balance to recent discourse emphasizing linkages between global and local economies' (1998: 300). To put this another way, the detail in cultures and stories is often held and told in matter. Small differences and particularities are evidenced in things rather than words. Van der Tuin (after Elizabeth Grosz) characterises new materialism as a means for locating 'the surprise of the future that we find in the past' (2015: 10). Similarly, Levi argues that religious '*objects* are not inert relics from the past but, on the contrary, *are active strategies for the present*' (1998: 300, emphasis added). Religious objects are strategies for the present and for subjectivation; they are constellation points that shape faith experiences. Religious objects inform what David Morgan (2015) calls 'the social life of feeling'. Morgan also agrees with this contention that the body and embodied engagements with material cultures of religion shape social imaginations. He suggests that:

> [t]o belong to a community is to participate, to take part, to perform a role, to find a place within the imagined whole, which I have called the social body. Belief, it is important to point out, is not simply assent to dogmatic principles or credal propositions, but also the embodied or material practices that enact belonging to the group. The feeling that one belongs takes the shape of many experiences, unfolds over time, and is mediated in many forms. Moreover, belonging is nurtured by the aesthetic practices that are designed to generate and refine feeling on the crossed axes of human relationships and human–divine interaction. (Morgan, 2015: 141)

Intra-action between material aesthetics, feeling and sociality is how we come to belong. Aesthetics is at the core of our experience, but ideas also shape how we interact with material worlds and need to be considered as one of the factors impacting affective states – people have faith in ideas as much as in things. There is, then, a sense in which studies of the visual and material cultures of religion reify the material realm for existing outside iconoclastic ideals or dogmatic structures. While this is largely true, engagements with material cultures can also be iconoclastic, dogmatic and are often popularly entwined with ideology. Any distinct split between the material and conceptual is a binary that cannot be upheld in everyday life. Bağlı (2015) explains the messy nature of the meanings of things by gesturing towards the slippery nature of the material world. The existential, the abstract, and the material are always enmeshed. Bağlı notes:

> The special case of religious symbols differs from the symbols in daily life like traffic signs, where we can make the connection between signifier and signified much easier. However in the case of religion, the metaphysical or 'unknown' nature of the signified (God) and the interconnectedness of the signifier ... make the process of analysis much harder and more complicated. (2015: 306)

What is God? How is God expressed in objects and actions? What sustains faith? How does faith animate human actions? Questions such as these require an approach that is so much more specific than a relationship between a sign and a signifier. The lived experience of having faith is a complex assemblage that is different for everyone who has faith. It is a complex and context-specific mixture of the material, the immaterial, community ritual and family history. Bağlı (2015) examines this slipperiness, or this complexity, as a new terrain in scholarship, reminding us that:

> [i]f we are to talk about the functionality of a religious object, it is usually directly related to an action as a part of a ritual or a practice, e.g., prayer beads (rosaries), prayer rugs, etc. The symbolic aspect, however, is more peripheral. It uses representation of some abstract values connected to the system of belief or certain religious figures mostly in the form of icons, without necessarily being connected to any religious practice. (306)

Indeed, Bağlı is not the only scholar to argue (see Wang, 2018) that reading symbols as being significant to religious experiences is a colonial importation, if not a racist imposition.

Islamic culture's preference for calligraphy, its choreographic work around the body in prayer and its attention to how praying bodies are positioned in space and time are significant. So too are the material rituals of washing, fasting and sharing meals. These are the organising material cultural aspects of the religion that hold power, rather than the focus on symbols that characterise Catholic, Christian, Hindu and Buddhist religions. We need to have an intra-active, mutable, reshapeable and engaged material-conceptual position on what a new materialist philosophy of faith might be. Faith is engendered by ideas, practices, places, rituals and symbols, and these intersect in ways that generate zones of relationality and inform experiences of faith.

In her 2009 piece 'Grasping the Elusive and Unknowable: Material Culture in Ritual Practice', Nicole Boivin argues that:

> [f]ollowing scholars like Clifford Geertz, many archaeologists have, indeed, seen religion as a 'system of symbols'. The recognition that many of these symbols are material ones, recoverable in the archaeological record, has helped to make ancient religion somewhat accessible to the trowels (and interpretive frameworks) of archaeologists. [However, she also cautions that] despite increased interest in recent years in the material dimension of religious practice, particularly within the discipline of archaeology, studies of the material and artifactual aspects of ritual continue largely to overlook the materiality of ritual objects and landscapes. (2009: 269)

Boivin shows that material systems of signification are remade, reinvented within the tangle of context-specific intra-action that constitutes practices of faith. Coding systems break down and are hacked and recoded in everyday life. She continues, explaining that:

> A recognition of the relevance of the physical qualities of material signs had often been implicit in structuralist analyses in archaeology ... and both anthropologists and archaeologists came to recognize more explicitly that the meaning of material signs was often motivated by their physical qualities. One early anthropological example of such a recognition can be found in the work of Victor Turner, whose extensive mid-1960s analysis of ritual symbols among the Ndembu of Zambia explored in some detail the links between material signifiers and the concepts they signify. (2009: 272)

Turner's work is but one early example of the shifting meanings that religious symbols can hold. The other point I make in framing intra-action above is that sharing food, drink and community togetherness is a key part of entanglements that create faith. This, too, is a point made consistently in the literature examining material cultures of religion. For example, Uri Kaplan (2017) argues that the individual nature of faith is co-constituted by consumption (food and drink) in material culture, explaining how:

> [e]ating and drinking (and abstention from which) play central roles in religious rites, where re-enacting mythologies jogs to life collective memories and re-confirms religious adhesion and distinctiveness ... facilitating communication between individuals and their communities, as well as with their ancestors and gods. (2017: 4)

Putting the question of transubstantiation aside for now, it is clear that there are many ways in which the consumption of food is part of faith-assemblages. So too are ritual performances, as characterised by Christiane Gruber:

> Dodging dogma as verbalized in prescriptive texts and modern curbs implemented in more-conservative milieus, votive practices and objects have long been a hallmark of creative activity among members of the global Muslim community. Early Arabic narrative sources tell us about devotees placing votive candles in shrines, while contemporary Muharram mourning ceremonies provide their participants with a rich *Gesamtkunstwerk*, blending processional and musical performances with votive objects and foods. (2017: 99)

Faith, then, is produced through daily life performances, involvement in material culture, ideology, belief and, more than anything, *context*.

Questions of scale

In this book, I respond to, and move in and out of, three scales across which faith entanglements and unconscious orientations articulate: macro, meso and micro. Both explicitly and implicitly, I argue that, on a macro level, geographies and networks of faith, material economies and worldviews impact substantially upon an individual's capacities to act. Geographies and material economies of faith are both political and world-making. For example, where people are born often influences the religion or belief system into which they are born, as do the economic and material conditions into which they are born. War, economies and associated rises and falls in opportunities for employment are global events, part of flows and assemblages which impact the creation and spread of flows of religious and secular faiths. For example, many of the Australian participants in the research had sought refuge in Australia as a result of either the conflict between Israel and Palestine, the war in Afghanistan or the West Papuan separatist conflict. My research participants in England had migrated largely from Africa (Eritrea, Nigeria, Democratic Republic of the Congo, Zimbabwe), India, Bangladesh, Pakistan and Sri Lanka. Similarly, civil war was a significant motivating factor behind these migration patterns. There are global, macro movements that shape the individual life and faith stories represented here.

On a meso level, educational systems and family are structures that bridge the global and the personal and which can reinforce religious faith, teach different religious faiths, question religious faiths and undoubtedly impact the ways that faith systems are maintained. The individual and community geographies of belonging that constitute people's everyday lives demonstrate the complex entanglements of matter and belief that make up lived faith worlds. An example of this is the national discourses about faith in participants' countries of residence and the religious organisations or school communities to which individuals belong, orient and inform their faith experiences. Medina from Adelaide draws a direct line between her national religion and her choice to invest in religion over ethnicity:

> *Beginning with my religious background, I'm Muslim, so I belong to the religion of Islam. I was, I would say, fortunately born into it, because my parents were both Muslims. They were Bangladeshi Muslim, so that's my ethnicity part. I belong to Bangladesh, it's a country in South-East Asia, very close to India, but it's a country of its own, and it has not just Islam as a religion, although the government runs on Islam ... it has Islamic inclusions in it. But there is Hinduism, there's Buddhism, and Christianity, but they are a minority. Yeah, but we actually did get a chance as a Bangladeshi to integrate into other religions as well. But, in my household we always try to keep our identity as a Muslim at a higher level than being a Bangladeshi, because there are points where religion and the Bangladeshi culture do clash, and ... my dad was always very firm with his belief in*

Islam and he taught us how to differentiate where it's going wrong, or where religion is not being accepted by the Bangladeshi culture because of their own background and historical events, that actually made some changes with how people follow Islam there. (Medina, south-west Adelaide focus group, 2019)

Medina primarily identifies with being Muslim above all other community attachments. At a micro level, Medina shows us how faith can be a form of what Spinoza (1996) would call 'joy', a feeling generated by an extension of the capacity to act. However, in other circumstances, faith is what Berlant (2011) calls 'cruel optimism'. That is, faith can be a deferral of the present based on a hope for other things. Educational and biographic experiences orient people towards their faith – be it religious or secular.

Faith as bodily affect

Having faith can increase, or alternatively decrease, a body's capacity to act. Value judgements about faith can stop a person from connecting with another, can cause rejection, and create a 'sharp edge' (Barad, 2003: 803). Faith can also provide the capacity to reach out to others, to be there for others, to keep people going. Many people in my research tell stories of moving across the world, living through wars and surviving change and separation from family, and their stories make clear the fact that faith can sustain people through very difficult times. Rafi, a Muslim man living in Melbourne, explains his journey to relative safety in Australia:

Ten years ago, I came from Christmas Island [an immigration detention centre]. I had only one T-shirt from Immigration. One small shirt. The shirt is from Immigration. Nothing else. And at the moment, I have a house, two, three cars. My life is not rich. Not the bottom. In the middle. Similar like someone who is born in Australia. We live the same way. It's the best country. I think it's the best, best country in the world. (Rafi, south-east Melbourne focus group, 2019)

Rafi had lived in Afghanistan until fleeing the war, and he arrived on Christmas Island in 2009. His Muslim faith sustained him not just through war, but through the difficult process of seeking asylum and the complex task of building a new life. He explains: 'All religion is looking for one way, to follow, to look for a God' (southeast Melbourne focus group, 2019). It seems to me that, as Rafi and many others suggest, this act of looking for a God can give bodies the capacity to keep going. Rafi and Ersheen, a mother in Manchester, whom I discuss in the chapter on incapacity, both went to great lengths to explain the similarities between Muslim and Christian relationships; they offered detailed academic accounts of these similarities that stood out from many other comments on the similarity of religions.

While these accounts illustrate faith as a way of extending people's capacities to act, my research has also shown that faith can generate embodied limits. For example, I was told I was 'going to hell' for believing that all religions are equal by an angry Christian minister's secretary in the religiously conservative outer west suburbs of Sydney. On some level, I think I am still recovering from her denunciation. Therefore, faith also creates (in)capacity, and can be thought of as both enabling and disabling. Another example of limits to acting is given by Joanie, who explains feeling rejected by Muslim mothers, one of whom said to her, 'You know what I mean' as a justification for why her daughter from a north Pakistani Muslim family and Joanie's white, English, secular daughter should not be friends.

Creating affect, faith aligns subjects to experience a moment in which 'the mind is assailed by any emotion, [and] the body is affected at the same time by a modification whereby its power of acting is either increased or diminished' (Spinoza, 1996: 148). Deleuze, and Deleuze and Guattari subsequently argue that *affect* refers to changes in bodily capacity. The body to which Deleuze refers is not necessarily human. It is a degree of power held within any given assemblage or *mixture*. Faith creates affects, in that it extends or decreases the limits of what a *body* – or *a given assemblage or mixture* – can do. An affect, then, is the margin of change in capacity: a material and/or conceptual bloc that articulates an increase or decrease in a body's capacity to act.

The term *faith* can, in fact, be employed in exchange with *affect* to refer to changing bodies: to what a body can do. The actual changes caused by the experience of faith are *affectus*, the empirical increase or decrease in subjective capacity made by an affect (Marrati, 2006; Clough, 2008; Hickey-Moody, 2009, 2013a, 2013b; Parr, 2010;

Duff, 2014). As I have explained elsewhere (Hickey-Moody, 2020), in *Spinoza, Practical Philosophy*, Deleuze says that an *affectus* is '[a]n increase or decrease of the power of acting, for the body and the mind alike' (1988: 49). He builds on this definition through arguing that *affectus* is different from emotion. While emotion is the psychological striation of affect, *affectus* is the way our experiences change our subjectivity; it is the virtuality and materiality of the increase or decrease effected in a body's power of acting. Objects such as religious icons, experiences of reciting a prayer, joining a community in praying or eating, are enculturating, enculturated, affective experiences. Deleuze explains:

> The affection refers to a state of the affected body and implies the presence of the affecting body, whereas the affectus refers to the passage [or movement] from one state to another ... there is a difference in nature between the image affections or ideas and the feeling affect. (1988: 49)

Thus, *affectus* is the materiality of change: it is *the passage from one state to another* which occurs in relation to *affecting bodies*. Image affections, or the 'ideas' to which Deleuze refers, can be the idea of a God, or gods, or an image of the religious deities or figures in which people believe. Increasing or decreasing one's capacity to act is the modulation of *affectus*: the virtual and material change that prompts affection or *feeling* in consciousness (Hickey-Moody, 2013a, 2013b). Faith attachments and the act of believing in something create virtual and material change that prompts affection or the *feeling of affect* in consciousness.

Deleuze's work on affect as changes in embodied capacities begins with his reading of Spinoza. In *Spinoza, Practical Philosophy*, Deleuze explains:

> The affections [*affectiones*] are the modes [forms of life] themselves. The modes are the affections of substance [matter, the universal] or of its attributes ... These affections are not necessarily active, since they are explained by the nature of God as adequate cause, and God cannot be acted upon. At a second level, the affections designate that which happens to the mode, the modifications of the mode [*affectus*], the effects of other modes on it. These affections are therefore images or corporeal traces first of all and their *ideas* involve both the nature of the affected body and that of the affecting external body. (1988: 48)

Deleuze reminds us of how feelings, and to this I would add beliefs, mark out our emotional geographies. This is Deleuze's Spinozist framework for thinking about the ways ideas and interactions can create conceptual and material changes. For Spinoza, substance is the stuff of which life is made. Substance is expressed in modes, which are changed (affected or *modulated*) by affections (*affectiones*). *Affectiones* are traces of interaction: residues of experience that live in thought and in the body. They make affects, modulations marked by our feelings. Faith, then – the belief that something is possible, or that something is inherently wrong – changes capacities in ways that are marked by feelings. Faith in religion, faith in social values or faith in science choreographs people, societies and relationalities. Following this understanding of assemblages of places, objects, people, beliefs, as ways of shaping patterns of feeling, we can see that faith can become a map, an internal–external set of coordinates that moves bodies to act and react in certain ways. This map is living; it is a dynamic, responsive, and very alive part of people's engagements with their contexts. In being responsive, faith is always being remade; it shapes streams of consciousness that flow across established patterns of feeling.

In the examples I give above, and indeed in much of my discussion in this book, the example of faith given is of religion; however, as Joanie's story, and as many other accounts of belief in secularism show, the experience of faith is bigger than (and extends beyond) the experience of religion. Indeed, as I have suggested, faith in science can also be seen as a form of religion.

Faith as joy

Faith can be a form of joy. Spinoza (1996) discusses different kinds of joy: active and passive joys that can arise from vicarious experience or from acting through good intent, which he calls 'good encounters'. Writing on good encounters, Deleuze explains that:

> Reason's only commandment ... is to link a maximum of passive joys with a maximum of active ones. For joy is the only passive affection that increases our power of action, and of all affections joy alone can be active. The slave may be recognized by his sad passions, and the free man by his joys, passive and active. The sense of joy is revealed

Faith: a new materialist approach / Creideamh

as the truly ethical sense; it is to the practical sphere what affirmation itself is to the speculative ... A philosophy of pure affirmation, the *Ethics* is also a philosophy of the joy corresponding to such affirmation. (1992b: 272)

Active joys are those we work for, rather than those we experience by chance. When faith is a way of extending the capacities of others to act, as well as extending one's own capacity to act, this affords the marriage of reason and passions and creates active joy. Deleuze continues, stating that 'joyful passions increase our power of action; reason is the power of understanding, the power of action belonging to the soul; so joyful passions agree with reason, and lead us to understand, or determine us to become reasonable' (1992b: 273–4). For many, their faith is a resource they use to survive and navigate difficult life changes: a source of reason. Faith is also a means of supporting their family and community: a way of increasing the power of acting. As a way of understanding differences, faith allows many to become reasonable.

Spinoza discusses three kinds of joy, two of which are accidental. Indirect and partial joys are experienced as a result of benefiting from the misfortune of others, or of being pleased by something that might give passing pleasure but might not actually extend our capacity to act. He here explains indirect and partial joys in Spinoza's work by saying that:

> We must also take account of other concrete factors, for the first sort of encounter, good encounters with bodies whose relation combines directly with our own, remains altogether hypothetical. The question is, once we exist, is *there any chance of us naturally having good encounters, and experiencing the joyful affections that follow from them?* The chances are in fact slight enough ... There is, then, very little chance of our naturally having good encounters. We seem to be determined to much contest, much hatred, and to the experience of only partial or indirect joys which do not sufficiently disrupt the chain of our sorrows and hatreds. Partial joys are 'titillations' which only ever increase our power of action at one point by reducing it everywhere else. Indirect joys are those we experience in seeing a hated object sad or destroyed; but such joys remain imprisoned in sadness. Hate is in fact a sadness, itself involving the sadness from which it derives; the joys of hatred mask this sadness and inhibit it, but can never eliminate it. (Deleuze, 1992b: 244–5)

Spinoza's sad reading of the natural orientation of human beings towards hate is quite an indictment on the human condition. He establishes the ethical orientation of his work – true joy entails increasing other people's, as well as one's own, capacity to act. Joy is achievable only when reason and intuition align. Deleuze further explains that:

> The primary question of the *Ethics* is thus: What must we do in order to be affected by a maximum of joyful passions? Nature does not favour us in this respect. But we should rely on the efforts of reason, the very slow empirical effort which finds in the City the conditions that make it possible: reason in the first principle of its development, or in its initial aspect, is the effort to organize encounters in such a way that we are affected by a maximum of joyful passions. For joyful passions increase our power of action; reason is the power of understanding, the power of action belonging to the soul; so joyful passions agree with reason, and lead us to understand, or determine us to become reasonable. (1992b: 273–4)

Here, Deleuze explains Spinoza's alignment between reason, intuition and action. This alignment is part of the work of 'becoming reasonable' and developing one's own capacity to act. Many of the accounts of religious and secular faith given in this book explain the tectonics of joyful passions: the ideas, actions, contexts and histories that inspire acts of *becoming reasonable* in relation to others, of increasing one's own – and other's – capacities to act. The production of joy can be identified as one of the dominant discourses of faith. It is, however, not the only 'big picture' story that faith cultures produce. While faith is usually a positive agent in people's lives, it can, as some of the stories discussed in chapters to come will show, also be a promise that operates as a form of cruel optimism, something that is never actually realised. Faith can be a series of sacrifices one makes in the hope they might be exchanged for a better future.

Faith as promise, object and exchange value

In *Cruel Optimism*, Lauren Berlant (2011) discusses the feelings of failure, and the process of what she calls 'slow death', that can arise from trying to change habits that are perhaps not in our best interest (think: smoking, eating too much, having unprotected sex with multiple partners). In this part of the chapter, I explore some of Berlant's astute observations about unrealised and impossible desire in a very different context, not in relation to people trying to change when social, biological, economic and institutional structures prevent this possibility, but rather in relation to religious faith as a form of slow death. In such instances, religious faith demonstrates 'the cruelty of optimism revealed to people without control over the material conditions of their lives' (2011: 46). Berlant examines unfulfillable promises, often embedded in objects of desire, as one example of cruel optimism. She also discusses the promise of exchange value as another form of cruel optimism. Each of these ways of thinking offers insight into some faith experiences.

Faith objects and surfaces

In some contexts, religious faith operates as a form of cruel optimism in which 'proximity to the object means proximity to the cluster of things that the object [symbolising faith] promises' (Berlant, 2011: 23). Faith in religion can, depending on its configuration, lead to believing in a 'cluster of promises ... embedded in a person, a thing, an institution, a text, a norm' (Berlant, 2011: 23). This is not necessarily a bad thing; as I show in the discussion above, the experience when an idea and practice come together (or intuition and reason meet) can be a joyful and sustaining experience. However, like all things, faith – either faith in medicine, science or religious faith – is not always able to be joyful and sustaining. It can be a set of impossibilities or refusals. Medicine cannot cure all ills. Science alone cannot stop climate change. Being religious does not necessarily make a person good or caring. In some instances, religious faith can be an endless deferral of pleasure which may never come to fruition, and which may value acts of pleasure deferral undertaken in relation to object attachments. Berlant explains this by stating, 'all attachments are optimistic. When we talk about an object of desire, we are really talking about a cluster of promises we want someone or something to make us and make possible for us' (2011: 23). All religions have faith objects: shrines to elders and their ghosts, images or statues of deities, prayer beads, holy books, the crucifix, a prayer mat, the Ka'bah; attachments to objects related to religious faith are part of the practices of orthodox and non-orthodox religious people in ways that facilitate attachments of different kinds. Like objects, surfaces also form sites of attachment: landscapes, the outsides of communities, physical and social edges, unexpected connections between people or places become things to believe in. Berlant explains:

> So many of the normative and singular objects made available for investing in the world are themselves threats to both the energy and the fantasy of ongoingness, namely, that people/collectivities face daily the cruelty not just of potentially relinquishing their objects or changing their lives, but of losing the binding that fantasy itself has allowed to what's potentially there in the risky domains of the yet untested and unlived life. (2011: 48)

People's attachments to objects or surfaces symbolising hopes and ideas are often more powerful than attachments to others or one's surroundings. Pilgrimages to holy places and attachments to religious icons or objects come to mind here. Each religion has its own version of faith object or place attachment, such as Virgin Mary shrines, rosary beads, Hajj, malas, temples and so on. Here, an object or surface stands in for the rewards or qualities that the believer holds dear. Berlant also discusses the promise of exchange value as another form of cruel optimism. This approach also offers insights into some faith experiences.

Prayer as exchange value

Cruel optimism is expressed in the possibility of exchange value, the kinds of intersubjective relationships that are cultivated through entertaining and voicing attachments to possibilities of promising qualities that are yet to materialise. Berlant examines the performance of investment in possible exchange value in ways that remind me of the act of prayer; namely a practice of annunciation spoken to a hearer who is not physically present:

> the condition of projected possibility, of a hearing that cannot take place in the terms of its annunciation ('you' are not here, 'you' are eternally belated to the conversation with you that I am imagining) creates a fake present moment of intersubjectivity in which, nonetheless, a performance of address can take place. (Berlant, 2011: 25)

Prayer can be seen as an imagined conversation with God, an imagined intersubjective moment. The above quote brought into my mind a mother, a Serbian refugee living in Melbourne, who explained she felt that she needed to save her attachment for the afterlife. Malina explains that:

> *I'm trying not to get too attached to recipes or things or places or anything. For me, they're not important to me. Sorry. For me it's like my prayer, my beliefs, it's like that's what I – I love my family and everything, but one day just my other friend she told me her husband just passed away. How? Like he was a perfectly looking, healthy young man. It's just – one day people are here, and another day they are gone. You know? It just makes you think they're here, that's my family. But how much is that important? It's like the next day you're just going to leave and leave everything there, even your friends and family. Nothing of that matters anymore.* (Malina, southeast Melbourne focus group, 2019)

Here, we see faith as exchange value, faith in the afterlife is exchanged for daily investment in her children or husband. Malina is living her life in the hope of other worlds.

Conclusion

In this chapter, I have situated this book in relation to the literature on materialism and religion while defining the remit of the book as considering faith as being larger than a focus on religion alone. I have drawn on the work of Spinoza, Deleuze and Berlant to think about faith as both positive and negative in the lives of my research participants. I have explored the micro, meso and macro scales across which faith articulates. I have tried to show that, in some ways, all those who have faith make it themselves, even if they do so unconsciously. Rituals, consumption practices and signification practices are citational modes that choreograph faith experiences.

The theoretical resources assembled in this chapter demonstrate my belief that any useful philosophical perspective on faith needs to be informed by interdisciplinary knowledge, since '[w]hen scholars of religion write on materiality … they generally benefit from an art historian's perspective, just as art historians with scant training in religious studies frameworks may benefit from the insights of a reader in that discipline' (Floyd and Promey, 2018: 267). In developing my own new materialist perspective on faith and drawing on interdisciplinary resources to think about the production of faith as an affective experience, I want to show the complex ways people are moved to believe. We all have faith in something. Our faith is both an expression of context and a political act. Faith, like the body, is a thermometer of social becomings and, wherever we are situated and whatever we profess, faith is the means by which we continue to become who we are. In moving forward, I investigate situated faith in its material-conceptual-social and historical complexity.

Note

1 Lauren Berlant (2011) explains this idea by noting the amount of women who defer the pleasure of eating in the hope of being rewarded by weight loss.

3

Mapping and making / *Ag déanamh*

Introduction

In this chapter, I explain my research methods. They primarily consist of a multi-sited ethnography, which I extend with arts-based methods for young research participants. Arts-based methods are an excellent way of communicating complex information. Life experiences are not always able to be expressed in words, and often my research participants speak languages other than English, but the artworks they create communicate affectively, regardless of language. In this book, I examine stories from my qualitative data only, while my extensive quantitative data is considered elsewhere (Hickey-Moody, Horn and Garg, 2023). In my ethnographic work, I look for everyday stories and experiences of belonging, faith attachment and 'what really matters'. These experiences are often expressed through images, words, memory, allegory, anecdote and collaborative exchanges. My approach to research, and to what is popularly termed 'data collection', is concerned with making space to recognise subjugated, non-mainstream knowledges. Making art with culturally and linguistically diverse children and talking to their parents is an everyday decolonising approach (Menon, Thapar-Björkert and Tlostanova, 2021) to a feminist, new materialist methodology (Coleman, Page and Palmer, 2019) concerned with the agency of experience, places, matter and things. My approach acknowledges the centrality and importance of vernacular culture (Fiske, 1989) and responds to the agency of matter and political landscapes that shape global flows of faith and local communities (see Harris, 2017).

My methodology recognises that meaning and communication are often non-verbal and are constituted in the vital present in ways that are shaped by complex political, social and cultural histories (Hickey-Moody, 2011, 2013, 2019). The methods I have developed de-centre dominant and, thus, often explicitly colonial stories, and physically and materially make space for affective communication through centring the voices that emerge from migrant communities. My materialist methods span a range of media and employ various making practices. These methods offer different articulations of my core theoretical position: that attachments and orientations are often experienced and performed unconsciously. Such methods may be best understood affectively, by working with the material and the unconscious. In what is to follow, firstly I explain my multi-sited ethnography as a feminist new materialist practice with a decolonial ethic. I then examine the methods – many of which are presented in the form of lesson or workshop plans – as a performance of my methodology. I also introduce the focus groups and interviews that I employed when working with adult research participants.

Multi-sited ethnography

Multi-sited ethnography is a set of practices popularised by George Marcus in 1995 to describe 'ethnographies … both in and of the world system' (95). Many scholars have taken up multi-sited ethnography as a method (Burawoy, 2000; Francisco-Menchavez, 2018; Kenway, Kraack and Hickey-Moody, 2006). The primary difference between what once might have been considered 'classic' ethnography and multi-sited ethnography is that multi-sited ethnography is a method for exploring relationships between communities across the globe. It enables researching global themes and patterns of experience, such as connections to religion or, in this case, faith. Multi-sited ethnography has been usefully critiqued by Ghassan Hage (2005) in a way that breathes life into the project of undertaking a multi-sited ethnography in transnational contexts. Hage makes some points of critique that I suggest can (perhaps unexpectedly) be read as explaining exactly why multi-sited ethnography might be useful. More than this, his perspective is grounded in practice in a way that brings the ethnographic experience to life. My eyes grew moist with tired recognition while reading Hage's (2005) discussion of jetlag, exhaustion and the practical difficulties of international multi-sited ethnography. Often the logistics of multi-sited ethnography require more from a person than they can give.

Before discussing this further, I want to introduce my reading of multi-sited ethnography. I sketch out some of the ways we might come to understand a multi-sited ethnography as a:

> less common mode of ethnographic research self-consciously embedded in a world system, now often associated with the wave of intellectual capital labelled postmodern, [that] moves out from the single sites and local situations of conventional ethnographic research designs to *examine the circulation of cultural meanings, objects and identities in diffuse space-time*. (Marcus, 1995: 96, emphasis added)

Multi-sited ethnography is embedded in more than one place. Ethnographic research is typically concerned with understanding culture from the 'inside' and developing site-specific knowledge about cultural meaning. In contrast to this, multi-sited ethnography looks for cultural meanings that are important in more than one place. It is a conversation between places that is made up of issues, attachments and experiences shared between sites. For example, all my research sites featured children who were worried about climate change, and parents who were interested in faith in unorthodox ways. Multi-sited ethnography finds resonances (and differences) across places, people, culture and things.

The central purpose of my ethnography is to map the circulation of cultural meanings, objects and identities in diffuse space-time. This purpose is explained by Hage's (2005) suggestion that when undertaking multi-sited ethnography, one must 'treat all these locations, dispersed as they [a]re, as just one site' (466). The global sites in which my ethnography is embedded are both world systems and lived experiences of cultural meanings of faith, objects, surfaces and identities. Systems of schooling, religions, the global politics of migration and associated migration services, are transnational structures that I have come to know through weeks and months of being embedded in their operations. Within and outside of these systems, I paid attention to the circulation of cultural meanings of belonging as well as meanings of faith, home and terrorism and of objects, such as the Virgin Mary, the headscarf, the altar and the prayer mat. The cultural meanings, objects and identities that led my inquiry were defined by my research participants. They are not necessarily what I was 'looking for' in understanding faith communities, so much as what I found. Across the book, I explore the themes of young identities as defined in relation to friendship, religion, soccer, the spectre of adolescence and climate change. Even though these stories are told by many different voices across a variety of social contexts and places, their similarities are striking.

Multi-sited ethnography is an ethnographic practice that traces cultural meanings across sites. Without initially intending to, I have conducted an ethnography of children's plans for combating climate change, as this theme came up as 'what really matters' to them. Therefore, I have explored this theme as part of an ethnography that explores faith, religion and belonging, community and attachment. All these themes characterise data from twelve sites and two countries. Multi-sited ethnography is a practice comprised of 'strategies of quite literally following connections, associations and putative relationships' (Marcus, 1995: 97). More than this, Marcus (2011) notes that multi-sited ethnography looks 'beyond the situated subjects of ethnography towards *the system of relations which define them*' (19, emphasis added), such as class, race, language, religion, gender and sexuality.

Class is expressed non-verbally through geography, taste and aspiration. Race articulates differently for everyone – there is no one way of being Bangladeshi-English or Palestinian-Australian. However, race is an enduring organising feature of subjectivity, religion and community life in the Australian and English communities in which I worked. Language, which is invariably tied closely to emotion, imagination and aspiration, is something I have worked to avoid relying on solely as a totalising system for exchanging information. I have tried to create ways of sharing information that also incorporate the non-discursive. The people involved in my project speak a wide variety of languages at home: Bengali, Urdu, Khmer, Vietnamese, Punjabi, Persian, Samoan, Rohingya, Arabic, Burmese, Maori, Bosnian, Tamil, Mandarin, Greek, Sinhalese, Filipino and Dinka, to name but a few. However, most people wanted to speak to me in English as much as possible, without interpreters. I was constantly told not to book interpreters, or I booked interpreters that participants did not want to use, as the opportunity to speak

English with a fluent English speaker was relished as an opportunity for language development. I protested that we should speak in the 'language you think and feel in', but, for the most part, my research participants did not care what I said – they wanted to practise their English with me and nothing was going to stop that from happening. They were understandably proud of the English they had acquired and preferred to talk using the few English words they had. Often, I left an interview or focus group trying to come up with a new strategy for involving interpreters in conversations.

The last three organising systems that I see as shaping research participants' experiences of their social and spiritual worlds are religion, gender and sexuality. Religion is fabulously diverse, not just in terms of the number of different religions that exist, but also in terms of what constitutes religion for those who are religious, and indeed for those who are not. Differences between religion and culture are as divergent as individual people. As I have argued, those who are not religious are still sustained by faith: faith in capitalism, faith in doing the right thing, faith that there is something else 'out there'. I went into this ethnography somewhat naive about how competitive some religious communities actually can be. Church and mosque communities are all very distinct – the church that was substantially involved in this ethnography is politically progressive and is very different from other churches I approached in my research. In no uncertain terms, the mosque communities in Australia and London were more welcoming and more genuinely interested in my work than the church communities. Within these communities, I have been part of really interesting conversations about differences and relationships between faith, religion and culture. Outside religious institutions, I have learnt about the porosity of religion in ways I never imagined. In writing this sentence I can see in my mind's eye several mothers who changed how I thought about what it means to be Muslim. For example, a mother in an inner Melbourne suburb wears a burqa, and when I asked her about her religious practices, she explained that she prays every day. Not five times a day, but every day. I asked her about praying at her local mosque and she said she did not have a mosque, but rather prayed at home. She lives in an area with many mosques, but clearly was not interested in leaving her home to pray. This was not the only woman who identified as Muslim but did not belong to a physical religious institution. A mother in south-east London offered a very similar account of her religious life, saying she prays at home, where she prepares food for her family and watches TV in her first language (Punjabi). She doesn't know the names of any of the local mosques, nor does she visit them. These women are connected to their spiritual practices and have strong religious identities, but they are not part of networks that extend beyond their homes. These examples of faith belonging stick to me: they are everyday, vernacular ways of believing and persisting that have been developed to suit people's characters and lives. These are the kinds of stories I found in abundance: stories that animate the unorthodox ways faith works in people's lives.

Very few of my research participants say that their religion is their culture; rather, for most, it is a set of practices that reflects their beliefs. However, sometimes people's religious lives occur almost entirely outside religious institutions. In west Sydney, I caught up for lunch with Reyhan, a research participant who had moved from Adelaide. I got to know her through my fieldwork in Adelaide and I would consider her to be a very religious person. Moving to Sydney had taken her away from her mosque community and introduced much longer commutes into her life: Sydney is a much larger city than Adelaide and is notoriously expensive. Reyhan explained to me that making prayer time was now much more difficult because she did not have a local mosque to which she was connected. She was having to bring a mat to work and pray there, and she missed having the community that a mosque brought with it, the community that her mosque south-west of Adelaide had been. Most of my Hindu research participants prayed at home with home altars, and those who were Buddhist or religiously hybrid (e.g. both Christian and Muslim), or 'spiritual but not religious', developed a sense of themselves as a spiritual person outside institutional life through reflection and intentional life practices. What struck me most when I began this work in 2016, and is accounted for by Ammerman's superb discussions of finding religion in everyday life (2014), are these independently religious people, whose identities are religious, and yet who are not part of an institutionalised group (Ammerman, 2013, 2014). Ammerman suggests that understanding these people is a scholarly project that requires a turn to thinking about materiality. The places in which people pray, the icons to which they pray, are their institutions. She explains, '[l]ooking for lived religion does mean that we look for the material, embodied aspects of religion as they occur in everyday life, in addition to listening for how people explain themselves' (2014: 190). I follow this approach in my interviews, focus groups and ethnographic observations.

My research participants are involved in diverse communities: some are religious and some are non-religious, but they nevertheless remain sustained by all kinds of faith. Family homes animate faith in all kinds of ways, every day. While I often joined in prayers in Adelaide, Sydney and Manchester, I also really wanted to pop over for home prayer with many of the participants I met through schools who did not pray in institutional settings. As I go on to discuss, for the children in the fieldwork, religion is a transversal space characterised mainly by other worlds, or the possibilities of other worlds. Children worry about climate change and how to stop it, they are connected to soccer, and many think about ice-cream as much as God. They hope for futures that involve faith-based pilgrimages and places of worship, alongside developing the skills to stop the destruction of the planet. Believing something is possible – be it seeing God, or stopping climate change – is a huge act of faith.

Gender is a fundamental organising feature of human life. Like all people's experiences of being human, for the children and adults involved in the study, gender shapes how they become who they are, how they relate to the world and form attachments to it. Gender orients people's relationships to religion and faith practices. For example, a caring and engaged father in a church community in Adelaide was left feeling uncomfortable after we went for prayers in a mosque, having been separated from his daughter for the duration of the prayer. She had come with me into the women's prayer area, but for him, parenting is closely linked to his spirituality, so praying is something best done with the family together. Another father in east London explained how his relationship with Islam deepened after his father died. For him, his religious identity was a way of feeling close to his father once he was no longer alive. He grew a beard and started wearing a *taqiyah* (Muslim cap). He took his son on a pilgrimage to Mecca. His masculinity and religion were very closely linked, as the way he had learnt to be a man, following his father, was to be a Muslim man. There are aligned stories to be told about women and the veil and the intimate relationship between the gendering of religious practice and identity. Suffice it to say, everyone's distinctive approach to religion or faith is intricately entwined with their gender identity.

Sexuality is the final organising factor that orients my participants' lives. I explore this, along with a discussion of class, race and digital community in the chapters to come. Here, I briefly introduce sexuality as an organising feature of both children's and adults' subjectivities. Children's sexualities are attitudes that shape how they take up space. They express their pleasures and desires in a sideways fashion (Bond Stockton, 2009). Their sexuality is ubiquitous. As 'adults' we are taught not to be interested in children's sexuality, because any such interest is assumed to be perverse. Therefore, it can be quite hard to put into words the non-sexual experiences of learning about nascent child sexuality. Religion and sexuality are closely linked, as both are expressions of a person's most intimate self. Stories about religion and sexuality that I have heard show that religion is almost a sexual experience for some, but also acknowledge how much more work needs to be undertaken in order for religious spaces to be able to accommodate and make space for discussions around sexuality (Rasmussen, 2017). Such conversations need to happen more often, as media discourses broadly construct sexuality as a secular concern, whereas my research, and indeed much other research on religious families and cultures (Ammerman, 2013, 2014), shows us that this is not the case: spirituality and sexuality are closely linked, regardless of religious and sexual orientation.

The organising features and contextual expressions of the world systems of class, race, language, religion, gender and sexuality create my sites of ethnographic investigation, along with the themes arising from the children of climate change solutions, football, friendship, intergenerational relationships and fear of homelessness. These themes are significant, as they point to other worlds, to relationships with adults, and identify a lack of trust in the adult world. The children's faith in the idea that another world is possible (a world where we can stop climate change and eat ice-cream) is one of the most significant acts of faith I discovered. A focus on themes differentiates a multi-sited ethnography from other forms of ethnography. Multi-sited ethnography is a study of themes or experiences, and only secondly a study of place and individual identities.

Marcus (2011) operationalises an 'understanding of the multi-sited field emerging from strategic collaborations with which fieldwork begins' (23). He looks to study 'distributed knowledge systems' (24) in which 'the object of ethnographic inquiry is ... moving' (25). For me, this 'moving object' of ethnographic inquiry is often a symbol, colour, pattern, idea, practice, orientation or mode of embodiment. Marcus's 'distributed knowledge systems' include school curricula, religious beliefs and practices and systems of governance (welfare, schooling, law). Ethnography therefore becomes, in part, the act of 'stage managing in collaboration with connected events of dialogue and independent inquiries around them' (Marcus, 2011: 28). This quote stood out to me because it explains the responsive nature of maintaining conversations across geographical places. Responsivity is critical when listening to resonances between children's voices, cultures and engagements with systems in the UK and Australia. Below, I briefly discuss some examples of global circulating cultural meanings that frame my research, before going on to situate the political nature of my inquiry.

Circulating meanings of community and belonging

People experience community and belonging in diverse ways. In my fieldwork these include attachments to queer culture, being part of online single-parenting communities, work communities and volunteering communities, ethnic and religious communities, local and diasporic geographic communities, school communities and football communities. I developed my research methods specifically to ask about and understand people's attachments to, and their experiences of, community, as well as to invite discussions of differences between perceived dominant discourses about lived cultures. Some of the many responses that parents offered when I asked them about their experiences of community include the following statements chosen from different research sites:

> I live in Atherton Gardens (an estate), so I feel like I'm in the local community ... all the kids there. Yeah, I grew up there, went to school there, came to this school too. (Kirsten, inner-north Melbourne focus group, 2019)

Religion is something that sticks with you, I guess – and you don't forget it. When you are taught it [religion], you just rely on it. And it does stick with you throughout the whole week and it doesn't change. In the community it's, let's say, a way of belonging when you're with other people, because I am Christian and Muslim. (Anna, west Sydney focus group, 2018)

I've been building a mums' network community, of which I'd say I was strongly part of, which is part of a group of mothers in the Greenwich Peninsula. I'm deliberately focused on doing that. And also a group in East Greenwich for isolated women. And I'm just about to join a community of parents with mixed-heritage children. Because the parents don't always have the heritage information, so it's to come together and work around supporting each other and also sharing. (Emily, south-east London focus group, 2018)

My mum was training to be a reverend, so I would say that the Church of England and going to church was something that we would always do. I was in that community, until I had to start working on Sundays, so I had to drop my involvement in that community a little bit to get some money. But my daughter very much goes to church. My dad wasn't very religious but he really gave support to mum, so I would say that's progressive faith in itself. I think their work ethic is crazy and that's rubbed off on me a little bit, so I would say that's a community I'm closest to. (Jackie, north-west Manchester focus group, 2018)

My dad's part of the Ahmadi Muslim community and they are hugely community-centred. So that is an absolute strength. There is this community focus, because it is largely Pakistani-dominated. I mean there are lots of converts from all around the world, it's growing very fast. But there is a really, really, really strong sense of community and giving and service … Like if you were to go to any event run by this church community, it is amazing. There are always older boys manning the gates and I mean, it tends to be very gendered, which I don't like. But there are girls just going automatically and helping with the cooking, kids and the minding. And there's this real sense of village. And I feel like that is hugely lacking in Australia as a culture. (Samia, inner-east Adelaide focus group, 2018)

For our community, we always do the open mosque day or something like that. We always open our hand, but we are afraid to go into like a general Australian like what they are doing. For us, because we want our kids to be brought up as an Aussie because they're living here,

Mapping and making / Ag déanamh 59

they have to be mingling with everybody. Not only in the Muslim community. So we put them in scouts which makes them able to interact with everybody, not only their friends, in their own groups. (Zahar, Canberra focus group, 2019)

These quotes give some indication of the diverse ways women – and in this instance, women from Melbourne, west Sydney, south-east London, Manchester, Adelaide and Canberra – experience community: through place, race, religion, family, history and recreation. A number of mothers taught ways of understanding cultural differences through food, like, for example, Sophie from Manchester who explains how her grocery-shopping experience has changed as a result of:

the amount of Black people, mixed-race people now because it makes it easier, you know to get yam, to get potato, cassava, things like that, okra. (Sophie, inner-south Manchester focus group, 2018)

More than anything else, I am interested in people's experiences of community and belonging. Discourses and experiences of community and belonging circulate across the ways that both adults and children respond to, and engage with, my research methods. I developed the methods to understand, express and explore people's experiences of community and belonging. Notably, community and belonging are different for everyone, and they are not something that people are always able to define explicitly: some might say they are an active member of the church, but until I ask about community, people often don't use the word 'community'. I read any sense of attachment to a collective as a form of community belonging, because while only some people will use the word community, everyone exists in relation to the communities to which they are attached (Hickey-Moody and Willcox, 2019). As collectives and experiences, community and belonging are as unique as identity. I define them through the words and artworks of my research participants, who express their own versions of community and belonging in myriad ways.

Children also develop a sense of community while working together through the collaborative methods I employ. An example of this can be found in my field notes from outer-east Adelaide:

Video making: The children paired up – one older and one younger – to make the videos introducing themselves and explaining their special objects and things that made them feel they belong. They moved around their refuge tents with pride.

They took to making the videos of each other's work very fluidly – while parents expressed concern that they would drop/throw the iPads, instead, they took care in choosing the camera angles. Pablo and Fraser used the zoom to focus in on their partners while they were explaining their artwork. This showed a clear engagement with the task and also an interest in recording each other's stories.

The children leading this exercise really had to take ownership of their spaces and listen to each other. They worked as a team, were engaged and very respectful of the equipment. This collaboration through partnered video making showed their willingness to rely on one another and seemed a positive step in working towards exploring their understanding of community and belonging. (Fieldwork notes, September 2019)

Children in my research expressed community and belonging through colours, symbols and sounds, and most adults broadly articulated their experiences of community and belonging in relation to place and/or religion. One parent in the Adelaide church group characterised her experience of community by saying:

What was really nice about joining my church was the storytelling and making sense of the world and those kinds of things that come from religion. So, we both really thought this was important, as refugees from other religions. This community has been a place to talk to others, with other people, around values and ethics. And those kinds of things, the lovely things about religion, without the dogmatic aspects of religion. (Inner-east Adelaide focus group, 2018)

An ocean away, in south-east London, a mother with a very different background and culture explained her belonging in terms of city geographies, ethnicities and heritage:

When people migrate they normally look for everywhere their community is. So like you said with Italy, the Italians have come to East London ... why don't they think of going somewhere in North London or somewhere, or South London? Because, you tend to find that people look for their own community. I've seen people who come from Australia, they look for South West London ... from South Africa, Australia, you see lots of people, but they look for their own community, so that's where their comfort zone is or what they're familiar with. (Samia, south-east London focus group, 2018)

Here, I have provided two examples in which community and belonging are defined by people of different races, ages, religions and communities across two different countries, and yet they share a focus on discussions of values, community and similar ethics. Community can be a region of a city in which you live, where people share your ethnic heritage. It might be a group of people with the same sexual orientation or a shared desire to discuss social and spiritual values. Community is all kinds of different forms of connection, and most people belong to multiple communities. 'Your people' may be those with whom you make meaning, or they may be those who hail from similar places. One Manchester mother expressed belonging in relation to a very broad sense of spirituality:

I don't follow an organised religion. I'm spiritual, and I believe there is something bigger, and there's a lot of similarities across ninety-nine per cent of religions. What I have an issue with is the way people in power use religion as a tool to make us fight against each other, when actually we've got a lot more in common than we've got difference. (Sandy, north-west Manchester focus group, 2017)

I saw a comparable sentiment in the words expressed by a Muslim man in Sydney who explained his belonging in relation to Islam and Muslim communities, while lamenting that Muslims as a collective are held accountable and scapegoated for the actions of those who do the 'wrong thing':

If one person is doing something wrong in the society, we shouldn't put blame on every individual … we have been advised by our religion to do the right thing. If one person is doing the wrong thing, we should blame him, not the whole community. We should not … pass it to everybody. We should not blame the whole community. (Abdul, west Sydney focus group, 2017)

Religion is clearly a site of belonging for many. There were, in many instances, quite mixed feelings resulting from the identification of religious communities or beliefs as a primary site of belonging and the perceived and actual judgement of secular others who believe religion is wrong. Secular people can enact a sense of superiority, which can make religious people feel embarrassed to identify their beliefs. Stephanie, a mother from Adelaide, explains this feeling:

> *I went to church and nobody else who we hung out with went to church, I was definitely excluded because I was a 'goody-two-shoes'. Because I was involved in the church, there was definitely a presumption about what I would do and wouldn't do and how people should act around me and stuff like that. I was a teenager then, and even now, I wanted to get my kids baptised, have a christening because that's how I'd kind of grown up. But then Brett wasn't religious at all and both of us didn't want to lie and so we didn't want to go up there and say those words, we will bring up our children in the Christian way … blah blah – and especially not lie in church, which is really wrong [laughs].* (Inner-east Adelaide focus group, 2018)

While this candid statement frames the superior position so often taken by secular people (Rasmussen, 2015), there are also thinly veiled assumptions made about race and class repeatedly in the ways Anglo communities in Australia and England respond to and frame religion.

Spirituality and a relationship to God were expressed in multiple ways by my research participants, and these often excluded, or differed from, traditional divides between secularism and religion. See, for example, the following two statements:

> *[I see] meaning as something that is, that's constructed in groups between people and that's what, if I was gonna use the word God, it's like that's where God is. Like when people get together to make meaning about the world and yeah. That's my storytelling and meaning making.* (Inner-east Adelaide focus group, 2018)

A mother from Manchester expressed the significance of spirituality:

> *We're bringing up Rose very much, if she asks, 'Is there a God?' we say, 'We've not got the arrogance to say we full [sic] know.' And I don't mean that in a bad way to anybody else, but we don't know.* (North-west Manchester focus group, 2017)

As these quotes show, conversations about the co-creation of meaning, geography, location, ethnicity, heritage, spirituality and religion are key factors in determining the ways community and belonging are experienced. I explore aspects of community and belonging in greater detail later in this book, especially through the lens of children's artwork and adults' narratives of religious subcultures. Children's art and their worlds, as uniquely expressed through their artwork and their identities, are core subjects that I examine across 'diffuse space-time' (Marcus, 1998: 79). I explore these themes through the idea of childworlds, and art as the medium through which childworlds are primarily constructed.

Childworlds

One of the most important operationalising concepts and practices in my methodology is to work towards being *in* children's worlds *with them*. Make-believe is often central to children's art practices. The capacity to invent imagined worlds and to reimagine their own realities is key to children's making and understanding, which facilitates the collaborative making process that is at the heart of my methodology for working with children. Inquiring into the ways child participants understand and negotiate place-based religious discourses and mediated representations usually prompts discussion regarding the extent and nature of young people's media engagement and mediated engagement practices. The increasing deindustrialisation and gentrification of a number of the fieldwork sites in both Australia and the UK prompt consideration of the ways children feel they identify/do not identify with their home and community (as evidenced through their own observations and artwork creation) and how and why this is potentially shifting. As this book progresses, I examine the collaborative works made by children in this light, mindful of Kitching's (2020) insightful observation that:

> children find various ways of negotiating differences, conflicts and ambiguities that are present both within and across religious and secular settings ... they grow 'sideways', finding creative ways of negotiating their own differences, knowns and unknowns within and beyond adults' religious/secular representation of the world. (25)

I continually question how I can best bring out the everyday cultural politics of the 'cultural meanings, objects and identities' (Marcus, 1995: 96) that matter to children from their artworks. With this as a primary and organising focus of my work, I have found that homelessness, climate change/global warming, soccer, friendship and ice-cream are the subjects and objects that matter the most to the largest number of children I have worked with across Australia and the UK. As I will go on to suggest, these topics and objects have more to do with faith, belonging and growing up than we might think.

Matter as method

The matter of making together brings into being shared visions of life made by children from often quite different cultural backgrounds. The matter of drawing can show intimate experiences in ways that cannot be codified into words. Doing and being both matter and *make matter* in ways that can consistently provide complex alternatives to contemporary 'legacies of coloniality' (Mignolo, 2007: 452). For Walter Mignolo (2000), the 'decolonial', as opposed to 'postcolonial', is a word he uses to describe oppositional practices by 'people of colour', 'Third-World intellectuals', and 'ethnic groups' (87). Mignolo (2007) defines decoloniality as a movement 'away and beyond the post-colonial' because 'decolonial criticism and theory is a project of scholarly transformation within the academy' (452). For Mignolo, decoloniality is a method for breaking away from 'contemporary legacies of coloniality' (452). However, he locates these practices in relation to a now historical concept of west Europe. The project of undertaking a 'programmatic de-linking from contemporary legacies of coloniality' (Mignolo, 2007: 452) needs to be undertaken in a fashion that is more context-specific than writing against Europe. As a citizen of the Republic of Ireland, I believe that Europe as it is currently defined certainly cannot be held synonymous with all colonial power. Europe is partly constituted by decolonising flows of migrant bodies and languages, which have agency and whose stories must be told. Ireland is a decolonised republic. I also see close relationships between the projects of postcolonialism and decolonialism and argue that they are complementary.

Consequently, my decolonial feminist new materialist methodology is unorthodox: drawing on Rosi Braidotti's (2018) affirmative ethics of generative scholarship, I bring together aspects of postcolonial politics and practices with a 'programmatic de-linking' (Mignolo, 2007: 452) of ideas that haunt Mignolo's suggestions that contemporary Europe as a whole can be held responsible for the colonial agenda, and that the postcolonial should be seen as distinct from the decolonial. I contend that the two positions bring complementary perspectives and can be mobilised in unison. After the thought-provoking work of Hinton et al. (2015) and Leppänen (2018), I take up Hinton's scholarly agenda that:

> race and the very processes through which racialized bodies come to matter (in both senses of the word) still have to be considered as areas that are underrepresented in many new materialist approaches. It appears that new materialisms still miss a strong link with post and de-colonial theories, as well as with critical race and migration studies. (2015: 1)

Hinton et al.'s call to embrace decolonial theory brings a much-needed perspective to both new materialism and decolonial theory, as new materialism needs to consistently address issues of race and intersectionality, and decolonial theory needs to avoid creating false binaries between a historicised 'Europe' and decolonial 'other'. Contemporary Europe is filled with migratory flows and non-white citizens. It is inaccurate to cast contemporary 'Europe', the European Union, as a white colonial entity. Parts of Europe, such as the Republic of Ireland, are constitutionally decolonial. Decolonial bodies and refugees map movements across Europe that call us to attend to their presence. Further, colonisation is not confined to Europe, and neither is all of Europe 'colonial'. Decolonial theory looks to break the reproduction of colonial power. In order to do this, we have to listen for the voices of decolonial subjects in both 'colonised' and 'colonising' places. I do this through a focus on material, geographic, cultural and sensory scapes created by, and bringing together, the largely non-white communities with which I have worked since 2016.

While postcolonial theory rose out of Indian scholarship and politics in Asia (Spivak, 1983; Chambers and Watkins, 2012), decolonial theory has emanated from South America and, more recently, the Republic of Ireland (Feldman, 2018; Gray, 2004; Ignatiev, 1995; Meaney, 2010; Ó Cuinneagáin, 2018) and France (Vergès, 2021). The central premise of postcolonial theory is aligned with the goals of decolonial theory and can be thought about as a way of redressing the cultural, political, aesthetic, economic and social impacts of colonial rule across the eighteenth and nineteenth centuries, and its impacts on contemporary life, values and subjectivities.

Bringing a new materialist lens to thinking about decolonising practices and communities, I have worked with the primary materiality of decoloniality: bodies, their physical objects of attachments, their places of belonging and, following on from this, their stories of diaspora. To avoid historically specific constructions of colonial Europe, the immigrant and migrant communities now living within and across the European Union need to be recognised along with the decolonising activities of Europeans, some of whom, such as those in the Irish Republic, have been resisting imperialist notions of colonialism for decades. In the context of Australia, Indigenous peoples and their long history and relationship with immigrants predates European invasion and needs to be acknowledged and given ownership. Colonisation is being contested in everyday ways in diverse communities and we all need to tell these stories of contestation, along with existing histories of successful revolts such as those fought on Aboriginal lands today. Some matter is inherently resistant to a colonial agenda – it can indeed be resistant to all agendas – instead remaining as an often-unifying connection across language, culture, past and present, and many geographic places. Across the materiality of making with children, and group and individual conversations with adults, I have listened for stories that decentre or question colonial or colonising dominant narratives. This is an everyday decolonising way of doing and making, new materialist research, the methodologies for which are detailed below.

Arts-based methods for working with children

Art offers a way for children to express themselves non-verbally but, more than this, making visual art creates a space for contemplative reflection and collaboration. Such a space can provide opportunity for critical thinking, and for expressing feelings and illustrating imagination in ways that conversation alone can fail to provide. Building on my work on affect as method (Hickey-Moody, 2011, 2013, 2015), I take socially engaged art practice as a cultural pedagogy or process, and as a text that has the capacity to change culture. My work (Hickey-Moody, 2009, 2013) has been inspired by an ethos of practice popularised by the phrase 'the social turn'. This name was first used around 2005 (Bishop, 2005) to describe the rise of socially engaged art that is collaborative, participatory and involves people as a medium or material. In her now classic 2005 essay 'The Social Turn: Collaboration and Its Discontents', historian Clare Bishop argues that art which operates under the umbrella of the social turn tends to happen outside museums or galleries, although this is not always the case. Because much of the art produced through socially engaged practice is collaborative and focuses on constructive social change, it is rarely commercial or object-based. Rather, it is about process, about making feelings, ideas and relationships. Social practice is ostensibly about making the social matter, and the artform is the practice of making the social into matter. Consequently, socially engaged art practice is more than an engaged aesthetic – it is an invaluable political resource. It is a means through which people and, in my work, children in particular, can communicate complex ideas. Art can make complicated issues visible, as it communicates through images, icons, feelings, colours, textures and sounds. It moves us to feel positively or negatively about subjects.

The arts practice workshops with children designed for the Interfaith Childhoods project were the first stage of my empirical data collection and were the way I developed relationships with communities. As I have suggested, the data collected from these workshops and parent focus groups forms the substantive focus of my analysis in this book. The arts workshops occurred in a location that was already embedded in the children's worlds – either their school, their religious institution or a local service provider. I designed the workshops to support children in thinking about and expressing their opinions and experiences individually, and then to develop collective visions of the future and community life.

In most instances, the workshops employed the same (or very similar) media in all the research sites and followed a similar order of events. Each workshop was prefaced by a plenary discussion in which I led the children through an exploration of their responses to (and existing knowledge of) the subject with which the day's workshop was concerned. The topics ranged from identity, belonging and values, to 'what really matters' and 'imagining a future city'. These discussions resulted in the children's main ideas being written on a whiteboard and then drawn on as a resource for art-making across the course of the workshop.

The workshops were broken into sections. Workshop one focused on expressing feelings visually through line, shape, form, tone, colour and texture. I began by asking the children to draw a self-portrait and to think about the ways that they could show their character, their history, and their culture by using symbols, colours, textures and so on. Often, I started by asking children to make some 'feeling pictures' – drawing feelings of 'happy', 'sad', 'angry' and so on. Then, taking their newly practised expressive drawing to their identity pictures, children were asked to represent visible and invisible parts of their identity. This included aspects of subjectivity or identity, such as language, heritage, religion, taste and personality. Children drew these things in all kinds of ways, and their modes of expression were significant: they expressed their imagined worlds, tastes and attachments.

After completing their self-portraits, the children were invited to work in pairs and to collaborate on drawing a 'values picture' examining 'what really matters' to them. These value pictures were 'doing' actions – they were about things like helping, caring and stopping climate change, whatever the children thought was most important. The work of sharing a page with someone else was quite difficult for many of the children, who were aged between five and twelve. Most, but not all, were used to drawing, but few had consciously shared a piece of paper and collaborated with another person to make a shared drawing or piece of art. The nature of the task required not just sharing a page but also collaborating in relation to the idea being drawn, navigating who drew what and where and so on. After the pictures were drawn with partners, I asked the children to make groups of between four and six, depending on the total size of the class or group. These groups were asked to bring all the things 'that really matter' together in one large group image of the future. This 'future' was painted collaboratively and comprised places and objects that the children chose. These included: a flying recycling station, a flying mosque, flying cars, streets that are rivers (in order to stop climate change), housing estates that have ice-cream machines, zoos, churches, temples, parks and airports.

Mapping and making / Ag déanamh   69

These world-making exercises were followed by discussions about why certain things were included in the cities, and the children's answers demonstrated visions for future civic practices. For example, children in Manchester defined value as 'love, respect, cooperation'. When I asked them what mattered most, they said 'friendship, education, family, different countries – some countries are different from others' (south-east London, 2017). The children identified the fact that 'kindness' was needed and 'generosity' was needed when some countries do not have enough food (north-west Manchester, 2017). Respect and understanding differences were brought up repeatedly by children when discussing what really matters in the community. These kinds of self-reflexive conversations were what my collaborative art projects were designed to create.

I explored three-dimensional art with children in the second round of workshops. The media I initially employed to work with three-dimensionally was changed in the later workshops. It began as papier-mâché but then moved on to tents and mobiles. My first attempt at papier-mâché three-dimensional shapes took place in summer in west Sydney, which is notoriously hot. We made globes: papier-mâché balloons that were again intended to result in imagined worlds made up of what mattered the most to the children. These papier-mâché balloons were painted in colours of the children's choosing, varnished and adorned with collaged symbols of 'what really matters'. These symbols were pictures, words and various semiotic forms of communicating values. I bought strings of LED lights to wrap around the globes so they could become bedroom decorations and night lights. There were rainbow-coloured globes, national flags, drawings of different places and imagined 'worlds', which included landscapes, symbols and people and animals. Covering the balloons with papier-mâché took hours. At home, I sat up late in my little local Airbnb loft bedroom trying to 'catch up' the balloons that needed more work, patch up errors and reinforce surfaces. Three-dimensional modelling clay has replaced papier-mâché in the craft world, and I wondered if I should have made modelling-clay globes. Even sourcing the materials for papier-mâché was difficult. Newspapers and PVA glue were not able to be procured from anywhere near the University of Sydney, where I was working at the time. I was distressed to discover that the young staff working in the university newsagent had not even heard of the university student magazine, let alone thought about stocking it. A large pile of Greek and Lebanese community newspapers from a grocer in west Sydney and four industrial-sized bottles of PVA glue from a craft superstore further out west finally solved my dilemma. This process stood in stark contrast to buying six canvases for the first workshop series, along with paper, paint and pastels, which was fabulously easy. At the community organisation where the fieldwork was taking place, children fell in love with the viscosity of PVA glue. While I had bought what I thought was enough to see me through most of my Australian fieldwork, and carefully poured what I thought was the appropriate amount out onto plastic plates, the children poured out more. They poured one liquid (glue) onto another (paint). They poured blended liquids onto balloons. They found and *emptied* bottles. They poured because they loved pouring. They squelched paper into the PVA and made globes that had accidental lumpy and spikey bits that I tried to smooth out. I sat the soaking wet creations in the sun and hoped they would dry. Some collapsed in on themselves and some survived. One would think I may have learnt my lesson and moved on slightly more quickly. However, it took even more time spent making papier-mâché balloons in an Airbnb in Manchester in a very wet and drizzly English 'summer' to establish my conviction that papier-mâché was untenable (see Hickey-Moody, 2019). Papier-mâché takes some time to dry in the Australian summer; however, it simply does not dry at all in the English equivalent. Looking for alternative options, I decided to try adorning tents with the symbols of what really matters, rather than decorating papier-mâché globes.

The tents brought with them new possibilities: interiors and exteriors, mobiles and play spaces. They brought a world with them. Tent cities speak of places of refuge, and I worked with the children around themes of refuge and home, but also empathy for others who have less than us. How do we make places that accept difference? What would an architecture of empathy look like? These were questions I asked the children and they responded through making. The tents also brought with them possibilities for play. Children filmed each other playing inside the tents, explaining their symbols about what really matters to them and why, and also living out their imagined worlds, which extend to gardens, views and broader community life. For example, Figure 3.1 depicts the home/

Mapping and making / Ag déanamh 71

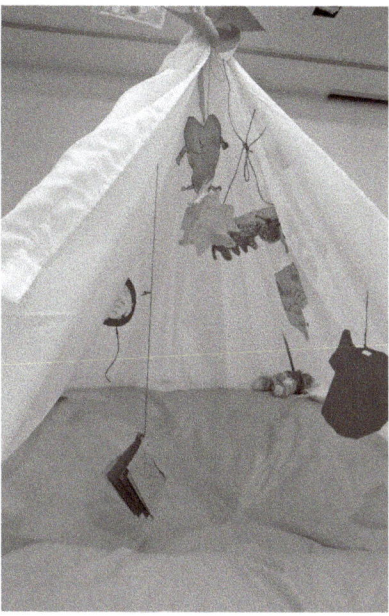

Figure 3.1 'Refuge' tent built by children in London, 2018

refuge decorated with symbols of 'what really matters', a vegetable garden built outside the home, and a 'view' that can be seen from the imagined home.

In the third and final round of workshops with children, I used textiles and digital animations. The textiles work was a process of making a quilt, a large colourful patchwork sheet comprised of children's stories of home. Developing these large patchworks took some time – each child usually practised what they wanted to draw onto the textiles on a sheet of paper first. The child artist was asked to choose a patchwork square in a colour they liked. After experimenting with different ways of decorating the fabric, I decided that drawing onto the fabric with felt-tip pens was the easiest way to create images and narrative. These pens came in a huge range of colours, so children could choose how they represented their geographies of belonging. The glitter pens were always in huge demand – especially the gold glitter pens (Coleman, 2020). Children drew maps of their favourite places and remade geographies of belonging that brought together their favourite places, people and activities on a square of

Figure 3.2 The first patchwork made in Sydney, 2017

material. I invented little homework packs that included a selection of decorative materials, a coloured fabric square and a worksheet for parents/carers and children to do together, exploring family stories of migration and mapping family history. Once each child had made two squares, one square alone and one with an adult, the fabric squares were stuck together on a sheet (see Figure 3.2). The co-location of everyone's belonging geography had a very powerful effect. Suddenly all the different stories were one: together but distinct.

In most instances, I followed the patchwork geographies of belonging with a workshop on digital animations about identity. Here, children returned to the themes of the visible and invisible aspects of their identity and explored what they felt makes them 'who they are'. Each child was given an iPad and a stylus, and the drawing happened using the application Procreate, which is designed specifically for digital art. Procreate records the drawing process, so once children finished drawing their 'identity picture', the application could play back the process of drawing, creating an animation of their identity story. I then worked with the children to write down the story of what they had drawn and recorded them narrating the story out loud. Exporting the animation and the narrative account of the animation into iMovie, I merged the two together to make a narrated digital animation. The children's voices brought their artworks to life with a depth and vivacity that is hard to communicate in written words.[1] The identity stories, conversations and imagined worlds generated through working with children form the focus of discussions in later chapters. The other key modes of qualitative data collection that have informed this book especially are the focus groups and follow-up interviews.

Focus groups and follow-up interviews

After completing at least three days' worth of collaborative making, children took home invitations for their parents to join me in a group discussion about community values. These focus groups were sometimes one of the only times parents met each other, and were again held in places that were embedded in the children's worlds, such as school staff rooms, classrooms or community spaces attached to a place of worship/religious building. The focus groups always featured food, and wherever possible this was a shared, halal meal. In Australia, I always started the focus groups with an acknowledgement of the traditional owners of the country, and in both Australia and the UK, I started the focus groups by acknowledging my own intersectionality and complex attachments to religion. I then asked participants to introduce themselves and include their name, country of origin, cultural background and their religion, if they had one. I then facilitated a themed discussion and tried to ask the following questions. I didn't always have time to ask each of these questions to the group; the number of questions I was able to ask depended on the number of people taking part in the focus group and the amount of discussion that took place. The questions were broadly organised around three themes: identity, community and belonging/exclusion. All focus groups were conducted in English with the support of interpreters.

1 Can you tell me what role religion plays in your life? For instance, does it influence how you organise your day or determine what your special places are and the significance of celebration dates?
2 What values do you share with people from different faith backgrounds?

3 Can you tell me if you feel like you belong to a community, or a few key communities, and if so, what they are? (They don't have to be Australian/British.)
4 Do you feel part of a broader Australian/British national identity? What does being Australian/British mean to you?
5 Have you experienced racism/exclusion because of your cultural or religious identity? Can you share an example with us?
6 What do you think will help us develop a more inclusive community that appreciates religious differences?

These questions were answered in very diverse ways, and I discuss the core themes that arose from the focus groups' discussions in the following chapters.

All of the research participants in the focus groups were also invited to undertake follow-up one-on-one interviews, and at least one person per focus group accepted this invitation, often more. Interviews took place in a location chosen by the participant. These ranged from their home to schools or their mosque. Through the interview questions, I explored religion, faith, identity, community and belonging. The questions that I asked were:

1 Can you tell me about what your ethnic or religious identity means to you?
2 How important is religion to you? Could you please elaborate?
3 How closely do you follow the traditional teachings of your religion/faith?
4 How would you describe yourself (e.g. strict, relaxed, orthodox, devout)?
5 What do you consider the most important values of your religion/faith to be?
6 Can you tell me about how religion is a part of your life? For instance, is it part of how you organise your day, what your special places, dates and celebrations are?
7 Does the internet/social media play a role in the way you practise/experience your religion?
8 What are some symbols that signify/represent your religious identity?
9 Can you tell me if you feel like you belong to a community or a few key communities and if so, what are they? (They don't have to be in Australia/Britain.)

10 What role does religion play in how you feel connected to communities?
11 Do you share values with people from different faith backgrounds? If so, what are they?
12 How comfortable do you feel engaging with people from different faith backgrounds?
13 What are some of the challenges of being a person from your faith background? Can you share a story with me?
14 Do you feel part of the broader Australian/British national identity? What does being Australian/British mean to you?
15 Have you experienced racism/exclusion because of your cultural/religious identity?
16 What do you think will help us develop a more inclusive community that appreciates religious differences?

The first five to eight of these questions formed the basis for the focus groups, and the second eight formed the basis for the interviews. Some overlap usually occurred in order to build on what had been discussed previously. In focus groups and interviews, I focused on trying to make space for connection. Sharing happens in lots of different ways, and I saw my role as holding space to create connections between people, especially between myself and others.

Conclusion

Often when I drop a pebble in a body of water, I notice how it makes a series of small ripples. As these ripples get larger, smaller, slower circles spread out from that initial point of contact. I imagine that my research methods make a similar pattern. The little stone I drop in the water is my ethnographic observations and collaborative art-making with children. But, by putting this detail into some sense-making context and adding perspective, focus group stories and individual interviews illustrate larger patterns of experience. Multi-sited ethnography is useful because it helps with finding common ground between diverse places. Art gives children ways of expressing complex experiences, and in focus groups and interviews I work to create space in which parents and carers can share 'what really matters' to them. In the following chapters, I explore resonant themes that run across children's stories from the arts workshops and the parents' stories from the focus groups and interviews, with a view to thinking about how methods enable thinking and making across sites.

Note

1 See www.interfaithchildhoods.com (accessed 19 October 2022) for some examples of the animations.

4

Affect and joy / *Áthas*

Introduction

Affect and joy are key themes that run through my data in a number of ways. Firstly, the research methods and the data communicate through affect. The children's artwork, both individual and collaborative, touches the feelings of its viewers and expresses the feelings of those who have made it. The artworks themselves are materialisations of feeling, communicated through line, shape, form, tone, imagination and matter. The adults' conversations are similarly drenched with affect. Faith is an emotional issue. What we believe in arises from our family history, our places of birth and residence, the languages we speak: our blood and the air we breathe. It is impossible for such intimate matters to be devoid of emotion and connectedness to others, both of which are defining aspects of affect. The *connectedness to others* which is both part of collaborative art-making and participating in a faith is what also creates joy as Spinoza explains it. Spinoza suggests that 'If a person has done anything which he imagines will affect others with joy, he will also be affected with joy, accompanied with an idea of himself as its cause; that is to say, he will look upon himself with joy' (2001: 121). He later concedes (on the same page) that such joy may, at times, be imagined. To the extent that acts of connection, empathy and support facilitated through faith practices are real, they bring joy to those who experience them. In this chapter, I explore affect and joy as created through children making artworks, as communicated in children's artworks and as themes that run through the parents' focus group discussions and interviews.

What really matters

As I noted earlier and expand upon in the following chapters, my data collection with children began by asking them 'what really matters?' Read collectively, their visual and material responses to this issue can be seen as a chorus of joyful affects. Indeed, making artworks can be a form of valuing something – a way of revering objects and experiences. Renold and Ivinson (2022: 4) suggest that 'becoming able to respond to "what matters" is an embodied and embedded ethical practice'. The embodied and expressive nature of the children's work substantiates this claim. An earlier example of this relationship between ethics, the body and feelings can be found in proposition nineteen of the 'Origin and Nature of the Affects', where Spinoza suggests that 'He who imagines that what he loves is destroyed will sorrow, but if he imagines that it is preserved he will rejoice' (2001: 114). The demonstration for this proposition continues, explaining that 'the mind endeavours as much as it can to imagine those things which increase or assist the body's power of action … that is to say, to imagine those things which it loves' (2001: 114). This sentiment can be taken as a map for approaching the way children engaged with the making tasks I gave them. The act of thinking about 'what really matters' for children became a way of imagining 'those things' which are loved (2001: 114). The images they drew, in the first instance, almost always featured family. Pets, favourite locations (a tree, a shoreline, grandma's house, the back garden, the Ka'bah, the Burj Khalifa) and special foods and symbols (flags and religious symbols) were the 'go-to' first images that children created: key constellation points for their feelings. These points (or objects and people) all exist in affective relationships with each other. They are the neighbourhood of what children hold tightly: a map of what animates their emotional worlds.

These things (family, pets, places, symbols) have affected the children who draw them. Thinking about why they matter is part of the joy of creating for the children. As I noted earlier, affect is the concept of changing in relation to an experience or encounter. Deleuze employs this term in changing ways across his career, and all of them apply to various stages of the children making and sharing the artworks. There is a difference in nature between *image affections* (ideas) and affects. Image affections might include the idea of belonging, the name of the country in which you have citizenship, but not the actual feeling of belonging. Affect (*affectus*) is the materiality of change, how the feeling of belonging changes your body, the empirical relations that the affected body has to affecting bodies. *Affectus* is analogous to what theorists such as Giroux (2010) call 'pedagogy', namely, a relational practice through which some kind of knowledge is produced. These ideas help to foreground the fact that small economies of change are essentially what the children are making with their artworks.

The children pass on the ways that 'what really matters' in their lives has changed them. *Affectus* is a rhythmic trace of the world written into the body, an expression of an encounter between a corporeal form and material forces that are not necessarily 'human'. Art-making – especially collaborative art-making – can create individual affective responses and generate *affectus*. In creating subjective change or a 'modulation' in the form of *affectus*, art materials become physical forces of change. Our environments, animals and objects are material pedagogies and they impact on us in pre-perceptive ways that are so small we don't necessarily notice them.

I now turn my focus from the joy found in making art about 'what really matters' to examining the joy that is communicated by art. Extending the possibilities for thinking through how matter impacts subjectivity, Deleuze and Guattari develop the ideas of the percept and affect in a chapter from *What is Philosophy?* (1996) as a nuanced theory of art's material agency. They argue that percepts are fragments of the perception of the world created in an artwork. Affects are the compounds of artistic techniques that make one feel a certain way in response to a work of art. The art children made explores the way that non-human things such as significant places, animals, beliefs, objects and rituals impact on their subjectivity and can enrich and extend their emotional worlds.

In explaining how art communicates, *What is Philosophy?* shows us that art is more than a mode of producing subjectivity and a way of modulating community. Deleuze and Guattari (1996: 24, 66, 163–99, 173, 177–84, 211–12) suggest that a percept is a physical fragment of the world imagined in and through the artwork. An affect is the sense, or feeling, that is enmeshed with the materiality of the artwork. Combined together in art, percepts and affects constitute what Deleuze and Guattari term a 'bloc of sensations' (1996:

176). Blocs of sensations are the language with which art speaks. They suggest:

> Art is the language of sensations. Art does not have opinions. Art undoes the triple organisation of perceptions, affections and opinions in order to substitute a monument composed of percepts, affects and blocs of sensations that take the place of language ... A monument does not commemorate or celebrate something that happened but confides to the ear of the future the persistent sensations that embody the event. (1996: 176–7)

Through art, knowledge is communicated in ways that exceed language, and often by things that are not human: by colours, textures, amalgams, lines or shapes. This is especially important in the case of children's work because often their vocabulary is limited and their expression comes from other sources, including the materiality of their art. The children's artworks are monuments 'composed of percepts, affects and blocs of sensations that take the place of language' (Deleuze and Guattari, 1996: 176). They propel the emotional geographies of those for whom they speak. In doing so, they create a new sensory landscape for their beholder. This act of creating a sensory landscape occurs *through* an artwork's affective potential. This is the way a work of art can make its observer feel; the connection(s) a work prompts its observer to make. The materiality of the artwork, the blocs of sensation from which it is composed, embody affects that are specific to the worlds and lives of the children who create them. Each bloc of sensation has its own affective force or quality. The materiality of art can readjust what a person is or is not able to understand, produce and connect to. This is not to say that a work of art necessarily *will* change viewers in prescribed ways, but rather that artworks *can* create new associations and habits of clustering emotion around new images. Art thinks with us; it machines thoughts and feelings.

Percepts and affects exist within a work of art, as part of a work of art, upon terms established by and situated within the work; terms that are specific to the *way* the work of art has been constructed. This kind of affect embedded in a work of art is a new milieu of sense, or series of personal associations, that are created in relation to percepts: 'Affects are precisely these nonhuman becomings of man [*sic*]' (Deleuze and Guattari, 1996: 169). Such transformations are more than human (or 'non-human' in this quote) because, although an affect is an embodied change in the respect that it is a readjustment of personal 'limit' or capacity, affect is produced in relation to the material product – the work – an artist has created. A work of art thus presents its viewer with a miniature universe that performs a pedagogic function through crafting and imbuing elements of experience, and experiential difference, upon its spectator. For example, children's artworks often featured places that were significant in the emotional geographies of their religious worlds, such as the Ka'bah, or their local church or mosque: symbols that show what they believe. The materiality of these symbolic expressions changed them and also brought them into the world in a way that allowed the children's images and what they represent to become part of the emotional economies of their beholders. The Ka'bah, expressed in paint, glitter and cardboard, both shows what it feels like to be drawn to something, to revere something and dream of it, and it also presents the Ka'bah as an actor in the centre of its own story. Who is praying outside the Ka'bah? What can they see? What stories, hopes and dreams do they bring on their pilgrimage? It is the materiality of the artwork, after being entangled with the child's imagination, that asks these questions.

Exploring the agency of matter in art, the term percept describes aspects of the physicality of the artwork in its completed form. Deleuze and Guattari suggest:

> a percept is material crafted into a sensation ... it is difficult to say where in fact the material ends and sensation begins; preparation of the canvas, the track of the brush's hair, and many other things besides are obviously part of the sensation. (1996: 166)

The liveness of making is embedded in the percept. New lived sensibilities, or personal vocabularies, are often the *products* of the artistic affects that percepts make. In describing this potential for the creation of newness and transformation, Deleuze and Guattari argue:

> 'Blocs' of percepts and affects are innovative by *nature*; they are not about preserving previous events or works of art, but are the creation of a new solidarity ... Even if the material only lasts for a few seconds it will give sensation the power to exist and be preserved in itself in the eternity that exists for that short duration. (1996: 166)

Hundreds of little 'faiths' are expressed in the children's artworks. What it means to have faith is remade in relation to the joys of what really matters in life and shared with others. Translating this sentiment into subjective or 'human' terms, the implications of what Deleuze and Guattari suggest are that the person who experiences the force produced by an affect can retain this force, and can also be changed as a result of their experience. The effect of the children's art is to give the viewer a piece of their world. Not just any piece: a treasured source of joy that expresses how they connect to community, to place, to family, to religion and so on. The following conversation from my work in the Greenwich primary school illustrates children's experiences of joy in relation to their choices of 'what really matters' in life. The natural environment and family celebrations stand out to them as the most important things in their lives and the primary reason for their spiritual beliefs:

> Anna: *The next picture that we're going to do is a picture about what really matters and you're going to work with somebody else to make the picture of what really matters. So, what are some things that really matter? Call them out.*
> Elise: *Flowers.*
> Anna: *Excellent, and why do flowers really matter?*
> Elise: *Maybe because they take in carbon and make oxygen.*
> Anna: *Oxygen, excellent. Flowers make oxygen, well done. Who was next?*
> Elise: *They keep us alive.*
> Anna: *Keep us alive. Yep, Simon?*
> Simon: *Flowers are also good because it's also good for the bees, bees get the nectar to make honey for us.*
> Anna: *Right, flowers, bees that make honey. And you know what? The bees also make flowers because the bees carry pollen between flowers. Yeah, they sprinkle it on the flowers. Yes …*
> Simon: *How about rain, even though you don't like it, it gets you wet, but it still helps you because it goes through the tap so you can drink it, and wash your hands with it?*
> Francesca: *Our bodies.*
> Anna: *And why do our bodies matter?*
> Francesca: *Because we need to look after our bodies, by not like eating sugar.*
> Anna: *Eat healthily, no sugar. So we had other hands too, didn't we, you haven't said anything yet. So, who else?*
> Otto: *Nature.*
> Samantha: *Lungs.*
> Anna: *Lungs, that's fantastic.*

Samantha: *They help us breathe, and mine don't work very well because I have asthma.*
Anna: *Oh, honey. Do you? That's a shame. Help us breathe. Yeah. Yeah, so what about religion? Hands up here who has a religion. And so, can we say what everyone's religion is?*
Francesca: *Christian.*
Anna: *Yeah, Christian, that's Francesca's religion. Is religion something that really matters?*
Abdul: *Yes.*
Anna: *And does your family have a religion?*
Abdul: *Christian, Muslim.*
Anna: *Is it Christian or is it Muslim?*
Abdul: *Muslim.*
Anna: *And Frank, does your family have a religion?*
Frank: *Christian.*
Anna: *Great. And what's yours?*
Divya: *Hindu.*
Anna: *Hindu, that's right, of course. So, I just want to have a talk because religion is kind of meant to embody what really matters in a lot of ways, and what we are interested in doing is thinking about what religion teaches us and thinking about how there might be some similarities between what religions teach us and some differences. So, maybe if everyone gives us one word about what their religion teaches them. If you were going to say what's the main message of Hinduism, what would you say?*
Divya: *Parties.*
Anna: *Parties, that's awesome. I love a good party. So, what's the main message of Christianity, you think?*
Tom: *Keeping the people safe, keeping the bugs safe.*
Anna: *Keeping people and insects safe.*
Francesca: *I was going to say the same thing.*
Anna: *And so, Abdul, if you were going to pick something that was one word about being Muslim, what would it be?*
Abdul: *Praying to Allah.*
Anna: *Praying to Allah, yes.*
Abdul: *Eid is my birthday.*
Anna: *You've only just finished Ramadan, haven't you? Oh, is Eid your birthday?*
Abdul: *And everybody's different.*
(South-east London Primary School, 2018)

Clearly, the children value and delight in the natural world. Flowers, bees, rain, insects: they are enamoured with nature and respect the role it plays in sustaining life. Religion at ages eight to nine is still primarily about celebration, ritual and the pleasure of family and community togetherness. Indeed, the conversation recounted above could be read as a shopping list of 'what kids love', as they remember things that bring them joy in life. Spinoza explains: 'Besides the joys and sorrows which are passions, there are other affects of joy and sorrow which are related to us in so far as we act' (Spinoza, 2001: 144). He continues, explaining that the mind 'endeavours to preserve its own being' (2001: 144). In primarily being motivated by joy, children's recounting of religion acknowledges it as a source of great happiness. Religion is also, as Abdul shows us, about relationality. 'Praying to Allah' is inherently relational and it requires the production of the self who prays. Abdul points towards the many layers of experience that comprise a relationship with religion: the relationship between self and God, celebrations, understanding and accepting cultural differences.

Unintentionally, celebrating joy became the focus of children's explorations of what really matters. In many of the children's minds, religion was alight with the colour, sound and spectacles of parties. One exception was the Muslim boy, Abdul, who understood his relationship with Allah as the central purpose of his religion. I would suggest he was the most religious child out of the few who featured in the discussion above, and this was why he had a more developed perspective on the matter. The main thing the discussion shows us is that joy – connectedness to nature and to other people – is a primary motivating factor for children, and it organises how they see the world. Their artworks communicate their joy through affect: through the percepts and affects that they create in being enmeshed with matter.

Of course, the way an affect is experienced, and the ways an affect works, will always be specific to the body in question. Indeed, whether a work of art is perceived as having affect at all is always specific to the body in question. Not all viewers respond in the same way. As Deleuze and Guattari contend:

> [A work of art] is no less independent of the viewer or hearer, who only experience it after, if they have the strength for it. (1996: 164)

Therefore, the power of percepts and affects must be seen as situated: as context-specific and highly subjective. The forces produced by works of art exist in relation to those who experience them, those who 'have the strength for it' (Deleuze and Guattari, 1996: 164), those who have the strength to share the joy. In my discussion so far, I have drawn attention to the ways children orient their worlds towards joy and also how they communicate joy through their artwork. Turning to examine the adults' worlds and the way affect communicates joy in their lives, the theme of empathy comes through as something that people feel they develop through their faith practice and also something they value as a result of their faith.

Empathy and religious identities

Practices of belonging are often based on resonances between individual identities. However, my research has found that individuals can have more in common with others who do not follow the same religious beliefs but have a similar orientation to faith. Both similarities and differences can provide pathways to empathy and identification with others, experiences which are mediated through affect and which bring joy by increasing the individual's capacity to understand others. Spinoza's joy arises from an increase in power, but not controlling power; rather, an increase in capacity: to understand, to witness, to help. Many participants were bonded by their shared experiences of difference. Spinoza explains that 'If a person has done anything which he imagines will affect others with joy, he also will be affected with joy, accompanied with an idea of himself as its cause; that is to say, he will look upon himself with joy' (2001: 121). Similarities between others can also create a feeling of joy, especially when experiential similarities are found across contextual differences.

Many examples of similarities between people creating empathy can be found in my focus group discussions and interviews. During these discussions in England and Australia it became clear that participants' lived experiences of being Muslim did not generally coincide with what they saw as public perceptions of Islam, especially ideas broadcast by popular media. Most Muslim participants felt that the general public did not understand the diversity within Islam and, further, felt the fact that religious identities only make up a small part of individual systems of belonging was ignored in popular representations. Participants felt religious identity needed to be considered alongside other factors such as being a mother or a father, a student, a professional, an amateur photographer, a cricket enthusiast and so on. Many participants had experienced discrimination – including discrimination on religious grounds – but some had also had experiences where people in the workplace went out of their way to respect their need to pray, or where others in public had been accepting of religious, ethnic or cultural minorities. Even still, most participants were critical of the media's role in representing their religion, especially after the 9/11 terrorist attacks.

Anti-Islam media bias is well documented in the academic literature (Aly, 2007; Aly and Green, 2008; Aly and Walker, 2007). So too is the fact that media representations affect popular opinion and attitudes (Ahmed and Matthes, 2017; Baugut and Neumann, 2019; Brown and Richards, 2016; Moore, Mason and Lewis, 2008). Several participants in focus groups and interviews commented on the negative way Islam was represented. Aquid spoke of his family being persecuted for their religious beliefs by fundamentalist groups. He felt that ignorance, rather than malice, had been the cause for his experience of racism in Australia, but he also thought that the media was responsible for negative and stereotypical representations of Islam:

> *The person in Australia who talked to me when asking what my belief is, the person doesn't recognise they are learning from the media. They are watching the media and don't know exactly what's the difference between these people and those people. We don't belong to those people. Because they only thinking about the religion: 'Muslim'. All Muslims are the same to them. I had two or three experiences, not only me as well, two or three of my friends as well. When they were walking with their family on the street, one time they were attacked with an egg, his wife and her family as well. 'Go back to your country. You are not Australian', is what was said to them. That's why when they see the media, they don't recognise we are suffering as well from those fundamentalist people. They think all Muslims are the same ... My five children are wearing the hijab. The only thing they understand is that all of the Muslim have a hijab and are the same.* (South-east Melbourne focus group, August 2018)

The angry white Australian citizens who confronted Aquid in the park, and who he characterises above, are led by media representations of terrorism. Here, communicating through affect has led to a reduction in capacity to act: they are not able to relate to or understand a Muslim man because the affective arrangement of their emotions caused by popular media has limited them. They have been taught to conflate being Muslim with being a terrorist. Understandably, Aquid was disappointed by the inaccurate public understanding and the way that the media focus on Islamic extremism has led to open hostility and aggression. However, sharing this sentiment in the focus group engendered a lot of understanding from other people – especially from Muslims who'd had similar experiences. Collective experiences of misrecognition have clearly become a way in which people's capacity to act is extended: they understand how it is that others come to have such an impoverished view of what it means to be Muslim and feel empathy for the ignorance and lack of capacity demonstrated by those who believe popular misrepresentations.

As I have suggested, many other participants also observed how media representations and public opinion had conflated Islam with fundamentalism (Ahmed and Matthes, 2017). For example, Bilal, who took part in a one-on-one interview in Manchester in 2018, had experienced people's fear of extremism, but had also developed some clear strategies to counter the broad lack of public awareness. Above all, he felt that the role of the media in guiding people's perceptions of Islam was important because it could be leveraged to either improve community understanding or foster negative stereotypes. Bilal specifically referred to the taxi drivers who helped victims and witnesses of the 2017 Manchester Arena terrorist attacks. As Bilal points out, narratives of predominantly Muslim taxi drivers helping their fellow Mancunians were also included in media coverage. He suggests:

> *I cannot blame Islam or Islamophobia in any way, it's natural. People fear terrorism. So I guess the important point is communication among and between key actors of each religion. Of course, we can learn from the Manchester Arena attack where the bomb happened. I've heard that these taxi drivers were Muslim in the majority. They volunteered to take the victims home, free of charge. I mean, this is the most effective way to, how do you say – promote that Islam does not have anything to do with that terrorist attack. These perpetrators are extreme. People don't understand that. We actually practise the real Islam here. So it's action and communication that is important. But the most important thing is action. Because that's what the*

media catches, that's what is in the media. The media covers a story about these taxi drivers helping people to get home. That is the point where people start to respect Islam as a peaceful religion. (Individual interview, Manchester, June 2018)

Bilal, like so many participants, felt that a lack of differentiation between extremist and everyday Muslims in the mainstream media, alongside a failure to represent the complexities of religious affiliation and the diversity of subgroups within Islam, has led to stereotypical and negative public perceptions of Muslims and Islam. Through mainstream media, the 'mind's power of acting is lessened' (Spinoza, 2001: 144). These stereotypes result in racist and discriminatory attitudes that are expressed in frightening and confrontational ways, such as Aquid's friends being attacked with an egg in the street. Other examples included a woman being told she was not fit to be a doctor because she was Muslim, and young white men pretending to shoot non-white Muslim children while the children's parents watched. The fact that people found ways to overcome these egregious acts of violence and, even more so, to understand why they happen, demonstrates the phenomenal power of the mind as cultivated through faith. Spinoza suggests that 'when the mind contemplates itself and its own power of acting, it rejoices, and it rejoices in proportion to the distinctness with which it imagines itself and its power of acting' (2001: 138). Understood in this way, the power of understanding where hate acts and speech come from and why they are used is not just a cause for solidarity among those who experience oppression, but this understanding, insight and empathy into the lack of capacity of so many people who believe mass media texts is a kind of joy: it extends the capacity to act of those who experience it. Indeed, some participants had chosen to develop their faith because of their empathy for the ways people were marginalised. One example of this can be found in Fatima from Adelaide's story of finding her faith identity:

> *Fatima: I had never prayed a day in my life when I was nine. So yeah – so I really struggled with my identity and proving myself growing up and I wanted to wear a headscarf from when I was 16, but my parents were really against it, because they were scared I was going to be discriminated against and, you know, I wouldn't*

> find a job or I wouldn't even find a partner. That's how scared they were. And then I got to the age of twenty-two and I was in my second-to-last year of uni and I was like 'I don't care anymore. I'm going to wear a headscarf', because it was really, really important to me to show my religion and to prove myself. I was sick of being asked why I couldn't go on pub crawl. So yeah, I was like 'Sorry, Mum and Dad', and put on the headscarf. Put the Facebook post up, so, you know, friends can't say 'Oh no, the family doesn't know yet, you can take it off still.' And yeah, I ended up working for Islamic organisation.
> Anna: Are your parents sort of all right with it now? Like have they changed how they feel?
> Fatima: I think they always have a fear. Like my parents – so my mum didn't start wearing a headscarf till she was in her fifties and, like, they own a fish and chip shop in an area that was a housing trust area. So they get racist comments all the time. So, like, to the point where we're telling one customer that we wanted to close our shop and their response was to throw a hotdog at us and tell us where to go. And like – so my brothers are very visibly Arab and they grew up in a post-9/11 era where their faces were being photoshopped on Osama bin Laden's body and posted all over the school. So there was very much a reason for their fear. Like there was racist comments all the time. So for me, I was quite oblivious to it because I'm the one really white blonde person in my family whereas the rest of my brothers are very obviously Arab.
>
> (South-west Adelaide focus group, 2018)

Fatima's story shows how her empathy for her brothers increased her resolve to live a Muslim life in public as well as in private. Many participants had strategies to deal with and try to alter negative stereotypes. Like Bilal, some participants argued that it was important to engage in personal conversations with people in the community and to establish relationships in order to create trust and understanding. These strategies provide a counter-narrative to those disseminated in the mainstream media, but also tie in closely with faith as a means of belonging and togetherness, as such conversations build bridges between people and also cement similarities that already exist. More than anything, religion was seen as an ethical and moral guide in focus groups and interviews, and this is partly how my research participants understood the work of dismantling inaccurate representations of Muslim culture.

Exploring the theme of joy as an extension of the self and a product of increasing one's capacity to act more broadly, there were many accounts of the ways faith practices help people grow. For example, Ramadan featured in discussions as an example of how faith teaches people to become more caring:

> *Danah: And during Ramadan, we also put more emphasis on charity. Charity is something we consider in Islam, but during Ramadan even the kids – even if it's ten dollars or five dollars, we, they would want to donate it like through their school or through a kid who is needy. Yeah, even the kids turn, 'Okay, when do this, we get rewarded for this. We are helping a kid who doesn't get to pay for it', because even last Ramadan our girls were also like, 'Can you please get this? I want to donate it to these group of kids.' I mean, 'Our school they are having this collection.' So it shouldn't be expensive, just something so you can bring the smile on somebody's face.*
>
> *Zahuk: Yeah, so in terms of like Ramadan, it helps to build empathy and one more thing I want to add, the Qur'an mentions that – Ramadan is like the training session. Like a one-month training session to do good, so that you can be good for the rest of the year. So, like military training or police training, they have a training session, or like the firefighter, they have a training session, so that they can work. Just like a training session for us for one month so that we can be good for the rest of the eleven months.*
>
> (South-west Adelaide focus group, 2019)

These focus group participants clearly state that, in their experience, Muslim faith has taught them how to have empathy for the poor, how to sacrifice, how to work hard and how to grow as a person. I delved further into these themes as part of a follow-up interview I undertook with one of the focus group participants a week later. I asked Danah if she felt that her religion focused on empathy and had taught her to focus on empathy. She responded by explaining that:

> *Danah: Yes, the Ramadan is a training period, as my husband was mentioning the other day, it's like one-month training period in the whole year, which will actually allow us to refocus ourselves, and yeah, like develop empathy for the less fortunate who don't have enough to eat, if you're starving you'll actually understand how the person who is not able to afford a decent meal, how they might*

feel, you'll actually think about taking a part of your income to donate it. Because, like, as I was growing up, I noticed that when I was in school, there were some kids who were very well-off, and they didn't actually understand the value of anything they had. So, to understand that value of something you have to lose it. You have to not have it in your life. And on empathy, actually we are supposed to be very sensitive towards not only human beings, but even animals. Like we have a story, it's a collection of events that happened earlier, and it's, there's one story where this woman, she fed water to the dog and that's why she was granted paradise.
(Danah, individual interview, north-west Manchester, 2019)

Acts of kindness are rewarded in other worlds. Danah's account of this is unequivocal, as is the justification of Ramadan as a training method for kindness and empathy. This theme echoed through the children's artwork as well: many pictures featured the word 'service' and explained both through images and through words how important it was to be of service to your community and your God. While these examples are specific to the Muslim faith, there were other examples from other faith backgrounds. For example, Amira's story from the church in Adelaide:

My dad's from Pakistan, my mum's from Australia, I was born in Nigeria. I was only there for the first couple of years of my life. But since then I've grown up Australian/Pakistani, I've never actually been able to comfortably call myself Australian, or call myself Pakistani. I don't quite know where I belong, I kind of hover in the space in the oceans, kind of thing, in between. And so, for the very first time, I've realised that what I love about my work, when, on a good day, is that I can exist in that limbo space. So, it's a community where you don't have to belong to a particular thing to belong, in a way, or where I find meaning and purpose by not belonging to any particular thing, and by not belonging to any one particular aspect, I am able to engage with my students, and have empathy for my students, in a way that I'm finding, more and more, a lot of those who, those white-bread, for lack of a better term, people who have only ever grown up Australian, their attitudes towards our students, it's really interesting to hear the undercurrent of cultural imperialism that comes across. (Amira, inner-east Adelaide focus group, 2019)

In a church in a middle-class Adelaide suburb, Amira echoes the sentiments of Aquid from south-east Melbourne and Bilal from inner-south Manchester, both of whom have negotiated vernacular and institutionalised forms of white imperialism and have had cause to think about how such ignorant white supremacy has come to be accepted as a form of 'common sense' in the mainstream colonial culture. The role played by mass media in perpetuating and distributing racism was lamented in related ways across all my research sites. Discussions with mothers in north-west Manchester also explored the theme. For example, Emily, a white English mother, also suggests racism is perpetuated by the media, stating that:

> *I think most racism is informed from a place, even though they say it's hatred. I don't. I think most racism is a place of ignorance and lack of understanding. You know what I mean? It's fair. If we all listen to the media, you know we will never speak to migrants whether they are white, Black, Asian or whatever ... We tend to cherry-pick bits of the media that are the most frightening and stick that in the forefront of our mind and then apply it, which is wrong really. We should take the media with a pinch of salt. I usually think anything they say is the opposite of the truth. If it's going to rain, yes it's gonna be sunny. But I mean just take it as the opposite and then it'll make life a lot more easy for people.* (Emily, north-west Manchester focus group, June 2018)

Across class, race and geographic differences, media was identified as a key source of racist beliefs by the majority of my research participants. As the discussions I have included above have also shown, faith has proved a resource that people who are persecuted draw on in order to better understand why racist hate occurs. I have suggested that the collective and individual project of developing empathy for people who demonstrate racist beliefs is a form of joy, as to understand the actions of someone so different from the self is an increase in what one can do: it is an increase in the power of action. Spinoza notes that 'since joy increases or assists a man's power of action, it is easily demonstrated' (2001: 126). Other discussions explored this theme in slightly different ways. For example, parents in inner-north Melbourne suggested the qualities that their faith had taught them:

> Aadila: Respect.
> Anna: Yes, I think respect is very important, isn't it.
> Bingwen: Tolerance.
> Anna: For me, yeah, I think respect is probably what I would say as well. I think respect is really important. Other thoughts in terms of values? What values are most important to you?

Farah: Understanding.
Anna: Yes, that's a really good one. Elizabeth, what do you think?
Elizabeth: The same, understanding.
(Inner-north Melbourne focus group, 2019)

Respect, tolerance and understanding are brought up as the most important things that religion teaches this multicultural community of many faiths. In a similar discussion in Sydney, a participant suggested that an important difference between her religion and her husband's religion was a way of teaching understanding:

And it's funny, like when we got married, we got married in the Uniting Church and just as a – not a formal marriage, just a matrimonial blessing, so I, you know, got all dressed up and went there and the priest blessed us and then we had a reception afterwards. And the priest was saying the most beautiful things about how, you know, my religion and his religion have come together and, you know, what a great example we are and moving forward, um, blessing our marriage with peace and understanding and blah, blah, blah. And so I really took that to heart, like yes, I want us to be Catholic and Muslim and show the world, 'Look at us, we are fusing these two religions together', but I don't feel like we are fusing them together and showing the world 'Look at us' because he's not so Muslimy! Does that make sense? (Philomena, west Sydney focus group, 2019)

Again, here we see the strength faith can build through extending what people are, or are not, able to understand. However, these forms of extending capacity to act are clearly a difficult form of joy – they are about negotiating difference, learning to sacrifice and develop empathy, and advocating for cultural change. Some other discussions of faith in relation to joy were more straightforward explanations of happiness. Samia from Canberra suggested that:

I'm always feeling that I'm a part of this Australia community ... we have good neighbours as well. In the second day, they come to us and during Ramadan we usually cook a lot and then we send some to other neighbours and at the end of Ramadan, they come, bring us bucketful of fruit and they said, 'We know that this is Ramadan finished, so we wanted to share the joy.' (Canberra focus group, 2019)

Bahija from Rusholme, Manchester, made a similar point:

We have that too because, the two biggest celebrations in Islam are both to eat ... So both, I mean if we talk about place I mean, the typical place where we are Muslims and the prayer is … pray together. And in Manchester, particularly near the place where I live in Rusholme, there's always a big event. The prayers are held at the platform part, where many, many Muslims from Manchester gathers and do the prayers out there. This is amazing. This is amazing I think so, I don't have any trouble with expressing our happiness in celebrating, doing the routines or the uh, traditions that we usually do back home in Indonesia. So yeah no problem doing this. (Bahija, inner-south Manchester focus group, 2018)

Conclusion

Celebration, community, togetherness, understanding difference, teaching empathy: clearly people's faith practices extend their capacities to act in many ways. In this chapter, I have examined the ways that faith is experienced and communicated through affect, in children's words and imaginations and art, and in adults' worlds. From feeling enthusiastic about insects and their role in maintaining ecosystems, to making artworks that tell stories of pilgrimage, to reflecting upon how religion teaches us to think differently about others and to put oneself in the shoes of the less fortunate, affect mediates joy in different ways across a lifetime. The complex relationships between joy and sorrow that are part of so many people of faith's experiences substantiate Spinoza's repeated observations (2021: 134–5) that hope and fear, joy and hatred are two sides of the same coin: different responses to the same phenomena. In this chapter, I have tried to show that faith practices can extend people's capacities to act, often in quite extraordinary ways. From a young age onwards, faith informs how people live with nature, feel part of community, celebrate and how they respond to prejudice.

5

Belonging / *Muintearas*

Another thing that always makes me feel at home is when you get north of Port Augusta and you see your first mesas, you know those flat-top landforms and the colour combination of blue, and red and grey, instead of green. I know that desert: the Flinders Ranges. I spent a considerable amount of my childhood at Leigh Creek, golden childhood years, year four to year seven, and I think that's why I feel so attached. To that and to local people, the Adnyamathanha. I can pick an Adnyamathanha person in the street to this day. (Jenny, outer-south Adelaide focus group, 2018)

And the second thing that popped into my head was the muezzin's call to prayer from the minaret, hearing that through my teenage years, and some of my childhood, through sort of the dusk and it would just echo around the neighbourhood, and then the third thing that popped into my head was the warble of a magpie. When I was overseas, the one thing that really brought me to tears and made me suddenly homesick … is that sound. (Kinza, inner-east Adelaide focus group, 2018)

These different stories of belonging illustrate complex attachments. They are from women who live in the same city, yet who demonstrate different emotional and material entanglements of belonging. Place, sound, smell, people, language, prayer: the things with which we become enmeshed are diverse and often involuntary. I am not great at 'belonging' to communities, and I have moved more than most people I know. Like many Australians, I grew up as an outsider: not entirely Australian, but not Irish either. I still don't completely belong in either of these countries. Like so many other children of migrants, living as the diaspora, a part of me always feels like I would be better placed somewhere else. How, then, can I speak about belonging? Specifically, how can I speak about other people's experiences of belonging? In this chapter, I collect the belonging stories that people have shared with me. They include a diverse range of ways that people find connection, community and belonging. For my research participants, community is a complex set of attachments to places, spaces, people and things: attachments that create a sense of belonging. These connections are variously found online, on a soccer field, through marriage or at a mosque or church, and they make people feel like they are part of something bigger. Furthermore, both online and offline communities are central to people's sense of self, and these communities often reflect people's faith, geography and sexuality. Migration stories and geographic community play central roles in determining community belonging, often followed by sexuality and career choices. Many participants who belong to church, for example, do so for the music, storytelling and community, as well as (or even instead of) faith and spirituality. Embedded in this search for and experience of community is often a history of being rejected by other communities. Many research participants are inside and outside communities that are online and offline, intertwined in both. Through the themes of belonging and community, this chapter shows religious and secular people have more they can claim in common than they claim as a point of difference. And as a result, those things to which we are attached, things that make us feel we belong, whether they be people, places, values or things, are of utmost importance in considering what makes a community.

Belonging on and offline

Social media platforms and messaging apps are key components of migrant communities and present a way to stay in contact with families and maintain strong transnational communities (Dekker, Belabas and Scholten, 2015; Lam and Smirnov, 2017; Mahmod, 2019; Marino, 2015; Martin, 2019; Nowicka, 2020; Samak, 2017). The emergence of online communities has led some observers to point to a diminishing place-based solidarity among some migrants, who, rather than developing a sense of belonging in their homes, establish transnational networks online. This can result in feelings of alienation and isolation from offline communities (Kastoryano, 2018). More broadly, digitally mediated communities are increasingly important for most people, particularly for those who identify with historically marginalised groups within mainstream society. Online communities provide important resources for minority groups who are marginalised or experience discrimination, for instance as a result of their sexuality (Brandt and Carmichael, 2020; Miller, 2017). Online networks can offer crucial support mechanisms and strategies to disseminate information. They also enable people in similar circumstances to share their experiences (Brandt and Carmichael, 2020; Pedersen and Lupton, 2018; Williams Veazey, 2018).

Among my participants, both online and offline support groups emerged as important sites of belonging. Participants were strategic about the ways they negotiated online and offline communities, and the reasons why they chose to belong to different groups. In one focus group discussion, Nicole, a mother from Adelaide, shared her experience of membership in an online group of single mothers:

> *Probably the main community I'm part of is an online group called 'Solo Mums by Choice'. Some of the mums identify as lesbians, some as heterosexual, some don't particularly put themselves in a box, some have had failed relationships and then got to an age where if they were going to have children, then it has to be then. I'm nearly forty-nine, and my children are six and seven, so I was definitely in the category of, if I'm going to have kids this is how it's going to have to happen.* (Inner-east Adelaide focus group, 2018)

For Nicole, membership in the online[1] group provides her with an important opportunity to meet others who have chosen to become single mothers. Like many other online communities, 'Solo Mums by Choice' is a community of people who might not have met in any other way because they are spatially disparate, and do not necessarily foreground their identity as single mothers by choice because of negative stereotypes in the community, as Nicole pointed out later in the discussion. In her words, 'the other thing we all have in common is a bit of dislike for the phrase "don't you think it's selfish to have a child by yourself?"' Going through similar experiences and facing a shared social stigma in particular is an important connection for these women that creates a feeling of being understood. As

Nicole also suggested, the members of the community have more in common than just their choice of becoming mothers on their own:

> *The other thing I like about 'Solo Mums by Choice' is that it tends to be older mothers who are professionals, and so just by choosing career over relationships perhaps through their thirties, they've then ended up in a situation where, if they want to have children at all, they need to have children by themselves.* (Inner-east Adelaide focus group, 2018)

Nicole has known some members of the group for years and feels like they are good friends, even though she has not met most of them in person. She has visited some of them and stayed in their homes, an indicator of the trust that she has established as a result of their online engagements. Nicole explains:

> *It's a national group and I've gone on holidays with my kids and we've met up with other donor-conceived kids whose parents we've met through this forum. The kids and I went to Tasmania for four weeks and met up with three kids there who aren't related to us at all, but I know the mothers because we were in the pregnancy group together, then in the baby group together, in the toddler group together, and then the school-aged kids group together … And so, I've known these mums for eight years online. So, when I said 'Hey, I'm coming to Tassie for a month, can I pitch a tent in your back-yard?' and they were like 'yeah, come and sleep in the living room'. And we went to Melbourne on these last holidays and house-sat again, this same situation. The little girl is a similar age to Sophie, so I've known the mum online for eight years.* (Inner-east Adelaide focus group, 2018)

The women in this online group are making major life choices: they are becoming pregnant or fostering children by themselves, and their choices are sometimes judged by their peers, including friends and relatives. In contrast, the online group represents a variety of different family constellations, and this diversity results in a non-judgemental approach towards other members' circumstances. Group members tend to find that they also have other things in common:

> *Two of the women in the group that I know fairly well, have created families through fostering, or fostering and biology in the case of one family that we stayed with in Tassie. So, I think that I would*

click with most of these women anyway, just in terms of the age, background, where we live, lifestyle choices, and then particularly the other mums who have children the same age as mine, I feel like they're my friends even though we haven't met face-to-face in some cases. (Inner-east Adelaide focus group, 2018)

Nicole is also a member of a church community; she attends with her children. As she points out, though, religiosity is not her main reason for being a member of the church: 'We are a nice, quirky, interesting group … We are a religious group that's not technically that religious.' For her, the more relevant education she hopes her children will receive is what she calls 'characters and values education':

I started coming two years ago because, as a homeschooler, I was looking for a centre for characters and values education. And we are not religious homeschoolers and for me, this provides a lot of structure because our family comes pretty much every Sunday and I like the sense of community. (Inner-east Adelaide focus group, 2018)

One of Nicole's main reasons for attending the church with her children was to support them in understanding the similarities between different religions:

Church … can springboard into conversations with my kids about similarities and differences amongst religions without putting one particular religion as being better than the others. So, just yesterday, we strolled past a barbershop near our house that is run by some Muslim men and a lot of their clients are Muslim men and I was chatting about how looking clean, being clean and looking neat and tidy, shows respect for religion and the religious beliefs. So the kids and I were able to have a conversation about how you show respect and what's important, what you value, and it was great that we could use our experiences meeting people of different colours, and different cultures and backgrounds here, in a non-judgemental way to sort of link the two, link the Muslim faith to sort of the things that we believe. (Inner-east Adelaide focus group, 2018)

Nicole's story is one of many that show how online and offline communities can serve different purposes and fulfil different needs. The 'Solo Mums by Choice' online community connects Nicole with other mothers who decided to have children on their own, while her church group connects her with families who share spiritual and ethical values. The church and the online mums' group are great examples of how Nicole negotiates different kinds of communities and establishes functional strategies around the need to belong, to be supported by others, and to feel accepted, skilfully combining both online and offline sites of attachment. Many other families bridge distance with technology and also find real-life community in mosques or churches, as the move between digital and offline as a strategy for everyday belonging has become seamlessly enmeshed in day-to-day life.

Surface attachments and outside belongings

In her 1996 book titled *Outside Belongings*, Elspeth Probyn characterises a sense of attachment to peripheries and surfaces, in contrast to identification with nationality and/or dominant models of heterosexual domestic life. Following Probyn, I want to suggest that the edges and surfaces of communities, organisations and belief systems are critically engaged spaces, and that they are needed more than ever with the continued global rise of the far right. Probyn explains the utility of thinking through belonging to surfaces:

> At the same time that the 'whatever' aspect of belonging on the surface forces us to relinquish the idea of guarding difference jealously as a personal possession whereby 'my difference' makes me better than you, it also works against a happy pluralism. For the question of 'being such that it always matters' constantly compels us within the processes of singularizing specificity. Conducted on the surface, this requires us to constantly place ourselves within relations of proximity of different forms of belonging. And at the edge of ourselves we mutate; we become other. (1996: 34)

Investigating mutating edges, I consider the politics of 'becoming other', of life at the peripheries of social formations: faith and race, outside belongings in/as family, and the significance and complexity of such attachments. While online communities can span countries and continents, many communities are more spatially situated, anchored in the places and institutions that support everyday lives, such as schools, shops, workplaces, leisure and sports facilities, and religious institutions, including churches, mosques and temples.

Research into the practices that enable affective attachments to community shows that it is the everyday spaces and personal encounters that can destabilise prejudice and stereotyping and allow for a sense of belonging to emerge (Askins, 2015, 2016; Grzymala-Kazlowska, 2018; Williamson, 2016). Faith plays an important part in this process, not just because faith communities are important in the everyday lives of many of my participants, but also because faith in others and a belief in the importance of diversity motivates many participants' engagements with people from other ethnic and cultural backgrounds. Most participants believe that people from different religions are honest, trustworthy and kind, and what is required for better interpersonal understanding is more personal knowledge about different faiths and cultural and religious values.

In spite of this broad sentiment attributing honesty to those who are religious, attachment to religious and faith communities also emerged as a complicated topic for many participants. Reyhan, who we met earlier and who moved from South Australia to west Sydney, explained how, in her new area, communities were segregated around ethnicity and religion, to the point of attending religious institutions according to their own background:

Community is not important, as important. But to me, it has its pros and cons in that like for me, like I said, like it's very community-based here in west Sydney, but they are very split – like you know, you will go to Merrylands, and you'll know that's where the Lebs [people from Lebanese background] are, or Bankstown is where the Muslim Lebs are. Merrylands is more Christian Lebanese, or the Turkish people will be in Auburn … Here, they don't intermingle as much as in Adelaide. Like here it's very much you know, this mosque is for the Turks, this mosque is for the Lebs or the Arabs, and this mosque is for you know, the Indian/Pakistani community. (Reyhan, west Sydney, interview, 2018)

Reyhan moved from being at the heart of a Muslim community in Adelaide to Sydney and is finding it hard to 'fit in'. My research participants did not necessarily feel that they had much in common with people just because they shared the same ethnic background or religion.

Personal notions of community also often diverge from assumed external constructs. This is particularly striking in cases where a sense of affiliation is presumed on the basis of a shared aspect of identity, for instance among what is sometimes termed the 'Muslim community' or the 'LGBTQIA+ community'. Such generalisations can be useful, for instance when trying to examine issues such as discrimination or racism, but more often than not, identity labels gloss over the internal diversity (and internal frictions) of these presumed communities. In the case of ethnic religious and minority religious groups, such stereotyping is also often framed in spatial terms, in particular where some areas within a city or region have higher rates of ethnic or religious minorities. This is reaffirmed when this is reflected in the environment, in the names of shops or the goods for sale, in the skin colour of residents, or in the languages spoken on the street.

Exploring the intersections of place, ethnicity and community as sites of belonging, Hussain (2014) explains how associations of place and ethnicity inform popular ideas of a political construct of 'the Muslim community', based on simplistic assumptions and stereotypes. Hussain considers how definitions of 'community' have been utilised by the ruling, generally white, political class to delineate specific 'bounded ethnic and racial groups conceived by liberal multiculturalism and practised through identity politics' (623). He also uses the instance of the Sparkbrook 'spy-cam affair'[2] to investigate how constructions of 'the Muslim community' have been 'used in local policy- and decision-making to locate and govern "other" groups – in this case Muslims' (2014: 623). Hussain contends that a dominant 'multicultural' model of place and community maps religions onto spatial areas where ethnic and religious minorities live. Hussain shows how dominant representations and public discourses tap into particular constructions of 'the Muslim community', namely as a 'homogenous [sic] group of outsiders' (623), but also create 'the Muslim community' as being spatially bound, such as to a suburb or ward. As the data from my ethnography clearly shows, and Hussain's argument corroborates, 'the Muslim community' is neither homogeneous nor spatially bound. Secular and religious communities are diverse, and part of their similarity lies in this diversity.

Against constructions of homogeneous Muslim communities, Hussain (2014) argues that we need to develop 'a more complicated

Belonging / Muintearas 103

Figure 5.1 Street photos from Claremont, 2019

picture of community as contested and created through space and in dialogue with notions of race, ethnicity and nation, and not determined by them' (623). He goes on to explain that 'What binds people together, in this case Muslims, is not an assumed idea of culture derived from ethnicity, but an assemblage of social, cultural and affective practices that produce relations between different ethnicities, generations and collectivities in the same area and beyond' (633). For Hussain, The Hub – a Muslim-led community arts space – is positioned as a place that 'materialises different ways in which Muslim identity and collectivity is felt' (2014: 633) and 'enables a making of Muslim identity in ways that challenge reductionist accounts framed in ethno-religious terms alone' (2014: 624). Indeed, this assemblage is how belonging is created across both the religious and secular communities with whom I worked. Martha from south-east London explained her belonging in relation to her church community:

> I belong to a strong church community and I would say that's both local, as in my immediate church community, but also larger, as I belong to the Anglican Church, so I would say I'd be quite linked to the Anglican Church in this diocese of the country. Perhaps worldwide, but I struggle with that because I don't always agree with it, but I obviously feel part of it, so that's quite interesting. And I sometimes do ministry in different parts of the world. So I've been to India and places like that on ministry trips, so I do feel kind of part of a worldwide sense of the, they call it Anglican but it's the Episcopal church. (South-east London focus group, 2018)

Martha is both outside and inside her church community, a theme that returns in many ways across participants' stories of belonging. Indeed, the complex nature of belonging and of the 'diverse ranges of social, cultural and affective practices that produce relations between different ethnicities, generations, and collectivities' (Hussain, 2014: 633) mean that being inside and outside communities simultaneously and learning to accept and value diversity are critical components in feeling belonging. For example, Meerab, a Muslim immigrant living in Canberra, explains valuing diversity as core to building community:

> Our heritage from our origin and country is not a good thing to lose. Because it is very important to carry these things on and if we can bring them here, the good things, then we can pass these things on. (Meerab, Canberra focus group, 2018)

Meerab felt we have to hold on to 'the good things' to form a community and keep heritage alive. He was afraid of losing his culture coming to Australia. She mentioned that there are always good and bad things, and that we can't judge a whole community based on a few bad people. As a Muslim, Meerab went on to refer to terrorism and the ways it has created prejudice or racism towards her community, leading to attitudes such as:

> Well, you know there might be a nice boy at your school and he finds out that your dad's a Muslim and then loses interest in you and goes back and tells his family: 'Oh, you know, stay away from her; her dad's Muslim.' (Meerab, Canberra focus group, 2018)

Meerab's experiences are not isolated. Iner (2015) has found very similar experiences in her work with young practising Muslim women in Australia. Iner worked with both those born in Australia and those who had relocated. These women experience belonging in relation to Islam, Australia, and their ethnic origin and had also experienced prejudice, often based on an unrealistic idea of their community or acts of violence that are extrapolated to represent their community. Interestingly, Iner argues for diverse and intersecting senses of belonging in her participants. She suggests that respondents displayed a sense of belonging to 'many worlds at once' (2015: 168). Iner found that this sense of belonging was a fluid and dynamic process in which 'the identity formation of the second generation is actually an active process of rebuilding, reassessing and redressing their sense of belonging with situationality' (168). Part of this situational responsivity is a requisite engagement with social stereotypes about Muslim culture.

Iner explores belonging as a component of identity, specifically the sociopolitical formation of a collective Muslim identity that is 'strongly felt especially among the Muslim immigrants in non-Muslim majority countries' (156). Iner identifies several 'inside' and 'outside' forces that contribute to the formation and characterisation of these group identities, such as the national identity of the host country, parental and familial pressures of loyalty, and national and ethnic heritage. Iner documents several instances in which young people worked to develop specific community identities around Islam and the national identity of the host country, stating emphatically that 'ethno-religious identities are not at odds with embracing a host country's national as well as cultural and sportive assets' (159). Yet the day-to-day life of Muslim people in Australia is too often crossed by having to justify themselves in the face of popular misconceptions about their religion, and indeed, their character.

Queer family belongings

Much has changed since Probyn published *Outside Belongings* (1996), including a vote for marriage equality not just in Australia but many other countries, notably the Republic of Ireland, and the accompanying rise and celebration of 'rainbow families'. *Outside*

Belongings came back into my mind in two very different fieldwork settings, in east London and Adelaide, when discussing social and community values with two different families that both consisted of white Christian lesbian mothers and a Black son. The feelings of outside belonging that organise family and attachment were articulated by these mothers in terms of nationality, class, race, gender and family, in insightful ways that resonated between my fieldwork sites.

One of these mothers was Martha, who has a powerful story of 'elective belonging' (see Jeffery, 2018), detailing her move from a very conservative family to a working-class area. Martha also shared stories of outside belonging, of creating new surfaces and points of intersection for isolated mothers, and of seeking communities of mothers of mixed-race children:

> *I've been building a mums' network community, of which I'd say I was strongly part of, which is part of a group of mothers in the Greenwich Peninsula ... I'm deliberately focused on doing that. And also some in East Greenwich for isolated women. And I'm just about to join a community of parents with mixed heritage children. Because the parents don't always have the heritage information, so it's to come together and work around supporting each other and also sharing.* (South-east London focus group, 2018)

Martha very much identifies with communities at the margins. While she is part of a range of different and often marginalised community groups, being a lesbian mother and a female church minister, she is also very grounded in her sense of belonging. She explained: 'When I say this community here, I would say I have a sense of living in quite a big area of Greenwich and [Charlton], it's not just up here, it's quite a bigger geographical area, but I definitely feel rooted here' (south-east London focus group, 2018).

While Martha expressed her need for support with the politics of being a mother of a mixed-race child, she did not explain how she intended to meet her children's needs when questions of racial prejudice and white privilege shaped her son's (and her daughter's) experiences of growing up. These issues were discussed a little more by Nancy and Louise, the two white lesbian mothers living in Adelaide. Senses of belonging and relationships with place are mediated by all kinds of things that extend beyond sexuality and relationships with community.

Nancy and Louise are a white lesbian couple who live in Adelaide with their son Jessie. Over some food at a church focus group in the Adelaide Hills, they explained the complications of belonging to a church as a lesbian couple and of parenting a Black boy in the racist climate of predominantly white Australia:

Anna: Nancy, what drew you to the church?
Nancy: Well, when I met Louise, she was going to a rather large Pentecostal church with Jessie quite regularly, and I was never very religious, I wasn't raised religious, I went to a public school, didn't have any kind of religious background at all, but obviously it was important to Louise, she went to a Christian school –
Louise: My school was an Anglican school –
Nancy: And Jessie was at an Anglican school at the time so it was obviously quite important to them, so I thought I'd go with them to support the family. But it was quite evident when I started coming with Jessie, that they weren't very, they weren't rude –
Louise: Nobody ever said anything, but –
Nancy: You just never really got the full sense of welcome that you expect.
Louise: And it was around the same time as the same-sex marriage laws were changing, they did the postal vote, and so –
Nancy: Yeah, so there were a few talks about that,
Louise: We liked to talk about it.
Nancy: They were like 'Make sure you stick with your values', and we were like 'We will', but you know, it wasn't the greatest fit so we just stopped going for a while. Then Jessie started saying that he wanted to go back to church, because at the church that he went to they would play video games and stuff, so he just wanted to be with the other kids again, but we couldn't really get past that just to go for him, and we didn't want to send him there to learn all these values as well, we were a little bit conflicted, so I think I ended up googling which religion is most accepting of same-sex families.
Louise: What she did was she googled 'top ten most accepting churches for same-sex couples'.
Nancy: And then we just started coming, and Jessie has just loved it. All different kinds of families that are here, and all different kinds of kids, it's very multicultural which is very good for him, him being raised by two white women but he's very clearly of African descent. It's important for him to be around people with different kinds of families.

(Outer-south Adelaide focus group, 2018)

While the journey to find a safe spiritual home led Louise and Nancy to a church where they and their son are very happy and accepted, the politics of race relations in Australia are an ongoing source of marginalisation for the family in some community settings. This is compounded for their son Jessie by the perspectives of many religious communities on same-sex families. Louise explained Jessie's feelings of outside belongings:

> Jessie struggles a lot, when we go out, people automatically assume he's adopted, and he's got quite a complex history with his dad's side, so that can be really hard for him, because he's wanting to be proud of his culture, but isn't really proud of his dad's side. So it's really quite conflicting, so a lot of time he just ends up saying he is adopted. (Outer-east Adelaide focus group, 2018)

The negotiations that Louise and Nancy explain as being core to Jessie's everyday life become even more complex when questions of race are considered. Nancy's family live in a country town in south Australia called Maitland, in which the racist treatment of Aboriginal people is explicit and normalised (see, for example, the work of Fowler, Roberts and Rigney, 2016; Liebelt, Roberts, O'Loughlin and Milera, 2016). The Aboriginal members of the community live on a mission adjacent to the township, racially separating the two communities. They explained the Aboriginal people in her parents' town:

> Nancy: They all live in the mission, no one [who is Aboriginal] lives in the town, and when we take Jessie back, everybody stares at you. And I got really scared, because from the back, he was wearing his helmet one day, scootering along, and from the back he looks like an Aboriginal boy because of his dark skin, and he was scootering off, and I thought, we've got to stay with him, because I was worried that someone was going to start yelling at him or something. Because even the Indigenous kids from the mission don't go to school in Maitland, they go to the Indigenous school, and so there is no integration. I was scared. We went to an Australia Day breakfast they had there, because that's what my grandparents do. My grandparents, they kind of like to stay away from all the bitterness in the town. There's all these little cliques, but my grandparents say, we do our own thing. And so grandparents are sitting there, they're already quite segregated in

the town, and they've got a lesbian grandchild, with their half-Black great-grandchild, and they're taking it in their stride, and everybody is staring.
Louise: The whole room is white, there's not a single person who was –
Nancy: Not a single person who was even tanned. Everybody is pale white, and there are all these old white men, with beards and balding. And it was the first time where I thought, I should feel at home here, but I don't, and I don't want to be there because I felt, 'What am I bringing Jessie into?' He's too little to really notice it, [but] he's almost old enough to be like 'No one here looks like me', and there's going to be a point where he's going to say, 'No one looks like me', and there'll be an Indigenous person walking on the street and everybody around them will be saying something, or the police will come and chat to them just because they're sitting there, and it's horrible. So, when you were talking about feeling Australian, I guess I, yeah, it's this weird thing inside me that makes me feel like I'm not.
(Outer-east Adelaide focus group, 2018)

Nancy's dis-identification with a racist country town in white Australia comes together with fear for her child's safety. She went on to explain feeling scared for Jessie's safety, and complained about the emotional pain he is forced to live with:

What makes me more Australian than Jessie is? And why is it that everyone asks him 'Where are you from?' and he's like 'Adelaide'. (Outer-east Adelaide focus group, 2018)

Being on the organising surface of Maitland soil made both Jessie and his mothers feel un-Australian. Space and whiteness were used to position Jessie as 'not from here', and the racist, homophobic community sentiment leads his parents to also feel outside the culture. I had the distinct feeling that 'all these old white men, with beards and balding' had brought their temporalities with them. Days of unquestioned colonial reign, of the White Australia Policy and unquestioned, dysfunctional patriarchal rule were kept alive in their social imaginations. This feeling of unbelonging is significant and must be read as important. As Probyn (1996) so astutely notes, 'desires for alternative relations and connections can only be considered superficial if seen through an optic that excludes their importance' (35). Nancy and Louise worked hard to find their inclusive church, and love attending Pride with their family. But in other significant spaces, such as their son's Christian school and their parents' country town, they really struggle to feel a sense of belonging.

Martha, on the other hand, who lives in a much more progressive and cosmopolitan city (London, as opposed to Adelaide), has had more opportunities to create community through her work as the youth minister for her community church, her local mothers' group, and a local lesbian community. Martha shared a vivid and warm story about her wedding that gives a clear sense of her skill at community-building:

> We had a civil partnership in 2006 and then when the law changed we converted our civil partnership to a marriage. But we did it on my wife's fiftieth birthday, because she'd asked me to marry her on her thirtieth. And then we had a bit kind of celebratory party and it was not quite a garden party, a kind of country fair. We borrowed one of the churches. Borrowed loads of hay bales and had people playing live music and it was a kind of real cake bake-off and it was just a fun time … We have a friend who does clowning who came. Another friend brought his circus equipment. It was a bit kind of fun, all-ranging celebration we had when we did that … For everybody and after all, that's what it's meant to be about really. You're not … when you get married you're not just marrying the other person. You're creating community and you're forging community and it's not just the families you're with. It's much bigger. (South-east London, interview, 2019)

It isn't at all surprising that Martha has managed to create a sense of community through her marriage, as she has moved away from her family of birth in order to build a religious community, her family and a strong local mothers' community. Martha really is a community-maker. While Martha and Nancy and Louise are all white lesbian parents of Black boys (Martha also has a little girl), they navigate their experiences of belonging in different ways. Martha does enjoy Pride, but her primary connection is to her religious community, and then to her mothers' group. Nancy and Louise, on the other hand, have a primary connection to their local queer community and then to their church, which, as their story makes plain, they have joined because of their son. Both families have worked hard to both find and create spaces of acceptance and to navigate the prejudice some people hold against them and their children.

Faith as community and culture

During focus group discussions and individual interviews, people in all my research sites acknowledged the interrelatedness of religion, ethnicity and culture. This has also emerged as a pattern in the academic literature in recent years, in particular among younger people (Halafoff et al., 2020; McGuire, 2008; Woodhead, 2011). Participants repeatedly commented that culture has a significant impact on how religion is practised, including on the way that they felt towards specific religious communities. Many participants suggested that culture, rather than religion, was what drew them to religious communities, because they wanted to pass specific values on to their children. These include kindness, being helpful and generous and being convivial and sociable. Alayah said that she misses the educational aspects of the Muslim culture in which she was raised, and explained that she worries her daughter does not always behave in the ways she would like. She is trying to teach her daughter to be more helpful towards others. Like many others, Alayah felt that what she calls the 'sense of village' is often lacking in her experience of community in Australia. Many parents wanted their children to develop specific character qualities (being friendly, caring and selfless) that were, in many ways, inseparable from religious communities. Alayah is drawn to her church because it provides a sense of village life. In raising her daughter, she brings together the ethical teachings of the Islamic religion in which she was raised with the sense of community her church provides.

Some parents were quite clear about wanting to replicate their own childhood experiences for their children. Another mother, Sarah, was adamant that her main reason for being a member of a church was to enjoy a sense of community and learn values, rather than to learn about God or to serve God. Sarah explained that her own 'growing away from religion' was the reason for introducing her son to a more liberal church community:

> *I've been coming to the church for two or three years. I was introduced by another friend and I thought, Giorgio is an only child and it's a great place for him to experience community, and also some*

> *good values. I was brought up in South India, in an Orthodox Christian family called Syrian Jacobites. My grandfather was a church minister, and although I've grown away from religion, I've felt there were values that I was taught that were useful, and I want Giorgio to get a similar kind of education and experience.* (Inner-east Adelaide focus group, 2018)

The reasons why Sarah came back to a church show clearly how participants choose religious communities based on a complex enmeshment of history, lived experience and culture. Seeking a sense of community or trying to replicate their own childhood experiences for their children were among the main reasons parents gave for joining faith-based communities. For some participants, the attraction to religion was the feeling of 'fitting in' that fostered a sense of belonging, a feeling of familiarity and tradition. For example, as Philomena explained, her family still attends the church in which her parents were married, even though it is now a significant distance from their current home. Whenever possible, her family makes the long journey from their home in the outer-west suburbs of Sydney to the inner-west location of the church, because they derive a sense of belonging from their involvement with this community:

> My parents still like to go, so I sometimes drive them to Leichhardt church, which is where they got married. All my kids were baptised there. My brother and my sister got married there, so we have a big history at that church. I know my parents' funerals will be there … maybe even mine. So, there is a – a calling there, a belonging there, a family there, a community there. So, when there is a – a festival there or a commemoration of some sort we're drawn to that. (West Sydney focus group, 2018)

Philomena's comments illustrate how memory lives on in a place. Her story demonstrates the appeal of continuity with/in place, where community is built through years and years of living with, and interacting with, each other – what Alayah above calls the 'sense of village'.

For others, the quest to 'fit in' manifested itself in more complex ways: aspirationally moving to a more affluent community, moving to a more diverse area as a political statement, travelling abroad for education or safety, and so on. In these diverse settings, religion is seen as a way to be a better person, to belong to more desirable people, a barrier between self and others, and a way to keep going despite hardship. One Australian participant, Marge, explained the educational value she gets from her Buddhist religious group, whose members are predominantly of Vietnamese origin:

> I've got a few communities that I currently belong to. One is our [government-funded] public school community: we volunteer, and the parents and the teachers, our child's in grade four now, and the longer we're there I think we both feel that sense of community and working together. The teachers say, 'It's great that your parents are switched on, because we can work together' etc. So that gives me a sense of community I guess, being part of the local school. The other thing for me is, back to my Buddhist group, which is run by a fellow psychologist, it's actually at the moment all Vietnamese people, who kindly translate. We are working on Sunyata Emptiness Meditation. So, when I go to that group, with such a wonderful bunch of people who are essentially non-judgemental and really supportive, I feel at home and really part of, I'm part of their community, I feel part of their community, even though at the moment I'm the only English-speaking person, or some of them speak English and Vietnamese. So I feel like I'm coming home when I'm there, and yet I'm not Vietnamese, I'm Russian Orthodox from early on. (Outer-east Adelaide focus group, 2018)

Not only does Marge feel most at home in a group that is totally different from the culture in which she was raised, among peers who do not speak the same language she does, but the group itself is also fairly removed from any mainstream religious school of thought, or as she puts it, operates without 'all the dogma and stuff in the way'. Marge's Buddhist community creates its own religious sub-culture based on the priorities and aspirations of its members and their personal spiritual philosophies. This theme of faith as a way of belonging to community and culture is an attraction for people who belong to religions, as well as those who never chose to belong, but who encountered religion through others or family (Woodhead, 2011). Martha from south-east London made a huge effort to find a church where she could belong:

> So now, for me, the Church of England church I go to is part of Inclusive Church, which is a church that accepts everybody on grounds that it doesn't matter what your gender is, financial situation, disability, sexuality. Basically, it's very clear that this is a church

for everybody. Normal people, basically ... The church will not discriminate on any of those grounds: you know, things like addiction, debt, blah blah. All those things. Whereas a lot of churches would say they are welcoming, but really, you might come through the door and people might tut or say, 'well, that's okay for you but we don't want your type [lesbians]'. (South-east London focus group, 2018)

While Martha sought out her inclusive church in London, Simone experienced a very different version of an inclusive church as a result of the rural location of her childhood home.

Bordered on two sides by a warm coral sea, the state of Queensland in Australia has an area of 1.853 million km². It is seven times the size of England. Simone's experience of church community is set in north Queensland, and is an expression of the limited resources her father's community had available:

My father grew up in a very small town in north Queensland, and there was no church, and his mother owned the only pub in town. Because they weren't open Sunday mornings, the pub would alternate between housing the different religions in town – everyone would have their church service in the pub. Every Sunday, everyone would go, whether they were a Protestant or a Catholic or something else, and each preacher would have a turn once a month giving a sermon. The whole town would just rock up and listen. Remembering that from my dad cracks me up, that's how the community came together. The rabbi, the priest, and the minister walked into a pub and gave a sermon. They took turns. That's how he grew up, at his mum's pub – which was also the local church. It was everyone's religion. The alcoholics and the religious folk, they all came together. Everyone got to learn about the other religions because they had to share a church and sermons. And it brought together their similarities, more than the differences. I guess, if anything, you learn that it's all pretty much the same and that stops any arguing, and if you have a question the minister's right there from a different religion, so go and find out. It created that opportunity that you don't get when everything has their own place to go to and it's all separate. (Simone, south-east Melbourne focus group, 2018)

The idea that different faith systems have more in common than they have separating them clearly runs through Simone's story, which positions alcoholics and religious folk as the two halves of a shared place-based faith community. Faith is often based on acceptance into a community, but it can also result in rejection from communities (think of Martha trying so hard to find a church that would accept her as a lesbian). In very different ways, people see faith as a pathway to happiness. Bringing out people's similarities rather than their differences was the primary value Simone identified in her father's experience of pub church. She clearly identifies that understanding 'sameness' across cultural and religious differences is a skill her father learnt through the experience of Sunday pub sermons. Themes of moral and ethical education clearly run across all religions.

One identifying feature that did not run across all religions was the fact that Muslim participants often suggested their religion was *misunderstood* in some way. Participants were adamant that Muslims are a diverse community, and that on an individual and a community level they have as much in common with non-Muslims as they have with other Muslims. In the next section, I explore some of the conversations I had with participants as examples of subcultures of Islam, along with the often-cited opinion that popular culture misrepresents Islam in ways that can lead to racist depictions of Muslim people. Muslim diversity and connections with secular cultures.

Participants came from a variety of backgrounds. As pointed out elsewhere, not all Muslims have dark skin and certainly not all Christians are white, even though the research participants found that this imagined racial division is a persistent stereotype. Cultural and ethnic traditions varied widely, and many participants had grown up in more than one cultural environment. There were also sizeable differences in age groups, education levels, and political attitudes. In focus group discussions, these different subgroups of education standards, political attitudes and age often showed much greater similarities in attitude and opinion than those based on religious beliefs. Many people are unaware of the diversity within religion, particularly the diversity within Islam, which seems to be what has led to a public perception of Islam as monolithic and unchanging. However, just like within the Christian faith, there are many subgroups that are religiously and culturally quite different.

Diversity within Islam

During focus groups and interviews, a number of Muslim participants said they perceived the general public's knowledge of Islam as quite low. This included knowledge of Muslim practices and traditions, distinctions between moderate and fundamentalist beliefs, and between the different Muslim schools of thought and denominations. Many felt that they were unjustly perceived as the same kinds of people who would carry out atrocities (such as Islamic State, also known as ISIS or Daesh), even though they had themselves suffered from fundamentalist groups, and in some cases had become refugees because of fundamentalist persecution. One participant, Rahmatollah, explained:

> *I think at the moment Muslim people have a lot of problems. Especially in the media ... We come from the same religion. But it's two different branches ... Like two different groups. I'm Shia Muslim. And most of the population is Sunni Muslim. But when on the media showing like, al-Qaeda, Daesh, and the Taliban, they are Muslim. The public don't recognise what's the difference between us and them. And when the people see news on the TV and after that they think oh, this [is] a Muslim. When I am asked about what's your religion, I'm Muslim, the first thing people are thinking about is I belonging to those people as well. To Daesh, to al-Qaeda, to the Taliban. For example, in the first year when I came to Australia ... in Tasmania, I had a very bad experience with one of the Australians, in the park where I was sitting. Some Australian people came and started talking and then asking where I come from. I said, 'I'm from Afghanistan.' 'Where, from Afghanistan? You're Muslim?' I said, 'Yeah.' 'Oh Daesh! Al Qaeda! Mullah Omar!' I said, 'I'm sorry I'm not Daesh. I'm not Al Qaeda. I'm not Mullah Omar.' 'Yeah, but you are Muslim! Those people are also Muslim.' The public in Australia don't know that the Taliban, Daesh, al-Qaeda don't love us. Those fundamentalist organisations are saying to us, 'You are not Muslim' ... That's why we become refugees.* (South-east Melbourne focus group, 2018)

This story of alienation, loss and fear is extreme, but is also similar to many stories told by Muslim refugee participants. The key piece of information that seems to be missing from the popular consciousness in both Australia and the UK is the fact that, in most cases, Muslim refugees and migrants have left their home countries because of persecution *by extremist Muslim groups* (Kabir, 2007).

Rahmatollah was not only forced to leave his home by extremist Muslim groups, but he was then forced to live through negative experiences with racism in Australia, in which he was made out to be the same as the extremists that had forced him out of his home in Afghanistan. Rahmatollah was forced to the periphery of

Australian culture, made to belong to the edges. He said this was particularly painful because he had already been forced to leave his home country because of the danger from fundamentalist groups:

> We are affected by fundamentalist groups because we are always persecuted by Taliban and al-Qaeda, Daesh. As you know in the media, because they are Sunni Muslim, and you are Shia, they don't believe in the Shia, they believe that Shia are not Muslim. They are saying, 'You have to change your religion if you want to stay in Afghanistan, you have to change your religion. Or if you don't change it, you have to leave Afghanistan.' (South-east Melbourne focus group, 2018)

As Rahmatollah pointed out, subgroups have developed in Islam that follow quite different traditions and schools of thought. More conservative or fundamentalist groups are often highly critical of more permissive or liberal Muslims, but this is not often discussed in the mainstream Australian media.

As is the case with all religions, being a Muslim is not an exclusive identity. People also form practices of belonging and identity around other aspects of their lives (Jeldtoft, 2011). Elements of individual identity, such as ethnicity and culture, age, gender, sexuality, tastes and hobbies all influence modes of belonging. Some subcultures of Islam are organised, such as geographic communities that share a mosque, while others are more casual, such as followers of Instagram pages on modest fashion. Besides the main formalised groups, more informal, non-organised practices also exist (Ammerman, 2016; Jeldtoft, 2011). These include Muslims who adhere less closely to rituals, or who make up their own rituals or practices based on traditional culture or on their own values and needs, and also Muslims who are at odds with mainstream ideologies for a range of reasons. For example, LGBTQIA+ Muslims often struggle for recognition, rights or acceptance within mainstream society (Rasmussen, 2016) and within the Islamic legal system.

Conclusion

The stories of being culturally or socially positioned outside a majority that are woven across people's accounts of online belonging, queer, intersectional family-making, searches for sobriety and refugee experience are striking. They range from single mothers who have found their belonging communities online because the nuclear family remains the norm offline, to Muslim Australians and migrants who are positioned as 'outsiders' by Australians who ignorantly assume Muslims are extremist (see Eddo-Lodge, 2017). For those who belong to the edges of cultural formations – or culture's 'outsides' – the surfaces that organise their relationships certainly have agentic power, whether people attach to surfaces – like Jenny's love for the Flinders Ranges – or, like Louise and Nancy in Maitland, feel rejected by them. Probyn (1996) suggests that 'the surface is not another metaphor nor yet another fad within intellectual circles: it is a profound reordering of how we conceive of the social' (1996: 34). My research suggests this is indeed true, although surfaces reject as often as they welcome those who seek to belong.

Notes

1 Research has shown that online communities and support groups can be beneficial for people who experience a range of issues, including depression, anxiety, post-traumatic stress disorder and eating disorders, but also for practical problems such as parenting support (Haslam, Tee and Baker, 2017).
2 In April 2010, as part of the UK Government's antiterrorism measures, hundreds of surveillance cameras were installed in Sparkbrook and Washwood Heath, two suburbs of Birmingham known for their Muslim populations. The cameras allowed police to track residents and were part of a move to monitor populations identified as 'at risk' of extremism (Lewis, 2012), which the counterterrorism agencies had identified as areas with predominantly Muslim populations (Lewis, 2012; see also Hussain, 2014).

6

Connections / *Naisc*

In this chapter, I explore some of the internal systems of connection that constitute joyful assemblages in the lives of my research participants. The examples brought together here are relatively closed systems. They create safety and provide physical, social, emotional and imaginative ecosystems in which people feel safe and in this safety they can flourish. In some respects, these systems of connection need to be read in relation to vulnerability. They provide protection from broader contexts of marginalisation. They offer platforms for visibility, identity and relationality that are built on recognition, community and creativity. They create contexts for affecting people with joy. Spinoza (2001, 121) explains that:

> If a person has done anything which he imagines will affect others with joy, he also will be affected with joy, accompanied with an idea of himself as its cause; that is to say, he will look upon himself with joy.

As we have seen, so many of my research participants are part of communities that have historically been marginalised, colonised, de-valued by global cultural processes. This broader context of historical marginalisation means that specific interiorities need to be created and inhabited. Interiorities that offer safe visibility. This chapter offers three of many possible examples. These are council housing estates as sites of class belonging, football as a global community that affirms superdiversity and digital games as creative imaginative platforms and resources for children.

Council estates as sites of class belonging

Some of my fieldwork sites are located adjacent to council estates, and many of the parents involved in my research live on these estates. Some parents had made the conscious decision to bring up their families on the estate, and they embraced the sense of community and belonging these locations provided. Others, who were born on an estate, had never imagined anything other than life on the estate, and had not thought much about the possibilities of another life. These participants' experiences of estate life could not be further from the terrifying discussions of Tony Blair's 'sink estates'[1] (see Hanley, 2012). Participants' shared belonging stories relate entirely to the estate as their place of connection:

> [I lived on the Cherry Orchard estate] till I was eight ... And I came to this school ... and Sherrington and then Kidbrooke. And my mum moved round to Hornfair Road, which is about three roads round, in a house, so I've always been in Charlton ... And then I just moved to Plumstead last year and now I'm moving back because I don't like it. I'm literally swapping with someone that was brought up in Plumstead and she wants to move back. I don't know, I just can't settle there, it's really strange ... You know your bubble, that's that, and now you've stepped outside your bubble you're like, no, definitely coming back here. And here, you walk down the road and it's 'Hi, hi, hi'. And in Plumstead I don't know anybody. (Ella, south-east London focus group, 2018)

This is one of the many times in which I heard the estate characterised in a positive way by different parents as a 'bubble'. Ella's home, the Cherry Orchard estate, is well known in the area, and a geographic landmark. White-clad frontage and green lawns fit with the appearance of the local school, whose name the estate shares. Like other participants, Ella acknowledges the estate as her 'bubble' that provides comfort and familiarity, but also presents some barriers to the possibility of social mobility or new experiences. In the same group discussion, Jean shared a similar story of familiarity and belonging within the estate:

> See, I grew up on [Bram High Plain] which is literally just outside the estate, down towards the bottom road, I grew up there, so I was like six or seven, and then my mum moved to Woolwich, so my mum's

still in that house. So I've only ever lived there. And then back into Charlton onto the estate where I've had all three of my children. (Jean, south-east London focus group, 2018)

The notion of the estate as a 'bubble' within which people feel comfortable and accepted resonated for many. While housing estates, and having grown up on housing estates, are often used as a way of explaining class belonging, they also clearly explain place belonging for many. Two estates were central to my ethnographic work, one in London and the other in Melbourne, and many other research participants lived in forms of council housing. Both estates are located next to schools. While the estate itself provided the location for many of these women's lives, there were also occasions and events that focused their sense of class and shaped their sense of belonging through the sociocultural markers of class. For example, Neve clearly felt a sense of place connection, which she explained by describing how people in her estate were brought together through their love of football during the World Cup:

> *I don't follow sport at all, I'm one of those that are sort of 'ugh?', but actually, at the start of the World Cup I was like, no, we're not going to get anywhere, anyway. But then, as it was going on, and I could see it building up and everyone was getting so excited and I was like, come on, let's go and watch it, let's go and watch it. And we'd sit, our group of friends, we all went in together: us, with our kids. The local pub shut off their car park so all the kids had space to run around and enjoy themselves. They had a barbeque. There was such a buzz. And everyone, I don't think I've ever in eight years of living on the estate, I don't think I've ever seen us all come together like that. I think we had such a buzz with the build-up that it became really exciting.* (Neve, south-east London focus group, 2017)

Neve's narrative about her affection for the estate community and their rallying around football as a shared experience shows how various practices and preferences are expressions of class belonging. Wellington boots, croquet and rowing are a world apart from kids playing in the pub car park while the parents watch football on TV, but both sets of practices respectively illustrate two different kinds of predominantly English class belonging. While the World Cup brought the community of Cherry Orchard together in new ways, it also illustrates Neve's sense of geographic and class belonging in the estate. She identifies with her own 'bubble'. Yet, she also thinks that people on and off her estate have more in common than they have as a point of difference. Neve used the example of contemporary transatlantic politics to explain:

> *I think probably most people of faith will, like I'm not asking people's views about Donald Trump, but I think there's probably people from all faiths who were in the [anti-Trump] demonstration on Friday. You know, there were some things that people come together for. And he's a pretty big one.* (Neve, south-east London focus group, 2019)

On the other side of the earth, Atherton Gardens, the Melbourne estate, is similarly imbricated in people's sense of place belonging, although in more complicated ways. Atherton Gardens is a primary site for refugee resettlement, and within the broader geographic and economic community, the estate is taken as a signifier of migration and poverty. Atherton Gardens was built by the Housing Commission of Victoria in the mid-1960s as part of the Victorian Government's long-running 'slum reclamation' program, which began with the *Housing Act 1937* and the *Slum Reclamation Act 1938*. The estate features distinctive, prefabricated concrete panels that were made in the Housing Commission's concrete factory. One of my main research sites was a primary school just a block or two down the same street. It is the school of choice for locals who cannot afford to send their children to private or Catholic schools. Layla, a local mother whose son attends the school, explained her place belonging by saying, 'I feel like I'm in the community at Atherton Gardens, I know all the kids there. Yeah, I grew up there, went to school there, came to this school.'

While Layla has a clear sense of community belonging, others feel ambiguous about belonging to Atherton Gardens. Not everyone feels okay about growing up on an estate, and experiences of class and race hierarchies play out differently for migrants who are people of colour, as compared to white people. I have written elsewhere about Abdul and Caleb, who are first-generation Australian boys from refugee families who fled Somalia and West Papua respectively before they were born (Hickey-Moody and Willcox, 2020). They also live in Atherton Gardens with their families. There is a class divide between those who live on the council housing estate and those who live in private housing in the area, which is highly desirable real estate close to Melbourne's central business district and an area buzzing with bars, nightclubs, fashionable restaurants and boutiques. While the housing estate serves a much-needed purpose of providing shelter, it also reinforces the difference between refugees, migrants and the very well-off professional families and young people in share houses who live in the area. This juxtaposition clearly illustrates 'the great class divide [that] opens up the possibility of a longing for expansion that not only has no economic possibility for expression but also equally has to be understood in terms of the psychosocial affective history of its production' (Walkerdine, 2017: 6). The hip homeware shops filled with Danish-style furniture that line the main streets of Fitzroy scream 'unaffordable white middle-class belonging' to passers-by, and are most certainly not shops for those who live in Atherton Gardens.

In a conversation we had at the beginning of a round of workshops on belonging, Caleb ironically asserted that he lived in the very affluent suburb of Toorak, and, claiming that his 'dad had a big house there', suggesting his family was financially well-off. I was amazed that someone would drive from Toorak to Fitzroy every morning to attend a government-funded school. I confirmed this wasn't true by checking with his teacher. Later that afternoon, when I was walking to the tram, I noticed the blue neon sign that reads 'Our home' installed on the side of Atherton Gardens. While this sign reads like a proud statement, it contrasts with the run-down building, pointing to the very limited reach of this gesture towards gentrification. As a symbol, in comparison to Caleb's imaginary home in Toorak, the neon sign seems to overlook the struggles refugee families go through when moving across oceans to find a safe home. I wondered if Caleb likes the sign, or if he thinks it is ironic.

Football

With football, it's part of pretty much everyone's lives really. Yeah. Depending on what club you support ... You could talk about football and have a laugh with it. (Muhammad, south-east London focus group, June 2019)

Figure 6.1 'Our home', blue fluorescent light art on Caleb and Abul's housing block, inner-north Melbourne, 2019

Football – called soccer in Australia – is a theme that is most passionately discussed by children in Melbourne, London and Manchester, and features heavily in their artwork. Investments in football are a way that children belong to, or participate in, global imagined communities. While the partial streetscape in Figure 6.2 – featuring the words 'RONALDO' and 'CR7' (Ronaldo's initials and jersey number) repeatedly scrawled across it – is from a school in Manchester, the children across six of twelve research sites were equally besotted with football (soccer). It is a primary vehicle for friendship, belonging and pleasure.

Playing, watching and following football are all ways of belonging to a global, multi-ethnic community, which is very appealing to many of the children with whom I work. In his early, field-defining article on English football, '"Football's coming home" but whose home? And do we want it?', Ben Carrington (1998) famously argued that football works to create a white national 'imagined community'. As expressions of global soccer communities, this whiteness is interpolated and radically diversified by my research participants. The term 'imagined community' was developed by Benedict Anderson (1983) as a shorthand for the way notions of citizenship and belonging are reconstructed by contemporary forms of

Figure 6.2 Children in north-west Manchester draw their streets filled with names of football players, mixed media on canvas, 2018

media, popular culture and governments, Anderson argues that feelings of national belonging, of being part of a national community, are largely symbolic. This is not to say that mediated belonging is less real than attachments formed away from the keyboard (Russell, 2020) or screen, but it emphasises a need to analyse popular media if we want to understand how appeals to national sentiments work. Sport is one of the key domains in which mediated forms of imagined community are made – not just through football, but all kinds of competitive sports. Carrington (1998) discusses how the imagined community of English football supporters intersects with axes of gender and race. Sport invites fans to join an imagined national community, but it is a community in which certain types of bodies and identities are favoured over others. Carrington (1998) explains:

> The symbolism of national sporting sides, and sport itself, has … acquired huge political significance, especially for the political right, in trying to foster certain narrow notions of what Britain's/England's … cultural identity should look like. (102)

Much of Carrington's argument is concerned with the ways that popular media, and particularly the entertainment genre of sports television, can try to promote a myth of white, pure Englishness. Indeed, the broader social contexts within which football and football entertainment exist are closely linked to the national imaginary. In Britain, football's series of racial and national exclusions (which have been continued in the racist vilification of players involved in the 2021 FIFA Club World Cup) have previously been thematically connected with whiteness as configured in such things as the Britpop movement of the mid-to-late 1990s:

> What we see here [in football culture, pop culture, etc.] is an attempt to promote a fixed, closed and racially homogenous [sic] sense of national cultural identity that actively excludes black representations from the national imaginary. (Carrington, 1998: 105)

This point has been built upon, extended and recapped in a variety of ways since the late 1990s. Jamie Cleland (2014) has examined sport as a site for the creation of myths about national identity and belonging, and argues that this myth addresses people differentially according to race and gender. By and large, the evidence used to substantiate this argument has been textual. In an Australian context, theorists such as Colin Tatz (1995) in 'Racism and sport in Australia' and Baker-Lewton et al. (2017) and Cleland (2014) similarly recount the racialised and gendered nature of sport. These studies show that the achievements of white male athletes are most highly valued. While it is certainly the case that much sports commentary in Australia and England has formed a vehicle for racist sentiment veiled as 'nationalism', the majority of children interested in sport in my project were interested in football, often enamoured with it, and were mostly children of colour. Underneath mediated surfaces of whiteness, football communities are superdiverse, intergenerational and embodied. My fieldwork notes are peppered with comments such as this:

> *There was some interesting discussion around whether children went to church, or mosque, with one boy saying that he didn't go to church this Easter but he had gone before, and the other one commenting that he would rather go play football. They all would rather play football.* (Fieldwork notes, inner-north Melbourne, 2019)

Football was as significant as religion in the lives of many of the children. Indeed, not just in the lives of children – one mother in

London recounted experiencing the most profound feeling of belonging ever during the World Cup. Her estate was covered in football flags, and everyone on the estate came out to be part of a party for the final match. In the transcript below, parents from London's south-east explain their attachment to football and suggest it arouses more passion than religion:

> Anna: Yeah. Yeah. I know ... that you can just support a team, and then you're connected to the whole community.
> Sahar: Especially when it's the World Cup or something.
> Sally: I've seen more resentment and arguing about football than religion. Definitely.
> Anna: What would you say?
> Sahar: There's so much. When you've got kids it's about entertaining them and keeping them happy. And I think your life gets too busy to concentrate on one thing. And teaching them the right and wrong things. And you don't want them to get in trouble and stuff. Like when you hear of these shootings and stabbings and things going on it's awful. Like that twenty-three-year-old boy that got really badly stabbed and was bleeding to death. And he really died ... The boy went to the shop to get something, and he was trying to help these two other boys because they were picking on the Muslim. But he got stabbed instead. It was really bad. He was a Muslim boy. But the guys who did it to him – I don't know. I don't know who they were ... They've got gangs and groups and stuff like that. I think reading all this and seeing it on the telly – I think that makes you feel threatened before you even go out and see anything happening.
> (South-east London focus group, June 2019)

Here, the similarity between religion and football is introduced, by a mother saying 'I've seen more resentment and arguing about football than religion', and then going on to discuss football and violence caused by religion. Expanding on this theme, Cleland's (2014) study also found that violence oriented at religious soccer fans was an issue. Yet the children in my ethnography overwhelmingly described football as an activity they love and a place where they feel happy. The image in Figure 6.3 of three girls playing soccer in their hijabs illustrates the role that soccer has in maintaining friendships.

The school soccer oval is packed at lunchtimes and is always filled with as many girls as boys. Before school, too, the pupils are

Figure 6.3 Three girls wearing hijabs and playing soccer, mixed media on paper, Melbourne, 2018

playing soccer on the field and in any available space on the tarmac. During fieldwork, I often had to hide the football so as to encourage focus on art-making rather than football-playing, so enduring was the love of the ball. It would be bounced around in class at any given opportunity.

Figure 6.4 was made collaboratively by two young girls in a Melbourne school. It depicts a giant flying football that has an ice-cream factory inside it. The picture is powerful because it clearly situates soccer within a landscape of pleasure, and this is overwhelmingly the case for my research participants. Not only does the soccer pitch fly, so that anyone can play soccer whenever they want, but players can also make themselves an ice-cream mid-match. The merging of sport and ice-cream in the flying ice-cream factory-*cum*-soccer pitch is a drawing about what really matters, identity and belonging. Made in pairs, this imagined world was no less real to the girls who made it than playing soccer at lunchtime. Who wouldn't want to live and play in an ice-cream-making mobile soccer field? Later in this chapter, I examine some of the children's explorations

Figure 6.4 'Flying soccer ice-cream factory', pencil and felt-tip pen on paper, Melbourne, 2019

of their gender identity through their pleasurable investments in ice-cream and the video game Fortnite. As children explored identity through animation and other media, it became clear to me that possessing some insight into children's imaginative worlds is critically important to understanding their worldviews and values. I was also reminded of the feminist adage that the personal is always political (Hanisch, 2000); that spaces of pleasure, such as online gaming environments and sensuous experiences like eating ice-cream, play a central and significant role in children's worlds and everyday lives and play (Knight, 2019; Moore, 2017).

Pleasure and the spectre of adolescence

Some of the children in the study are approaching adolescence, and even those who are not quite of that age can often be seen exploring their gender and the sensual nature of their body through an enduring obsession with ice-cream and the computer game Fortnite. I read both the love of ice-cream and the fascination with – or addiction to – Fortnite as relating to the spectre of adolescence and the development and performance of gendered identities.

A childhood passion, an enduring vehicle for pleasure and friendship, ice-cream brings with it the possibility of wish fulfilment, the child-food assemblage of messy cone-sticky hands-lips-cold-sweet, the tongue dance of licking the drips, the acknowledgement of a happy intergenerational moment (Kim, 2019). Ice-cream can mean many things all at once.

It took repeated, unprompted discussions of ice-cream and countless artworks about ice-cream to bring me to the point of approaching an academic discussion of children's love for ice-cream. Does the fact that children made artwork about ice-cream more often than anything else really matter? If so, why? From a psychoanalytic perspective, I could say that the visceral oral pleasure of consuming ice-cream is a precursor to sexual pleasure, a brief return to the oral phase, or part of a budding gender performance (Blaise, 2010; Mechling, 2000; Renold, 2005). Ice-cream is a treat to which children gain access through their parents, so it brings with it a sense of approval, reward and celebration. Pleasure is a key means through which children become who they are (Bond Stockton, 2009; Rasmussen, 2006; Renold, 2005). In this instance, geographies of pleasure form around ice-cream. The children's fascination with ice-cream was introduced to me in north-west Manchester in 2017, when the collaboratively produced future city populated by high-rise estates featured 'an ice-cream maker in every home' (northwest Manchester girl, 2017). At the time I tried to play down this comment, saying that everyone having a home and everyone having an ice-cream maker were issues of very different importance. To my adult mind, they were not comparable. However, the ubiquity and consistency of children's work on ice-cream eventually made it worthy of consideration. Here are some examples of the many ways that children in very different contexts have, unprompted, brought ice-cream into their work, and what I think it might mean.

Figure 6.5 is an image of a collaborative painting made by children in Manchester in 2017. It is the work in which 'everyone has a home' and there is also an 'ice-cream maker in every home'. I have written about this image elsewhere (Hickey-Moody, 2018, 2019) because, as I noted above, it also shows a vision of the future that models sustainable urban developments, such as 'all the streets are rivers', a glass

Figure 6.5 'Future City', acrylic paint on board, Manchester, 2017

dome protecting the environment and a flying mosque. The ice-cream maker in every home then reappeared in different forms of abundion with ice-cream, some of which included animated pink ice-cream as part of an identity story (in an Adelaide mosque), and the flying ice-cream factory with a football pitch inside, which is shown above.

Many other children made various representations of ice-cream in relation to fun, identity and friendship. As well as being an identity resource and a source of pleasure, ice-cream signifies financial success and security because it is a luxury item, and can also be used to say, 'I love you' (Mechling, 2000). Ice-cream is a sign the basics are covered: a treat. For example, a news story by *Quartz* magazine reports on how class structures in Cuba are rated by the types of ice-cream people can consume (Feinberg and Padrón Cueto, 2018). Poorer people have access to a diluted, mass-produced brand called Coppelia. Coppelia is also a place, a park where people can come to get ice-cream and sit in an open-air market park to publicly demonstrate their access to ice-cream. However, with eighty per cent of people living on US$30 a month, and a government hold placed on certain ingredients, only the remaining 20 per cent of the

Figure 6.6 'I love ice cream', screenshot of digital animation, south-west Adelaide, 2018

population can afford the substantially higher-priced and harder to find premium gelato (Feinberg and Padrón Cueto, 2018). The authors remind the reader that, for the communist state, this is a form of governmental control, and the direct linking of class to ingredients shows how children's portrayal of ice-cream makers in every home expresses a fantasy of abundance, pleasure and enjoyment for everyone, despite financial constraints. A refugee mother in west Sydney explained ice-cream to me as an example of the safety of their secure and successful life in Australia:

> Oh yeah, the world is a very dirty place and every country is trying to protect their own interest. Every country. I still feel guilty and sad, but you know, I'm here with a beautiful life and they're [my family] over there suffering, they don't know where their next meal is going to come from, it's terrible ... Like today, watching my kids eat waffles makes me happy. That would make any mother happy, to be able to put a dollop of ice-cream on top of a waffle and hand it to them. I was so sad I didn't have a banana for them. Can you imagine not – that feeling, like – not being able to provide – it's so sad. So sad.
> (West Sydney, interview, May 2018)

A sign of prosperity, security, intergenerational pleasure and unformed sexuality, as well as a delicious experience, the enjoyment of ice-cream is a moment that, for children, 'really matters', because it means a range of things. Another seemingly banal feature of everyday life that was a site of connection and engagement repeatedly referred to by the children in my study was the online game Fortnite, which I contextualise in the next section.

Fortnite: Battle Royale, world-making and drawing about world-making

A noticeable number of boys in the study played the video game Fortnite. No girls in the study made art about a computer game, although girls did make art about media culture broadly – such as the 'TARDIS' from *Doctor Who*, and art featuring their computer or their iPad. A number of boys made artwork about games other than Fortnite, such as Minecraft and Roblox but, for the most part, when representing or drawing media culture and games, boys aged nine to thirteen made art about Fortnite. Only a few boys per group would draw Fortnite, but the ubiquitous interest in the game (and the fact that it was used as an example of something that 'really matters') stuck with me and led me to realise I needed to think seriously about the appeal of this experience.

Gaming is a powerful form of experiential learning in which children invent and test system hypotheses (Apperley, 2010: 101–13). For example, 'I think if I enter that room this way, I will have access to my target', 'I think if I attack my enemy this way, it will kill them' and so on. Strategic thinking and experiential learning are always central to using the 'toy' or a 'key' feature in a given video game, which in Fortnite is a weapon. The game of Fortnite also has diegetic 'toys', which are props, such as sports equipment, that players can earn. Fortnite is an online multiplayer game (Marlatt, 2020), which is highly social (users play each other and chat with each other as they play), and it also mobilises dance. The characters in the game dance, and children and youth playing the game often learn 'Fortnite dances' from their avatars.

Avatars and toys in Fortnite were constantly reproduced by boys in the project as symbols of 'what really matters' to them. Children in the church community in Adelaide decorated their refuge tents with symbols of 'what really matters', which, in this instance included a purple Fortnite piñata and a yellow mobile featuring three characters (or 'skins') and toys from Fortnite. Other symbols of 'what really matters' included family members and favourite books, songs and places. What has stood out to me across the years of undertaking this fieldwork is the consistency with which some boys in each group will choose this game as an example of what really matters. This makes me think it is related to learning masculinity. In the game, boys get to dress up in different avatars: they try on a selection of 'skins', or ways of looking, and this freedom to imagine and to be whomever they want to be is clearly very appealing to them.

The idea that children's engagement with gaming is drawn along gendered lines is a statement that might sound reductionist, but it is an accurate empirical account of the children in my study who made art about Fortnite. None of the girls in the study said that they played Fortnite, or indeed enjoyed gaming, which of course is not to say there aren't millions of girls all over the world who love gaming – they just did not happen to be in my ethnography.

As an adult it was, at the very least, alarming to see boys make images and characters from Fortnite as their expressions of 'what really matters'. I found it nearly impossible to believe that a character from an invented world can really matter as much as family or a religion. At the same time, I had to believe that it *does matter*, because the boys were adamant that, for them, it does. Many children play Fortnite with people they know offline, or have online friends with whom they often play – like a pen-pal they never meet, largely for geographic reasons. Primarily, the social aspect is engaging for these boys, but there is also something appealing about the nature of the imagined world they inhabit – they learn, and often master, dances that are built into the game of Fortnite. During one of the creative methods workshops in Adelaide, where we built refuges and decorated them with 'what really matters', boys made small stuffed animals and mobiles that represented Fortnite characters and danced Fortnite routines together. It was clear that the game was a vehicle for friendship and a means of feeling secure in oneself.

Fortnite also offers the opportunity of becoming and being all kinds of people by wearing different 'skins'. The everyday reproductions of Fortnite characters and weapons as artworks and dances were ways of demonstrating friendship and developing an identity on social media (e.g. TikTok). The boys desired the socially sanctioned opportunity to switch gender and to enjoy dance that is offered by Fortnite moves and skins. They can change how they appear from within the relatively safe confines of a virtual world in which everyone else in that world is 'playing along', i.e. suspending their disbelief. The 'collaborative collage' in Figure 6.7 shows 'what really matters' to two boys in Melbourne, and presents us with a drawing of the 'legendary pickaxe' that has been hastily and carelessly turned into a 'collage' through the application of a roughly cut strip of felt. Pickaxes are a tool in Fortnite, also known as a 'harvesting tool': a device that can mine substances and break barriers, and cause damage to enemies. Different pickaxe skins are divided into 'Legendary/Epic' skins, 'Rare/Uncommon' skins and 'Common' skins.

Fortnite characters, practices and dance moves bleed into children's creative spaces and are vehicles for pleasure, friendship and identity construction. These observations are echoed by other scholars as well. As a teacher-educator studying how multiliteracies cultivated in social settings can be leveraged towards academic success, Rick Marlatt (2020) undertook research into Fortnite. He had two objectives: to examine how Fortnite players operate within their digital community, and to explore what relationships may be established between the game's social literacy contexts and formal literacy learning. Marlatt attended a public Fortnite 'Battle Royale'

Figure 6.7 'Legendary pickaxe', mixed media on paper, inner-north Melbourne, 2019

on his university campus. For twelve hours on a Saturday, he conducted informal observations of gameplay and digital literacy, watching and listening as twenty-five university students competed for prizes in a standing-room-only computer lab. His two primary research questions were:

(1) How might Fortnite gamers operate within a digital community of practice?
(2) What intersections, if any, are visible between the game's social literacy practices and academic achievement in school settings?

Marlatt argues that, '[s]imilar to academic textual activity, the multiliteracies of Fortnite operate equally in cognitive and physical realms, where physical moves in corporeal and digital spaces are supported by applied conceptions of language and textual operations' (9). Marlatt usefully develops a framework for understanding the discourse and literacy practices generated by Fortnite players. Marlatt's work helped me to leverage my analysis of how Fortnite operates in the physical and mental realms of young boys' lives. There are pleasure and risk factors involved in putting on different skins and being encouraged to dance. Such experiments are part of a broader process of social engagement that demonstrates an experiment of masculinity and dominance among peers, which shows why Fortnite characters are ultimately 'what really matter' in many young boys' lives across the fieldwork sites.

Another research project on Fortnite was undertaken by Beate Hygen and colleagues (2019), who also note the ubiquity of electronic games and the extensive amount of time children spend on this activity. As the first study to examine children and social development in relation to Fortnite, Hygen and colleagues investigated whether the *quantity* of time children spend on gaming is related to their social development. They examined relations between time spent gaming and social competence in a sample of Norwegian six-year-olds who were followed up with at the ages eight, ten and twelve. Results suggest that, among girls, greater social competence at both eight and ten years predicted less gaming in two years' time, and that more gaming at age ten predicted less social competence at age twelve. They also found that the impacts of gaming are particularly gendered, suggesting that spending more time gaming seems to have a detrimental effect on the social competence of girls but not boys. Girls tend to play video games in smaller groups than boys, and their relationships offline are often more intimate (Archer and Lloyd, 2002: 79; Richardson, Hjorth and Davies, 2022). It might be that girls who game lose out on something very influential: more intimate interactions with close friends. In other words, given the differences in boys' and girls' social lives with peers, time spent gaming may carry less of a developmental 'cost' for boys (Hygen et al., 2019: 10). While boys spend substantially more time gaming than girls, gaming is more integrated into boys' play culture, and therefore easier to integrate into their social development.

What is clear, both from the studies cited above and my own findings, is that gaming is a significant form of social connection for all children who play. On one level, gaming can be seen as a form of escapism: children who struggle socially may turn to gaming as an escape. However, gaming is also an inherently social activity, and can form an extension of social activities for people who are gregarious offline (Apperley, 2010; Kowert, 2014; Richardson, Hjorth and Davies, 2022). Gaming can fulfil the need for mastery and accomplishment: by playing games – and thereby taking part in the gaming community – children may come to feel more competent and accomplished than would otherwise be the case.

A major theme that runs through the data on pleasure relating to football and gaming is the close relationship between pleasure and friendship. Children really enjoy football and gaming with friends. Indeed, online multiplayer games provide a context in which children are presented with a selection of possible new friends. The images in Figures 6.3 and 6.4, showing friends playing football together and friends standing next to a giant football which is also an ice-cream factory, make it explicitly clear that football, like Fortnite, is a social activity. Outside these three particular examples of vehicles for new friendship, the continuation of existing friendships is also, clearly, a very important part of the children's creative work. An excerpt from my fieldwork notes below shows an interwoven context for how play, space and games emerge from workshops that ask about values, belonging and what really matters:

Outer-east Adelaide, day two:

Andrew, Spiro and John made a 'skate park' and a playground in the middle of the tent city as the central area that connected all of the tents together. They gathered sticks and bush materials from around the building and experimented with arranging them in the middle of the tents, like a giant bonfire. This imagining of communal space echoes the designs of the earlier collaborative large canvases. The playground/skate park is a space which is generally designed for children and so it seems a sensible choice for the boys to create. Playgrounds and skate parks are places where you hang out with friends. It's important that they see this (friendship through doing) as being in the centre of their community. I wonder, too, if this is a space which is associated with certain kinds of play and several of the 'special objects' that they made are also associated with play – such as the tools you need to have fun?

Outer-east Adelaide, day three:

The workshop ended with a vibrant 'dance off' in the middle of the tent city. This was a great chance for the kids to show off their Fortnite moves, and also to get into their body in creative ways. It felt like there was a sense of pride and ownership over the space (physical tents and made objects). The kids had made their own city then chosen how they wanted to inhabit it. There was an impromptu 'gallery' started by Esther, where she took some of the adults – specifically, her mum – on a tour of the tents and proudly narrated the meaning behind the artworks decorating each tent. Each artwork provides a window into the world of the child artist, most specifically, into the things that the child artist loves and what really matters to them.
(Fieldwork notes, outer-east Adelaide, 2018)

These excerpts from my fieldwork notes show that friendship, pleasure and intergenerational relationships are key to how children engaged with the tasks I asked them to complete. The politics of friendship (who is friends with whom, why and what the implications of this are for the children involved) is something that my research was not originally designed to explore, but in seeing the larger role friendship plays in 'what really matters' to the children, I started to consider it more. Often children either write the word 'friends' into their artworks, or draw their friends with them, to show how important they are. For example, two boys attending primary school in south-east London made an animation together about 'what really matters', which for them was a spiritual pilgrimage and the striking architecture of the Middle East (Figure 6.8). The boys drew the Burj Khalifa in Saudi Arabia and the Ka'bah,

Figure 6.8 Screen capture from an animation of Burj Khalifa and friendship, south-east London, 2019

where they had been lucky enough to have been on Hajj visits with their fathers. They spoke enthusiastically about how they couldn't wait until they were old enough to go on Hajj together. They practised saying that sentence in perfect unison. It was an affirmation of their present friendship, the significant role that faith plays in their life and their intention to carry on that friendship through faith.

What is ultimately so striking about this animation of the Ka'bah, and the Fortnite drawings, is the idea that religion and faith are entangled with elements of fear, pleasure and friendship, which reveal themselves in almost all of the workshops. Whether it's a tent city decorated with purple piñatas copied from a video game, a Hajj pilgrimage, a mother's fear of football and religious violence, or creatively imagined solutions to climate change, there is never any singular succinct location or matter through which faith resonates. Faith is just there. Through friendship, through kindness, through fear, faith appears through a realisation that there is something bigger than just the confines of this moment. The lick of an ice-cream that demonstrates a parent's love for their child, the hung flags of a football team across an overpopulated housing estate express community and belonging – all these things are united by, and create, faith. Whether it be a god, a football field or a video game, we all are sustained by faith and, for children, this is a great source of pleasure.

Conclusion

The examples of connection and coming together explored here have been chosen because they are extremely prevalent in my data. They needed to be discussed. Overall, they provide architectures for connections between people that extend people's capacities to act, but, as my discussion of the Atherton Gardens estate demonstrates, these are never simple equations. Some limiting factors are part of all landscapes and too often these are racialised, gendered and classed. To differing extents, housing estates, football, ice-cream, gaming and art-making all constitute figures of attachment:

> Is it a wisdom or a religion – it does not matter which. It is only from this point of view that Chinese hexagrams, Hindu mandalas, Jewish sephiroth, Islamic 'imaginals', and Christian icons can be considered together: thinking through figures. (Deleuze and Guattari, 1996: 89)

I want to suggest that in some contexts, the 'figures' through which my research participants primarily think are not obviously identifiable as relating to faith. However, these figures are often expressions of faith for both religious and secular people. They show connection to community and/or demonstrate God's love. They express identity and belonging and/or God's will. They express ways of being in relation to others that have global, multifaced purposes.

Note

1 In 1998, Britain's then-Prime Minister Tony Blair famously called London's Aylesbury estate a 'sink estate' in a speech to Parliament.

7

Incapacity / *Neamhábaltacht*

Colonial power either constitutes or haunts the contexts in which this research takes place. This book is written on the lands of the Wurundjeri people of the Kulin nation, lands that are unceded and rightfully owned by Koorie Aboriginal peoples. I am a newcomer to these lands, the first person in my family born in Australia. I was born on Kaurna land and, after moving across the world and back again, I now live on lands owned by Koorie peoples. I acknowledge the Elders, past and present, of this community.

The racist foundations on which contemporary Australia has been constructed, and on which it still operates, overlay the ethnographic work I have undertaken in Sydney, Melbourne, Canberra and Adelaide. I write to the sound of crickets chirping through the dark blue light that is settling in after the sun has set and the sense of a long darkness ahead. Marcia Langton explains the Aboriginal world as having a very different space-time from white worlds:

> The idea of 'Old People' corresponds to the perception of the stars as being representations of the past. The Old People are encountered in the landscape, just as we see stars when we gaze at the night sky. We know that stars are what can still be seen now of some cataclysmic event in the universe many thousands of light years ago. That is, the light of the explosion emanating through time and visible to our eyes in the present. Likewise, Aboriginal people perceive the spiritual presence of Elders in the landscape as what has emanated through time since the ancestor died. (Langton, 2018: 205)

Time-space matter is configured in particular ways in Aboriginal Australia, and arguably all places have unique space-time assemblages. The role of the white anti-racist ally in such spaces is complex and often irreconcilable with the views of the white majority. This was one of the first lessons I learnt when studying social anthropology.

False promises of colonisation: Part I

In 1997 I was still living on Kaurna land, studying social anthropology and performing arts at the University of Adelaide. Through some of my social anthropology courses, I was learning about Tarntanya (red kangaroo place – Adelaide) and Karrawirra Pari (red gum forest river – the River Torrens). I would ride my bike to the city early every morning for yoga and stay back late for dance rehearsals. My white American anthropology lecturer used to spit all over me, the nerd, sitting in the front row. His overuse of the phrase 'rituals of Balinese cockfighting' spattered little American man droplets all over me. I had five casual waitressing jobs, two cleaning jobs and a cash envelope for each major life expense (rent, electrics, food), which I kept under my mattress.

1997 was the year I started thinking in earnest about the complicated ways that men and patriarchal knowledge systems can tell women that their knowledge does not matter via means that are so persuasive that the rest of the world believes them. I already knew this, and lived in the shadow of this truth. The Ngarrindjeri women of the Coorong had to experience this fact as a vehicle for racism, on a global stage. They had to sacrifice Kumarangk, their fertility lands, because material histories and embodied knowledges can be maligned with words. White 'land-owners' and aspiring property developers convinced the white government to give them money to build a bridge out to an island that had been renamed after a white man. The sacred women's place of Kumarangk was renamed 'Hindmarsh Island' (Simons, 2003).

Kumarangk sits at the mouth of the Murray River, facing the Great Australian Bight and with its back to the tiny coastal town of Goolwa, one hour south of Adelaide. A significant area around the island and the Murray estuary was designated as a protected wetland site in 1985. When a plan to build an AU$6 million bridge linking Goolwa with Kumarangk arose in the 1990s, Ngarrindjeri women complained about the desecration that would be caused to their sacred site. The land matter held stories that were part of who they were, knowledges that were embodied and inherited and enmeshed with place.

The developers complained. The white people knew nothing about this secret site. The white men had never heard of the secret women's business. There were at least twelve separate aspects to the claim of 'secret women's business' identified during the course of the resulting Hindmarsh Island Bridge Royal Commission. This knowledge was ancient and passed only to a small number of properly initiated women, hence the prior ignorance of anthropologists. The island is a fertility site. Its shape and that of the surrounding wetlands resembles the female reproductive system. The Ngarrindjeri name for the island, Kumarangk, is similar to the word for pregnancy, or woman. The island had to remain separate from the mainland because it would be disastrous if two separate bodily organs were connected together when they were not supposed to be. The proposed bridge would interfere with the 'meeting of the waters', the mixing of salt and fresh water in the Goolwa estuary, which is the source of Ngarrindjeri fertility. The waters of the Goolwa channel need uninterrupted views of the sky, particularly the Seven Sisters constellation, which is part of a number of Dreaming stories. Archaeological evidence also suggests that the site was used for ritual burials (Langton, 1996; Simons, 2003).

The *Hindmarsh Island Bridge Act 1997* expressly removed Kumarangk and the area surrounding it from the *Racial Discrimination Act 1975*, which outlawed racial discrimination (Simons, 2003). I watched this racist debate about the impossibility of material knowledges happen across the local newspapers and in the conversations between white anthropologists (see Bell, 1998). It was a giant and crippling version of the racist and sexist 'knowledge politics' we have to live every day. The *Hindmarsh Island Bridge Act 1997* exemplifies one of the biggest lessons I learnt while at university, a lesson that still shapes the ways academic institutions operate: white, patriarchal knowledge systems do not have the capacity to respect embodied and material knowledge, particularly women's knowledge and knowledges from non-white cultures. At the time, newspapers and white men made jokes about 'secret women's business'. At times, they still do.

In 2019, I was running a multi-sited ethnography across six cities and two countries. My head was mainly full of other people's stories, feelings and expressions. Any spare space was full of logistics: what needed to be brought where and when. I was collecting community stories told through art for this research. When I came home from communities, I would go to bed and lie there, trying to quieten my mind and remember myself. Sometimes, if I was going away again soon, I would not unpack my bags until the next trip. They were ready to go. I wanted to use embodied knowledge – memories, feelings, movement patterns, associations we make when watching bodies move – as a key knowledge source and a way of understanding orientations to faith. Two white academics wrote to me and told me I was racist. They were the only white Australians allowed to talk to Muslims because they belonged to the Critical Race Studies group and I did not. A female Muslim academic wrote to me and told me I was racist because I was not Muslim. I am quite good friends with many of the Muslim women in my research. From all my participants, the overwhelming majority of whom are not white, no one asked to withdraw, no one disputed my account of events or even vaguely insinuated I am racist. Muslim mothers brought me food and stayed to chat. We wanted to get to know each other. Some Muslim women spoke to the Australian national broadcaster, the ABC, with me and we had a feature published on their experiences of racism (Hanifie, 2019). I am warmly welcomed back into the communities with whom I have worked since 2016. And I am not a race scholar; and this is not a critical race studies book. I am an arts-based anthropologist who thinks critically, through feminist new materialism. But that does not make me racist. My whiteness does not mean I cannot hear. It means I am the site for other people's anger, and an ally who first and foremost works in and with diverse communities.

Long histories in both Australia and England of colonial trauma, multi-religious relationships and multicultural,[1] superdiverse[2] success and failure inform the contexts in which my fieldwork takes place. Both Australia and England are colonial places. Australia is a constitutional monarchy built on colonialism and England still proudly positions itself as the heart of Britain: a geographic and legal assemblage composed of the spoils of colonial bloodshed. Scotland, Wales and Ireland were, of course, independent countries before England attacked and invaded them. The colonial histories of both places frame my research, as well as bringing with them the continuation of a need for long-standing redress of issues surrounding imperialist cultural norms and the normalisation of white power. These cultural and political aspects of local research sites and countries are difficult to change, as while on one level they are constitutional, legal, institutionalised and normalised, on other levels they are unconscious and affective, articulated through pleasure, desire, taste and style. Following is another example of the affective and often unconscious normalisation of white privilege, this time from England.

Black panics: objects of fear

In my 2013 book, *Youth, Arts and Education*, I characterised the 'black panics' about Aboriginal youth and Sudanese refugee boys that were sweeping across the Australian media. These panics continue in relatively unchanged forms. Drawing on Cohen's (1972) classic theory of media moral panics and the creation of projected and internalised deviancy, I argued that 'Media moral panics suggest Aboriginal and Sudanese people living in Australia are a disadvantage: they are a threat to peaceful forms of social cohesion and do not have value' (Hickey-Moody, 2013: 52). Similar arguments can be made in relation to Muslim, Chinese and, to a lesser extent, Hindu communities in Australia and the UK.

During fieldwork between 2016 and 2019, experiences of racism were clearly articulated by many research participants, although, strikingly, this was the case more than twice as often in Australia as in England. Communities in Australia and England both live with the wounds of colonial power and the ghosts of empire, as institutionalised and lived continuations of empire constitute social and cultural contexts in enduringly problematic ways. In Australia, discourses of Islamophobia and racism have become part of everyday life in many places. In both Australia and England, civilians are repeatedly reminded to beware of potential terrorists, or of bombs 'disguised' as unattended baggage on public transport. Public announcements repeatedly remind commuters to look out for 'anything suspicious' and to report such unspecified suspiciousness immediately. Everything from a forgotten bag of shopping to a religious woman in a burqa reading a book, and an imagined vast terrain of inanimate objects in between, may potentially put one's life at risk. Quite an anxiety-inducing proposition indeed.

In 2016, in the Parliament of Australia – whose proceedings are screened on national television – far-right senator Pauline Hanson warned white Australians that they were at 'risk' of being 'taken over' by Muslims. In 2010, just a few years before this declaration of a plague of 'Muslim people', Hanson told the Australian public they were at risk of being swamped by Asian people. The linking concern here is contagion: fear of bodies that are not white and therefore represent an imagined threat. Human rights are violated daily in Australian offshore detention centres in Nauru and Papua New Guinea, sending a message to asylum seekers to 'stay out' of Australia (Human Rights Law Centre, 2015). Media discourses of Islamophobia and racism are accompanied by more institutionalised strategies for governance. Even proposals for ostensibly progressive policy, such as the document produced by the Counter Terrorism Policy Centre at the Australian Strategic Policy Institute (ASPI) think tank, *Strategy: 18 Years and Counting* (Kfir, 2019), can be seen as legitimising punitive forms of governance and feeding the culture of fear and xenophobia accepted as part of Australian public culture. However, the policy recommendation in the ASPI report does specifically note that there should be a move away from discussions of 'radicalisation', stating:

> It's important to move away from the castigation of Salafi-jihadism as a radical ideology and focus on it as an extremist ideology that wants to overthrow the established order through non-democratic means – violence. The need for the distinction stems from the basic fact that 'radicalism' is a relative concept and that, historically, being a radical wasn't necessarily a bad thing, as many early radicals fought for positive social, political and economic change. (Kfir, 2019: 20)

The broad frame of radicalisation might be thought of as reinforcing the stereotypical construction of radical Islam I have so fervently argued against (Hickey-Moody, 2018). A comparable form of institutionalised racism can be found in the fact that the UK Government spends forty million pounds every year on the Prevent strategy. This is one strand of the UK Government's counterterrorism policy, which has four strands – designed to Pursue, Protect, Prepare and Prevent terrorism (UK Home Office, 2015). This is a very particular way of trying to bridge different cultural beliefs, and one that has been rightly criticised based on racial profiling (Awan, 2012; Heath-Kelly, 2013; Sian, 2017). Nonetheless, this substantial financial investment made by the UK Government illustrates the urgency with which these issues need to be attended.

Aislinn O'Donnell (2016, 2018) has written on the educational implications of the Prevent agenda in the UK. She focuses on what she characterises as the associated deployments of epidemiological logics of contagion, infection, risk and bodily threat. O'Donnell contends that such narrow social imaginaries, and the prohibitions that they legitimise, shape and limit forms of community engagement. This needs to change, because a community in which young people from different cultural backgrounds thrive together cannot be founded on xenophobia. O'Donnell shows how the concept of 'radicalisation', which is mobilised as a rationale for Prevent, is inherently problematic. There remains an enduring lack of clarity concerning what exactly 'radicalisation' is, and numerous methodological problems associated with ideas of how people might *become radical*. Rhetorics of Islamophobia, fears of cultural contagion, and xenophobia remain the dominant discourses through which the politicisation of refugees and asylum seekers is justified.

Circulating meanings of terrorism and memorialisation

Dominant media discourses repeatedly reiterate connections between terrorism and religion (Kabir, 2006). As I noted earlier, this is incredibly problematic for numerous reasons, not least of which is because many very religious people are seriously persecuted as a result of different interpretations of religion. The embodied cultural affects of this were expressed by one of my research participants, Abiha from inner-east Adelaide:

> After 9/11 happened, I noticed a big difference when I would pull out my ID card, or I pull out my bank card, and it has Ahmed on the end of it. I really noticed. Or I'd be on the phone saying my name, it's just this pause that wasn't there before ... It's not so bad now. There was a period of time after that happened in Australia, where it was just ... And so many people I knew. And speaking about this current merge in Australian identity and whatever, I work with migrants and refugees and I have had a number of times that I've had to help students that had been assaulted and harassed [because of racism]. (Inner-east Adelaide focus group, 2018)

Much has been written about the damage that 9/11 caused Islamic communities and the continuing damage caused by popular and mediated conflation of terrorism and religion (Abu-Ras and Suarez, 2009; Lankala, 2006; Tindongan, 2011). The nature of my fieldwork sites mandated an ongoing engagement with circulating discourses of terror and associated practices of memorialisation. As I have noted elsewhere (Hickey-Moody, 2018, 2019), I undertook my first fieldwork in the UK during the time of the Manchester Arena bombing on 22 May 2017, and the subsequent London fieldwork during the London Bridge terrorist attack on 3 June 2017. This led to a pronounced focus in the children's art on flags and nationalism, as children sought to affirm their place identity.

Place identity, as defined by Proshansky, Fabian and Kaminoff (1983) is a set of positively and negatively balanced cognitions of physical settings, as the authors emphasise that 'it is in the home, school, and neighbourhood settings that the child learns some of his/her most significant social roles' (57). Manchester children repeatedly drew the Mancunian worker bee, which is a symbol of local working-class pride. One of the Manchester schools in which I was working at the time had a diverse multi-faith school group, and the children all possessed a strong awareness of a range of different religious celebrations and figures such as Ganesh, Lakshmi, the Ka'bah, and Muslim, Christian and Jewish symbols – to use the children's words, they know about: 'the star and the moon [the Islamic star and crescent]', 'the cross', or the 'Star of David'. For each of these children, the attack on Manchester Arena was experienced very much as an attack *on Manchester*. Their symbolic refutation of this act can be seen in their drawings of worker bees, the Union Flag, and in the attention given to the memorialisation of the event. Figures 7.1 and 7.2 are images of worker bees drawn by these children as symbols of 'what really matters'.

The worker bee became a symbol of Manchester during the Industrial Revolution, a time when the city took a leading role in new forms of mass production (Zeybek, 2020: 65) and became what was cast as a 'hive' of activity. Expressing the role of bees in place identity, the University of Manchester's coat of arms also features three bees. Various other public iterations of the symbol are well known; for example, the Manchester football team wore a bee-inspired kit during their away matches in the 2009–10 season. Since

Incapacity / Neamhábaltacht 149

Figure 7.1 The Manchester Bee 1, drawn by children in Manchester as a symbol of 'what really matters' directly after the Manchester Arena bombing in 2017

the Arena bombing, the streetscapes of Manchester have become self-consciously populated by images of worker bees, as murals on walls and decorated light poles affirm a proud sense of place identity (Abbit, 2017). Bee tattoos also gained popularity as a signifier of place attachment (Abbit, 2017).

One of the most obvious ways this fieldwork site spoke back to the experience of terrorism was through practices of memorialisation, and this practice is of particular interest in the ways it shows up the gendered nature of the attack.

A public shrine in Manchester was created to honour those killed in the Manchester Arena bombing. My initial (and enduring) response to the shrine was to marvel at the feminised nature of this collection of objects. It was a sea of pink that stretched on as far as the eye could see. When I first saw it, I thought of a tween girl's bedroom, but then, the more I thought about it, the more it looked like the morning after a teenage girl's birthday party. The victims

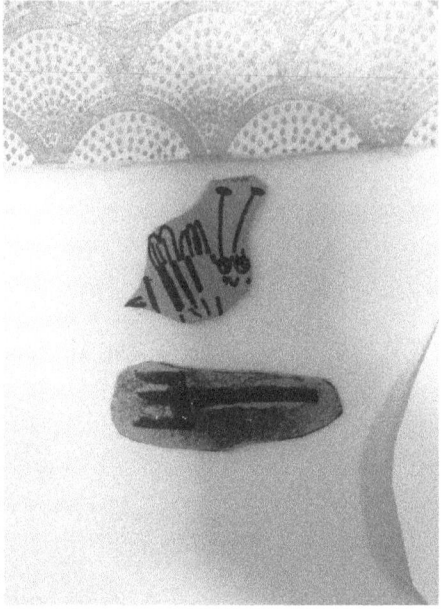

Figure 7.2 The Manchester Bee 2, drawn by children in Manchester as a symbol of 'what really matters' directly after the Manchester Arena bombing in 2017

of this senseless attack were predominantly young women, and the violence was perpetrated by a man in a feminised space (the concert of pop star Ariana Grande, whose very publicised event was the target of the bombing, has a predominantly female-identifying fan base). The subsequent, unrelated attack in London, and the other contemporaneous acts of terror that were perpetrated in Paris, Sydney, Christchurch and many other locations, were, notably, all perpetrated by men. Not all attacks are undertaken as men 'acting against women', or against a figure who symbolises femininity, as we see so clearly in the case of the Manchester Arena bombing. What is striking here, though, is that while the figure of the 'terrorist' and the spectre of 'terrorism' circulates across the spaces in which my research was undertaken, and was discussed by some parents involved in the research in relation to media representations of Muslim communities, the actual acts of terror can be read most clearly in gendered terms. Each was undertaken by a man and each

Incapacity / Neamhábaltacht   151

was a performance of some form of protest masculinity, in which a man expressed extreme anger and garnered attention by undertaking fatal acts of violence. A reading of this as a performative act must surely begin with a gendered lens. Gender is inseparable not just from my data, but from everyday life. The gendered nature of these attacks, among other things, shows the great extent to which moral panics surrounding terrorism are misplaced, and should rather be read as violent performances of protest masculinity.

Miles away, in Melbourne, my introductory discussion of the project again returns to discussions of terrorism:

Field notes, 15 May 2019: Inner-north Melbourne primary school introduction to the project.

The teacher gathered the class in the yoga room adjacent to the arts classroom for the introduction to the work. The children listened attentively, some were talkative and some were reluctant to speak up. One boy, Frankie, contributed loudly, with comments that were at times provoking. It was an attempt to arouse reactions. His comment on what was necessary in a future city was: 'Terrorists'. The other children seemed used to him and one commented that soldiers were also needed to keep in check the terrorists. 'Do we really need terrorists, though Frankie?' I ask him. 'Or do you just think the future will have terrorists in it?' He seems unsure.

I asked Frankie why we need terrorists. It seems that, rather than needing them, Frankie thought the future was destined to include terrorists. Discussions of religion are shadowed by discussions of terrorism because of the popular media links that are being made consistently between them. As I argued earlier, discourses of terror should be approached through a focus on gender, by researchers explicitly considering the gendered nature of acts and discourses associated with terrorism. It seems terrorism is a set of practices associated with masculinity, not with religion.

False promises of colonisation: Part II

Ersheen and Rafi didn't have long; Aadhil, their son, needed to be picked up from childcare before their daughter's school day was up. South-east London traffic is impossible after half-past three. Rafi was hoping to get back out in the cab before prayer time at the mosque, too. 'Why did Asda keep moving their halal meats section? It used to be here,' they complained to each other as they scoured the long refrigerator.

Ersheen moved to avoid a man with a shaved head wearing a black duffle coat. He mirrored her body, moving back in front of her. 'Whatcha wearing that for?' he spat, gesturing angrily up and down her niqab. Ersheen couldn't understand his hastily blurted words, but she could see he was angry, and his body language made his point for him. She asked Rafi to explain for her, which Rafi did, despite his anxiety about time.

'A niqab helps women dress modestly', Rafi explained, continuing: 'Face veiling is not a requirement of Islam; however, if women choose to, they can cover their faces in public.'

'Well, you're not in Iraq anymore, are ya? Dress like a Londoner!' the white man spat back. Rafi thought about mentioning that they were from Bangladesh, as he put his arm around Ersheen and ushered her past the angry white man, further along the aisle. 'Let's go?' he asked her, heading for the checkout. They could make do with the provisions in the house for dinner tonight, and tomorrow was a new day.

Six months later, Ersheen was sitting with me in her daughter's school, taking part in a focus group I ran in 2019. The group consisted of parents of the children I had worked with making collaborative art for nearly three years. I had met most of the parents numerous times, but not all of them. There were ten parents, two researchers and an interpreter in the room and we were discussing racism, because one of the questions I asked in focus groups was whether parents have experienced any racism or religious prejudice. Most parents said they had not experienced racism or prejudice, except Ersheen. Wearing her niqab and speaking through an interpreter, she told us the story related above, of how she had been shopping with her husband at Asda. Ersheen brought up this attack in response to my question regarding racism and prejudice. Before I could respond, Sarah, a white working-class mother, who was sitting between two white mothers – the only three white parents in the group – chimed in, 'But that's not really *assault* though, is it? You can't say that's assault, can you?' Up to this point, no one had mentioned assault. I couldn't understand where the focus on assault came from. The broader conversation that came before this exchange was as follows:

> Sarah: Religion's always existed ... But people have always got along. I think with events around the world, some people ask questions like, 'What's going on? Why do people behave like this?' And some people – intelligent people – they look into it and look for answers, rather than just go with the trend and not fully understand what's happening around the world. But people have always got along and have been accepted. We look different, we dress different, but we all get along ... I think it's in the way people feel threatened or attacked. I mean, you'll probably get people that might look at you differently or probably choose not to talk to you or probably just come and ask you a question.
> Ersheen: Because there's quite a large Bengali community everyone gets along. So it's not a small number. It's a large number, so everyone kind of integrates and gets on –
> Madge: And all the children as well play together as well. They're not bothered.
> Ersheen: I have had one experience of prejudice. There was a man in Asda questioning me, 'Why do you wear this? Why'd you come here?'
> Sarah: That's not really assault though, is it? You can't say that's assault, can you?
> Madge: He asked her why she wore it. Yeah. That's not an assault.

(South-east London focus group, 2019)

Sarah and Madge were white English mothers. The conversation included above did not begin with assault; it began by discussing prejudice. As our conversation continued, I interjected, explaining that it wouldn't seem right if people in Asda were questioning me for wearing an 'I love New York' t-shirt – I suggested we would all be thinking 'I can wear what I like!' Sarah, the white mother who was arguing that religious prejudice was only problematic if it was expressed as assault, went bright red after speaking, perhaps experiencing shame, anger, embarrassment or all these feelings. She said little else.

Earlier in the focus group, Sarah had been clear how proud she was of her child, and all the children at the school, for 'getting along with everyone', explaining how kids 'these days' all learn to accept and get along with each other. Her identification of generational differences also made it clear that this group of accepting children were schooled in *new ways*, and were different from her generation.

After the discussion of racism and prejudice, I asked the group whether there was a certain meal, place, smell or object that expressed their place belonging and identity. Sarah said that, for her, this is an English Christmas roast dinner. For me, the affective and symbolic communication here is really important. Sarah's blushing, later on, suggested she felt regret or confusion about her assertion that 'That's not really *assault* though, is it?' The traditional roast Christmas dinner seemed to symbolise the bounty of the Empire, as well as the popular celebration of the Christian religion. Interestingly, during this discussion, Ersheen, the mother who was confronted in Asda about wearing the niqab, made a point of raising, explaining and discussing the relationships between Mary (the Christian Mother of God) and Maryam (the Arabic name for the sister of Moses). The birth of Maryam is narrated in the Qur'an. Maryam's father is Imran, the equivalent of Joachim, who is Mary's father in some apocryphal Christian writings. Her mother is Hannah, the equivalent of Christianity's Saint Anne, who is sometimes referred to as Joachim's wife and Mary's mother. This discussion of closeness between Islam and Christianity was unprompted and was clearly a means of showing the relationships not only between the Christian and Muslim religions, but also the people who are associated with, or believe in, these religions. This short excerpt gives some insight into Ersheen's thinking:

> We believe that Mary is Maryam. Through her we learnt to cover ourselves, dress modestly. So she said, 'We think it's quite important.' So we take that. It's like Christianity thought 'we will believe in that'. Then Islam came in. So we know we follow the religion that came before … we've taken our religion, our religion came in, so we follow it. Veiling is not just something Islam just invented. We've taken on things from Christianity. (South-east London focus group, 2019)

The earlier exchange between the mothers is complex. At first, I thought it was an expression of Sarah's racism, but then I wondered if she was actually trying to smooth over what she experienced as a difficult situation. I saw Ersheen make an obvious attempt to appease the perpetrator of racism in her response that linked Christianity and Islam. I was taken aback by the overt nature of the racist comment, 'That's not really *assault* though, is it?', and noted that this comment 'spilt' out of Sarah, seemingly involuntarily. She appeared to have no way of holding it inside or thinking critically about the sentiments she was expressing. It was a raw feeling.

While I tried to create space for further exchange, I wasn't convinced that Sarah, the mum who felt that English Christmas lunch symbolised home and belonging had understood, or even heard, the discussion about Mary and Maryam and the similarities between Christianity and Islam. The implied suggestion that 'putting up' with racism in Asda should be somehow 'okay' stuck with me, very uncomfortably. Ersheen was clearly not implying that Sarah should put up with anything. One of the questions arising from this exchange for me was: can I do anything to change this involuntary response to cultural difference? I also wondered if this response came from fear of difference rather than curiosity. I tried to organise a follow-up interview with Sarah, but she declined. Moments such as these are scattered throughout the years between 2016 and 2020, years I spent living in places away from home, making art with kids and talking to their parents about 'what really matters'. There are some patterns and stories that emerge, but also many loose ends, like the above exchange, which I was never able to resolve.

In an attempt to redress the cultural normalisation of white power that leads to exchanges such as those explained above, and the fact that I am a white woman writing on Koorie lands, I draw inspiration from the political orientations of decolonial theorists who work towards a '"programmatic" of de-linking from contemporary legacies of coloniality' (Mignolo, 2007: 452). Many of the participants and collaborators in my research are living in Australia or England because they needed to escape war and have been, or are in the process of being, granted refuge from Syria, Palestine, Iran, Iraq, Afghanistan, Serbia, West Papua and many other countries. Many Australian refugee participants came via refugee detention centres, having travelled to Australia by boat. To quote one Melbourne father, he arrived from Christmas Island with no more than 'the shirt on my back'. Others in the UK have been granted citizenship or temporary residence for similar reasons. A father in Manchester told me emphatically: 'England is a safer place to be a Muslim than any Muslim country' (inner-south Manchester focus group, 2019). The same sentiment was expressed by members of the Islamic community in focus groups in Adelaide and Canberra. The causes of the wars from which these people have fled are complex assemblages of politics, capitalism, religion, racism and empire. They can't be equated solely with European and British colonisation, although in most instances, the broader context of colonisation has led to the stigmatisation of cultural and religious practices that are not historically English (or British).

Australia's history of racial discrimination, beginning with white settlement in the eighteenth century and the introduction of the White Australia Policy in 1901, was formed on the basis of racist ideologies privileging 'whiteness'. Australia's shift to multicultural social policies in the 1970s made space for the appreciation and recognition of diversity and difference, particularly for non-white migrants. However, social relations in both contemporary multicultural Australia and Britain continue to be informed by legacies of colonialism, in which race and racism are used as organising systems that re-inscribe white racial privilege (Hage, 2003, 2005; Noble, 2005).

Pauline Hanson provides the foremost example of using white privilege in an attempt to inform Australian policy. Hanson is an Australian politician who rose to infamy with her notably xenophobic and nationalist campaign for the Liberal Party[3] of Australia in the 1996 federal election. Despite being disendorsed by the party shortly before the election, she won and became a Member of Parliament, first as an independent and then as a member of the far-right One Nation party, which she founded in 1997. After losing her seat in the 1998 election, Hanson was elected to the Senate as the leader of One Nation in 2016. One Nation is a right-wing populist party, with strong white-nationalist platforms formed against First Nations Australians and in response to the 'invasion' of immigrants in Australia and the 'threat' they pose to 'white Australia'. These views came to a head in 2017, when Hanson, who is not a Muslim, wore a burqa to a session of the Senate, claiming it 'oppresses women' and calling for its ban in public places in Australia.

Similar sentiments can be seen in contemporary Britain's Prevent counterterrorism strategy. Prevent is one of four streams that comprise the UK's *Counter-Terrorism and Security Act 2015*. It is aimed at identifying and stopping individuals and groups who might be 'drawn into terrorism' (UK Home Office, 2015). Along

Incapacity / Neamhábaltacht   157

with providing police with increased powers to restrict movement and behaviour, the Prevent strand of the Act is notable in that it anticipates individuals and groups who are likely to be 'drawn' into terrorism, rather than punishing them after they have *actually committed* a terrorist act. Prevent has been criticised for encouraging the formulation of 'suspect communities', which are often characterised as existing around particular ideologies, religions (usually Islam), and races (usually non-white) (Qurashi, 2016). It has been criticised for inciting Islamophobia, restricting the freedoms of British citizens, and stigmatising and alienating Muslims in the UK (Awan, 2012; Heath-Kelly, 2013; Sian, 2017). Similarly, Pauline Hanson could easily be compared to UK nationalist politician Nigel Farage, as both Brexit and the Prevent agenda reflect the fact that there are echoes of a more recent kind of white historical displacement haunting Britain, performed in Sarah's assertion that 'That's not really *assault* though, is it?' and, more broadly, through the Brexit vote.

Feelings of uselessness lead to frustration, even rage. My mother's family owned an English sweet shop in Stanmore, London. It was passed through the family for generations. But when it came time for my great uncle to retire, his sons wanted nothing to do with the shop. Glass jars of boiled sweets had long been replaced by plastic packets of Haribo soft gummy bear candies from Germany, and corner stores were all Indian-owned businesses. An Indian family bought the shop and transformed it from neat rows of sweets in glass jars into a sell-all corner store overflowing with items ranging from hardware to cigarettes. My uncle and aunt didn't know how to explain their sadness about this in words. They felt like generations of meaning had lost their place in the world and no one cared. Their own icons, the coloured boiled sweets in glass jars, had been replaced by others: baskets of plantain and stockings on special. Their children didn't see anything wrong with that – it is the new way. Not long after, my uncle had a fall while riding a bike and passed away, and Aunt Madge moved to a nursing home in Plymouth to be nearer her son. She voted for Brexit. She voted for Brexit because there is not enough space created in England (or Australia for that matter) to bring together value systems of different old and new worlds. Those boiled sweets in glass jars symbolised family, inheritance and belonging for my great uncle and aunt. It is still a great sadness to my aunt that generations of meaning lost their place, that World War II – the war to keep England safe, in which so many of her friends had died – was a fight for an England that does not exist anymore. In political terms, I could respond by telling Madge that England was built on wealth stolen from others and it was always already overextended, built on slavery and exploitation, a cruel enterprise deserving of its troubles. This truth has, however, been proffered by younger generations for years, and what it completely ignores is the great feeling of sadness. Aunt Madge's special icons have lost their meaning; indeed, they have gone, and no one cares. This is not just about Aunt Madge; it is also Sarah, the mother from south-east London, and most of the Brexit 'leave' vote, who have been told for years that their feelings don't matter. Systems of attachment, old and new, can't simply be discarded or replaced. Somewhere in the middle of the cultural mixtures that make up contemporary everyday life, we need to make more space for valuing diverse old and new systems of meaning and bringing them together.

I also believe that the broader multicultural histories of colonised countries need to be taught and appreciated, rather than the versions of history so often institutionalised in curricula. In Australia, historical narratives can still, at times, begin with white settlement, and in the UK, history places the British Empire on a pedestal in ways that fail to recognise the damage caused by colonisation. One example of Australia's multicultural history that could feature more prominently in the school curriculum is the fact that Turkish Muslims traded peacefully with Indigenous Australian people prior to British colonisation (Ganter, 2012; Hersi, 2018). There is also significant evidence of the role that Muslim camel traders played in supporting expeditions such as Burke and Wills' journey across inland Australia (Jones and Kenny, 2010). Townships such as Alice Springs in Central Australia and the city of Darwin feature identifiably Muslim place names, particularly street names, which testify to the role that Muslim community members played in building these places. Despite this, and other, long-standing histories, practices of othering and the negative portrayal of Muslims have a long history in Australia (Aly, 2007; Brasted, 2001) and also in the UK. These practices of othering are deeply seated in historical colonial beliefs and continually represent Muslims in a negative light (Aly, 2007; Noble, 2008; Said, 1979).

Incapacity / Neamhábaltacht 159

Even in light of this, there are a lot of fulfilled religious people in my study, living safe and engaging lives. I read a book recently called *It's Not About the Burqa*, a collection of essays edited by Mariam Khan (2020). Some of the stories in this book are amazing: Yassmin Abdel-Magied, a Sudanese-Australian woman, tells of her experience working as an engineer on oil fields and combating sexism and racism, and Jamilla Hekmoun offers an incredibly moving account of struggles with mental health in Muslim culture. Yet other contributions are angry manifestos about the 'awful plight of the Muslim women' in fashion, feminism, and various other contexts that are shaped by class privilege. While clearly anger and outrage are key resources for these young women, I was left thinking about the hundreds of Muslim mums in my study, many of whom have lived through extremely traumatising experiences but are, for the most part, often genuinely happy, despite the huge complexities of forced migration, religion and racism. I want to tell their stories of everyday lives, lives that are complex, and include sadness, but are liveable and happy enough. This is not to downplay serious issues, but to suggest we need to celebrate everyday, 'ordinary' success stories in all their diversity more than texts like *It's Not About the Burqa* (Khan, 2020) might suggest.

Philomena has spent her life feeling left out. At school she was called the 'wog' kid and her parents really wanted her to marry a nice Italian man. When she married a Muslim, she thought they would never recover. Now here she is, fifteen years later, still being left out. She feels like the only parent who doesn't speak Dari and is completely overlooked in the principal's address at her own daughters' primary school. Why didn't he talk to all the school parents? Why only address 'new Australians'? Her mum and dad were new Australians not that long ago. They still think of themselves as new Australians. Her girls had to learn to get along. They could fit in at the mosque, at church, with her husband's culture and her own culture. Sometimes it felt like the Afghan women didn't want her to fit in or get to know anyone who didn't speak Dari. Or maybe it was just that she is always going to be the odd one out, the person who ended up alone. Intersections between race, class, gender and religion teach us a lot about shifting landscapes of inclusion, exclusion, belonging and unbelonging. These feelings make up spaces of everyday life for the people in my ethnography. So many of my participants are between lines of race, class, sexuality and religion, in ways that lead them to feel like they are outsiders. Lines of inclusion and exclusion are also created in literature that discusses class, which is often only applicable to communities who have lived in places for longer than one generation. Further, discussions of religion often focus on families of one religion only. Migration, global inequality, education markets, economic and social class, and religion create interiors, exteriors and intersections that can leave people in between dominant lines of identification and belonging. These are complicated issues that are mobile and diverse: intersections of religion and class are different from intersections of migration and inequality, and include education markets. However, they are brought together by the feeling of being left out that people experience when they are outside changing contours of culture. The process of engaging with, and coming to understand experiences of being between lines, or 'outside belongings' (Probyn, 1996), has also led me to interrogate my own experiences of outside belonging, in terms of class, ethnicity, sexuality and religion, alongside those of my research participants.

Eyes and eyes look out at me from council housing. Flats packed alongside and on top of each other tower over either side of the street. The vibrant blue London summer sky shines between the green-and-white-clad towers. I can feel my own class mobility. The poverty of my grandparents' farm in County Cork is not visible on my well-presented, if under-rested, façade. I remember my father's stories about working to make a 'better life', stories I would now say are classist. But at the time, the child 'me' tried to empathise with him. There was no work for him in Dublin, so he left to find work, to become 'better', to make a better life. Trying to cope with the contradictions his life then embodied, he taught us Irish and wore an Akubra hat.

My family was unquestionably aspirational in educational terms. The north side of Dublin is not known for its wealth, although my father won an academic scholarship for financially disadvantaged families to attend the best boys' school in Dublin: Belvedere College. The school still has a strong social mobility scholarship program. The oldest boy of four children (two boys and two girls), my father was the only one in his family to attend a fee-paying school, and this was because the fees were paid for by the scholarship. After graduation, he was accepted to study at Trinity College Dublin. He then left Dublin to find work, and met my mother in Cambridge. She was his boss, having attended university, unlike her parents. The 1970s saw her working in the social work department at Fulbourn psychiatric hospital. When I reread the literature on social and economic class, I can see that my father and my mother were very much the immigrants who were 'pushed to leave' (Archer, Hollingworth and Halsall, 2007; Ferro, 2006; Preece, 2020; Walkerdine and Lucey, 1989; Willis, 1978), skilled and able to look for work away from home. My mother's stories of poverty in England still echo in my memory: her recollection of crying from the pain of cold fingers while cutting potatoes in the freezing English winter. Before I was born, my parents left their damp white stone cottage with its wet thatched roof in Cambridge and emigrated to Australia, settling in Kaurna country. They protested for Aboriginal land rights and denuclearisation and learnt the names of eucalyptus trees. My mother found work at a hospital, and could not believe her first pay cheque was accurate, it seemed so large to her. They had a new life, where mum could afford a 'whole bottle' of wine with every pay and where the fire did not smoke out the house. My father went back to university for postgraduate study. They were becoming somebody. But, even as 'ordinarily' who wore Akubra hats and flannelette shirts, nothing ever eased my father's pain of leaving Ireland. His pain was expressed continuously through his overinvestment in our life 'being better' than his life had been, and his ongoing, awkward attempts at class distinction. I remember trying to understand the sadness embedded in the long explanations he gave me as a child between the difference in our family's neat photos in frames and his childhood home where the photos were 'just stuck up' on the wall. The photos in frames did not make him happy, but they were a way for him to express his class aspiration, and gave him some kind of unhappy satisfaction. I still feel his huge sadness, having grown up with it, and I think I always will.

In the middle of this very hot London summer day, under the very blue sky, I am trying to leave this sadness behind. I, too, am aspirational, but I aspire to leave behind the pain of my father that I carry with me. The women who live on the estate flick long ashes off their cigarettes and chat on their front steps. Clean washing flutters in the wind across balconies. I am a stranger to them as they watch me walk down their road, surrounded on either side by their estate. They also want their kids to become somebody, perhaps somebody just like them, perhaps somebody quite different. My mind wanders back to a conversation I had with one of the mothers from the estate when she attended the exhibition of her children's artwork I held at Goldsmiths College, with her two young daughters in tow. She was explaining to them how, although this was their first time at university, they would be coming back, they were both going to attend university. She herself had gone to the University of Greenwich to study social work as a mature-age student and single mother of two. It had taken an enormous amount of work and perseverance. After the first time I met her children, I asked their school principal if everything at home was okay, because they had explained their belonging and home stories as featuring their mum 'who is always angry and yells at us and punches me in the face'. The face punch turned out to be an absolute exaggeration, but the strain of studying, working and parenting was clearly impacting the whole family. How could it not?

Standing in the haze of the estate mothers' smoking, I wondered if life in one place is ever really happier than life in another. It might be safer. It might be better paid, or have better weather. I wondered at the extent to which being taught to look towards other places all the time – and to distance yourself from your past – was worth the pain of loss and rejection. One of the other mums on the estate contentedly explained her life to me as a bubble: 'I've grown up on a council estate as well, so that is my world … we're all very close-knit. I'm not someone who's majorly into the royal family, I don't follow politics. I keep myself to myself and I'm in my little bubble, and: "everyone, stay out!". If you don't agree with me, you stay outside my bubble' (Neve, south-east London, 2018). The bubble seems like a pretty good place to be. Neve's stories are not concerned with 'becoming respectable' (Skeggs, 2002), or any form of searching for approval from others outside her bubble. The residents of the estate are largely white, and I can't help but think of the stark differences between Neve's place and class belonging, and the unhappy relationships that some of the Sudanese refugee children living in the Atherton Gardens estate in Melbourne have with their home. Is Neve's bubble a happy place because she is white? Reflecting on Neve's bubble, and other accounts of class, ways of

Incapacity / Neamhábaltacht   163

understanding religion, ways of being religious while not professing to understand religion, and the very racialised systems of value we are born into, I have come to see many 'outsides' to stories of class in academic work that are largely concerned with white communities, yet do not present their work as studies of whiteness per se (Peel, 2003; Reay and Lucey, 2000; Thomson, 2002; Willis, 1978). Theories of aspirational mobility (Archer, Hollingworth and Halsall, 2007; Ferro, 2006) and understandings of how 'working-class kids get working-class jobs' (Willis, 1978) tell us much about how class works in some contexts, but these contexts are largely white. As I have suggested, this literature makes a lot of sense in understanding my own family's struggles, but it leaves out the loss of belonging inherent in experiences of class mobility and the stinging rejections of those who feel 'left behind'. It also does not extend to the shifting worlds experienced by the hundreds of migrants with whom I work, many of whom have university degrees that do not translate into the English language, or who speak and write multiple languages fluently and yet are financially punished for not being educated in English. The spaces between these roughly defined collective experiences create new outsides, some of which I explore in what follows.

Class belonging is physical and practical as much as it is conceptual or ideological. The in-between spaces, the unbelonging and loss associated with class and spatial mobility, the sad photo frames, stories of overstretched mothers who had returned to study being angry at home, Uber drivers with multiple degrees in languages other than English, need to be accounted for. Skeggs explains these struggles for women, saying, 'The real working-class for these women is something from which they are desperately trying to escape. It is why they are doing college courses. They want to be seen as different' (Skeggs, 2002: 76). Class is expressed in the kinds of identity and community assemblages people make and the ways they experience affinity, success, failure, happiness and unhappiness. Making new mixtures doesn't always work and is often very uncomfortable. Similarly, the family stories of many non-white families with whom I work, from cosmopolitan migrant and cosmopolitan refugee backgrounds, show how class articulates differently across cultures. Class does not easily translate between cultures. This is exemplified by the high numbers of Indian and Pakistani migrants with multiple degrees in their first language who are now driving cabs or Ubers in Australia or England.

Despite my discomfort with these gaps, my fieldwork has taught me repeatedly that class is the most significant factor that shapes the ways people see the world, even if academic literature on the subject doesn't always explain this in a manner that aligns with my experiences. In instances in which people are religious, I have found that class significantly informs why and how people are religious, and can also factor into whether or not they were born into religion or whether they chose religion for personal development. Ethnicity, and then class, tends to be the most significant influencing factor in whether people are born into religion or choose religion for themselves. Class is expressed through attachment to material objects and places (for example, Hunter wellington boots and housing estates), and how conflicts are lived between and across generations of migrants. There are limits to multiculturalism for white families who have tried to belong to these communities. I share some of many stories of cosmopolitan migration in which families from the Middle East have moved to Australia, and unpack their work in finding diverse communities that acknowledge their worldly cultural capital: a process that shows the limits of some studies of class in terms of mainly applying to white, non-migrant communities.

Class, materiality and whiteness

As I have suggested, class is a significant factor in the way people have faith, how they understand their faith, and what faith means to them. Class, faith and belonging are entangled in how people reflect on their experiences of belonging and unbelonging, and those of the people and communities around them. Class is often inherent in spatial and geographical arrangements: the housing estates towering on either side of me make a case in point. Class is reflected in the environments we inhabit and is therefore implicated in people's day-to-day activities. It contains people at the same time as it provides comfort, identity and structure (Jeffery, 2018). Class is implicit in how my participants narrated their experiences of belonging, even though it is often expressed in terms other than the word 'class', through geographic belonging, values, or levels of education. Upon reflection and analysis, class emerged in people's descriptions of material goods, in people's habits and practices, and in their expectations and aspirations. Class may be somewhat hidden within their descriptions, but on closer scrutiny it becomes clear that class is a fundamental organising aspect of their identities and lives.

Many of my participants with white Anglo-Saxon backgrounds thought deeply about class and about their own class belonging in ways that align with the literature on class (Peel, 2003; Reay, 2006; Savage, 2015; Thomson, 2002; Willis, 1978). Overall, the explicit and insightful conversations I had about class were largely conversations between white people, and I wonder at the extent to which reflexive discussions about class are a form of performative whiteness (Frankenberg, 1993) at times. Several participants were highly critical of the way class plays out in their lives and that of their families. Some felt uncomfortable with the way that class is expressed in objects, practices and desires. As Martha explained, for her family, being upper-class and English entails:

> *a stronger identification with a Boris Johnson-style of Britishness. Hunter wellingtons, croquet, rowing. That is it. And there was a certain expectation, totally an expectation of what you do, the sort of jobs you go into, what your leisure activities would be, how you sound, how you speak, what your children do. Blah blah blah. There are elements of what is British in their view. So the Barbour jacket, the green wellies, the foxhound dog, blah blah blah, that is my family. Hunting, shooting, fishing.* (Martha, south-east London, 2018)

Martha's words express upper-class England poetically, and, invoking notions of empire, she refers to 'Britain' and 'Britishness'. Although Martha was born on the island of England (and her family are English), she is well positioned to criticise empire and class because she was born into a well-to-do family as one of five children. Her four siblings were sent to fee-paying schools, and she attended a government-funded school. Whether or not this choice was Martha's or her parents' was not clear to me, although Martha did not seem to harbour resentment about being treated differently. She explained:

> *I know that I experienced a very different education from my siblings, which is quite interesting, because I'm one of five and they all went to public [independent fee-paying] schools and so did my*

> *cousins, but I didn't. And that was quite interesting … They think I'm the disadvantaged one … But it is very different in terms of schooling and in terms of values, the way values are put across. And expectation. And duty.* (South-east London focus group, 2018)

Martha moved to London from the countryside and chose to live in a working-class area of London, a community that seemed the right fit for her in terms of values. This choice, and her exquisite articulation of the way class shapes expectations and taste, is also an expression of her birth into an upper-class family, both worlds and miles away from her current life. Martha can explain class clearly partly because she has been afforded the resources with which to do so.

Martha's childhood, as the only sibling in an upper-class family to attend a government school, and her decision to bring up her family in a working-class community, informs her perspective on how class systems reinforce inequality. Martha explains how her ambiguity about her family's class was an issue for her family from childhood onwards. She starts by explaining the kinds of friends she made at her school being compared to her siblings' friends:

> *There is definitely something about the public school education which is … I can unpick it because I've sort of lived it without being 'in' it. And there was something about the expectation of my parents, which was quite difficult for them when obviously I wasn't in that system and my friends were just everybody locally in the community, and were not the sort of friends that my parents were used to having in their home … my friends would be anybody, where my siblings' friends would be from an international background or had a certain element of privilege, or their families were living abroad or they were in the armed forces.* (South-east London focus group, 2018)

Martha politely expresses her own criticism of class privilege, when she explains how her siblings and their classmates were able to avoid entrance exams because of their attendance at expensive private institutions:

> *so you have to pass an exam depending on what type of school you go to at eleven, except my siblings didn't because they all did something called common entrance, for the public school.* (South-east London focus group, 2018)

Martha's critique of the English[4] class system was also expressed by other white English participants. Like Martha's discussion of Hunter wellingtons and a 'Boris Johnson-style of Britishness' as a symbol of class, other participants also brought class together with nationality and ethnicity. Some white English participants felt quite ambiguous about nationality as a means of identification because of the ways that class is embedded in Englishness. Joanie, for example, a participant from Manchester, felt that her identity as a white British woman was cause for a sense of shame as much as a sense of community:

> I didn't come from a rich family ... you know, I'm one of five. Um, so I know me mum and dad would've struggled when we were younger. But we've all got a really strong work ethic from that, and that sense of family which you know I've now got with my little family ... What does [being] British mean to me? Absolutely nothing. It's an imperial thing that's gone back hundreds of years. I think as a nation you can only judge a nation, or in particular the government, based on how they treat their most vulnerable in society, and we are shocking. So as a British person, I am appalled by what my country does ... So yeah, obviously I'm British and I happen to be white. And I know they have those things on forms because it's a tick-box exercise for 'oh well look at us', you know. 'We're now employing an increased number in this particular ethnic community.' Um, but I just, I just think it's [Britishness] a very old, old way ... it's just an alien thing. (Manchester, interview, 2018)

Through characterising classed, racialised Britishness as 'an alien thing', Joanie is distancing herself from what she perceives as the problems of colonial Britain. The white fragility (DiAngelo, 2018) embedded in attempts at diversification is a reminder of Britain's colonial past, which Joanie temporally distinguishes herself from, by describing it as 'very old'. Colonisation is both very old and contemporary. It happens again and again in all kinds of ways; for example, I would suggest that English people referring to themselves as British can be an act of colonisation, or claiming territories that are not their own place. Joanie's and Martha's stories show the entanglement of class and whiteness that is specific to many popular ways of thinking about how 'class' operates in England.

Like Martha and Joanie, some white parents among my participants had made the decision to live in relatively working-class, ethnically superdiverse neighbourhoods, framing their decision to do so as an effort towards living in a more inclusive society. The decision to move and settle in a specific location is a performance of what Savage et al. (2010) has termed a sense of 'elective belonging' that arises out of people's perception of place and their ability to choose where to settle. Savage and colleagues define elective belonging as 'the way that middle-class people claimed moral rights over place through their capacity to move to, and put down roots in, a specific place which was not just functionally important to them but which also mattered symbolically' (116). While Martha's family was very involved in her church and had settled into south-east London life, Joanie still felt she was not accepted by migrant families at her daughter's Manchester school. For Joanie, there was certainly a sense that the other parents at her school resented the apparent ease with which white families can move. Indeed, the difference in migration stories is stark, and includes people who have spent seven to eleven years in Italy after fleeing war in Afghanistan, and now live in England with an Italian passport, to others who have travelled across the sea from Afghanistan on a refugee boat and been detained on Christmas Island, before being released to live in Melbourne, to others who have fled religious persecution in Palestine, Bosnia or Iraq. Joanie's and Martha's white mobility stories also stand in stark contrast to some of my other English participants who had been born in, and lived their whole lives, within working-class council estates, and could not imagine moving even just a short distance away.

Conclusion

In this chapter, I have examined some of the many causes that lead to an incapacity to understand religious and cultural differences. Biased media representations, classed upbringings, gendered violence, racism and histories of colonial violence are interwoven in creating the reasons that often lead to or result in prejudice. Religious identity can be often only a minor part of individual identity, but it is one that allows or prohibits the formation of a range of affiliations and solidarities with individuals and groups. In my discussions above I have worked to highlight diversity within Islam as a departure point for discussing Muslim culture as rich and hybrid. This broad terrain of ways of engaging with religion consists of countless examples of personal religious identities, many of which are omitted from popular representations. I have also examined colonial histories, and affective scapes of class as ways of orienting bodies away from non-west religions and their associated affective scapes.

Notes

1 The term multiculturalism holds a variety of meanings in policy and social research and has been both widely endorsed and critiqued (Levrau and Loobuyck, 2018). In the 1970s and 1980s, multiculturalism emerged as a way forward for societies with high levels of immigration (Modood, 2007). The idea was that different groups should be able to practise their cultural traditions and speak the languages of their places of origin while also identifying with their new country of residence (Foster, 1988). Underlying this approach was a cultural relativism of the time that allowed for the equivalence of different cultural traditions. More recently, however, critics have argued that multiculturalism appears as a tokenistic exoticising of otherness (Prato, 2016). As a result of growing collective anxieties around radicalisation, and following terrorist attacks in Europe and other regions of the world in which migrants and the children of migrants have been implicated, multiculturalism and its outcomes have come under increased media scrutiny. It has become clear that many countries struggle with the lack of social inclusion of immigrant groups, and that the limited integration even of second-generation migrants has led to lower outcomes in terms of education and socioeconomic status.
2 The term 'superdiversity' was coined by Vertovec (2005a, 2005b), in which he discusses the findings of several census-based projects on migrant identities. He describes the changing nature of UK immigration and make-up of migrant communities, away from two or three established countries with deep roots to the UK as a result of colonial histories and towards a more diverse range of countries and constituencies. Diversity has increased within migrant communities, which as a result have become less homogeneous.

3 The Australian Liberal Party is a centre-right conservative party akin to the Tories and Republicans, not a 'small l' liberal (i.e. progressive) party in the modern sense of the word.
4 Many of my research participants refer to themselves as British, although all my British participants were born in England, not in Scotland, Wales or Northern Ireland. I have referred to these participants as English, not British, and find the acquiescence to colonial history that I associate with the word 'British' unfortunate and something I would like to change.

8

Other worlds / *Neamhshaolta*

Faith and children's art are a means through which people create and explore the possibilities of other worlds. Both faith and art are interested in how things might be better, both in this world and after our death. Cusak suggests that 'many stories have the potential to be read as transcendent and uniquely meaningful (as mythology, theology or other explanatory narrative) by certain individuals and groups' (2016: 575). This statement brings together old and new faith systems and creative art practices. For example, children often make art about popular cultural stories (video games, fictional characters) and these artworks might simultaneously include comments about the way they wish the world was. For example, they often imagine a world in which we can actually stop climate change, or a world where housing is not a problem. Faith has often served similar functions in the respect that it can be a way of hoping for a better life during trying times. In this chapter, I explore the theme of other worlds, as it explains why people maintain their faith and what children often make art about. I examine the appeal of faith as a way to imagine a better life: both a life after death and a better way of having life now. I then move on to consider the roles that other worlds play in children's artwork: both fantasy worlds that children wish were real, and the act of making art as a way of envisaging changes that could be undertaken to make our world a better place.

Faith in other worlds

In what follows I explore parents' sentiments about the ways their faith connects them to other worlds, and/or is a resource on which they draw in order to reconnect to their world.

> *Ahmed: Being in God's hand is like that, sometimes in your life, your parents put you into God's hand and then you practise God, you go to the church, you go to mosque and then sometimes you fall out of that area because you're following the wrong people. Then comes a stage of your life where you realise 'ah, I've been [off], I need to go back to the same spot, I need to reconnect'. So you reconnect. [...]*
> *Philomena: It gives you calm, it makes you relax, that's important –*
> *Ahmed: Absolutely. There's a bigger picture than what we see –*
> *Philomena: You rely on someone stronger, someone out there, you ask them what about happiness? Okay, don't worry, I'm in safe hands, I'm in a safe place.*
> (Philomena and Ahmed, west Sydney focus group 2018)

Philomena and Ahmed's discussion shows us that they rely very much on their relationship with more than 'what we see'. Indeed, their happiness comes from being in the 'safe hands' of a God that neither they, nor anyone, can see. This relationship with the unseeable God also shapes their relationship with death. Ahmed and Philomena are not alone here, as this subject was picked up in other focus group discussions:

> *Rahmatollah: The thing is that following religion, especially for me, makes it more meaningful and gives me more motivation to live, it's more meaningful, my life. When I think about life after death, it makes me a little bit of sadness. It's very depressing. But when I think about the war, about the universe, everything, everything, it's like everything is like, must be controlled by some very strong person like God.*
> (South-east Melbourne focus group, 2018)

Rahmatollah deals with his fear of death by believing in God. More than this, for Rahmatollah, God helps him reconcile injustices that otherwise cause him great distress (such as war). The idea of a 'very strong person like God' is clearly not only sustaining, but it is also required to combat the sadness or depression that can accompany contemporary life. Similar experiences were shared by women from the same community, who felt not only that their relationship with God was sustaining, but a range of kinds of spiritual practices supported their day-to-day life in different ways:

> Patrizia: I used to go to a [yoga] class, to a lady in Glen Waverley. She was very good and she was very spiritual. It was a good grounding experience, you know?
> Maria: I think death is really interesting in terms of spirituality, because I think sometimes when people are dead, they're not there anymore but you feel like they're still there.
> Patrizia: Yes.
> Maria: And that's really a funny feeling.
> Patrizia: For me, they've gone back to God. Yeah, it is a funny feeling. And if you really think about that, it's that funny feeling with God as well. And it's hard to describe. It's a presence. It's a presence.
> Anna: When people aren't here, can you still feel their presence?
> Patrizia: Yeah, you feel their presence. And I suppose it's now I'm wanting to feel the presence of God more. Whereas before, I was too busy. I was too busy. And I still am, but I think, like the lady said, it's nice to find that time. That time where it's just peaceful and it's just grim. And sometimes I mean just close my eyes on the train and it's just – I block everything out. It doesn't matter where you are; you can pray anywhere, I think.
> (South-east Melbourne focus group, 2019)

The idea that 'It doesn't matter where you are; you can pray anywhere' is very powerful. Trains, workplaces, homes, religious spaces, parks – all become possible sanctuaries. Such an approach means that, regardless of social alienation within colonised or colonising contexts, acceptance and protection are assumed to be embedded in all places. One only has to 'block everything out'.

Parents from Anglo backgrounds in England discussed near-death experiences and how coming close to death had inspired faith in them: not faith in a particular God, but faith in an unseen, or unseeable, 'bigger picture' and the accompanying ideas that everything happens for a reason and there is more to life than what we can see. Others discussed family trees and the act of tracing their heritage across generations as a way of being connected to their spirituality and the aspects of their existence that extends beyond what we can see, hear or touch. One of the other significant themes running through the data is children's fears about what the world might become. For many children, the hope that other worlds are indeed possible was accompanied by the fear that if we don't act now to minimise climate change, then the world of their future will be extremely different to how it is now – in a way that they want to avoid. Children's art depicted 'other worlds' they imagine, and some which they see but do not necessarily inhabit.

Climate change and other worlds

The most pronounced theme that runs throughout the visual data from children (the artworks they made) is their fear of climate change. I have discussed this fear in detail and my approaches to it elsewhere (Hickey-Moody, Horn and Willcox, 2019; Hickey-Moody, Knight and Florence, 2021). Worlds that include technologies designed to ward off climate change, or worlds that have been even more severely impacted by climate change than our own, feature centrally in the artworks created by children, so it would be remiss of me not to discuss this here. Discussions of climate change began, somewhat unexpectedly, in my research in 2017 in Manchester, where children painted a collaborative future city made up of everything they thought 'really mattered'. The city featured a range of novel ways of responding to climate change, such as streets that were rivers of seawater designed as a tactical intervention into city life. The rivers were designed as transport systems that promoted biodiversity and keep the ocean fish alive while allowing people to get around. This city also featured a glass dome that protected the environment's flora and a flying mosque. This painting is reproduced below (Figure 8.1).

Protecting their future city with a glass dome designed to regulate the climate and protect wildlife is a good example of the inventive responses that children come up with when trying to mitigate their fear of climate change. Consistently, children in London, Sydney, Melbourne, Manchester, Adelaide and Canberra expressed the fear that climate change would ruin the world and posited creative alternative ways of stopping such disasters. At an inner-north Melbourne school, two years after I was presented with streets

Figure 8.1 'All the streets are rivers', Manchester, 2017

made out of rivers of seawater in Manchester, my introduction to the project, which asks the children 'what really matters?', was met with immediate concern about global warming, climate change and environmental pollution. In my plenary group discussion before we started making, the children brought up their concerns. Climate change was their primary example of 'what really matters' for the future: stopping climate change. An excerpt from my fieldwork notes further illustrates this point:

Field notes, inner-north Melbourne

Everyone seemed motivated and set out immediately on drawing their component of the future city. Two boys started creating a recycling factory, and the environment, climate change and pollution came up as topics several times. The children are clearly aware of these issues. Two other boys in the other group started with the idea to put all the national flags of the country of origin of their families together, but somehow then got side-tracked and did something totally different, which was a beautiful tree with some rivers and bridges across the river. One of the boys (his family was Burmese, asked me to check the flag) has a talent for drawing and explained how he wanted to include rivers and a park etc. (Fieldwork notes, inner-north Melbourne, 2019)

The children immediately drew future inventions that would stop climate change or were designed to restore versions of our increasingly damaged climate. Children in Canberra, Sydney and Adelaide showed similar concerns. Fieldwork notes from Adelaide show children's first responses to the question of 'what really matters', which included the environment:

> *Simon made an image of a green leafy tree with the word 'environment' written in capital letters. When asked about it, he said that the environment was really important: it is what really matters most to him.* (Fieldwork notes, Adelaide, 2019)

I have a huge number of images produced by the children that relate to climate change in different ways (Hickey-Moody, Horn and Willcox, 2019; Hickey-Moody, Knight and Florence, 2021). For now, I want to flag it as a motivating reason to create other worlds. As suggested by a painting depicting a future city being designed around what was called a 'tree of life' by the children, future worlds need to be different. This city has all the things one needs to live, including a hospital, school, housing, an airport, a mosque, parks and a pool, and all roads lead to the tree. This focus on the environment was ever-present in this fieldwork site, as was the fear that the world would end if action wasn't taken to recycle, clean the ocean or develop green solutions to transport.

All of the future cities that children created featured technological and imaginative inventions designed to stop climate change. They also featured low-cost, affordable housing, as a fear of homelessness is a theme that runs across many of my research sites. The need for futures characterised by low-cost, affordable housing features most notably in the artworks made by children in Manchester, Sydney and London. Discussions and representations of this theme began in 2017 in Manchester, where children painted multiple high-rise flats in their future cities comprised of 'what really matters'. They then explained these architectural choices (featuring only high-rises) by stating that it is very important that 'everyone has a home'. In recent years, groups of homeless people have camped out

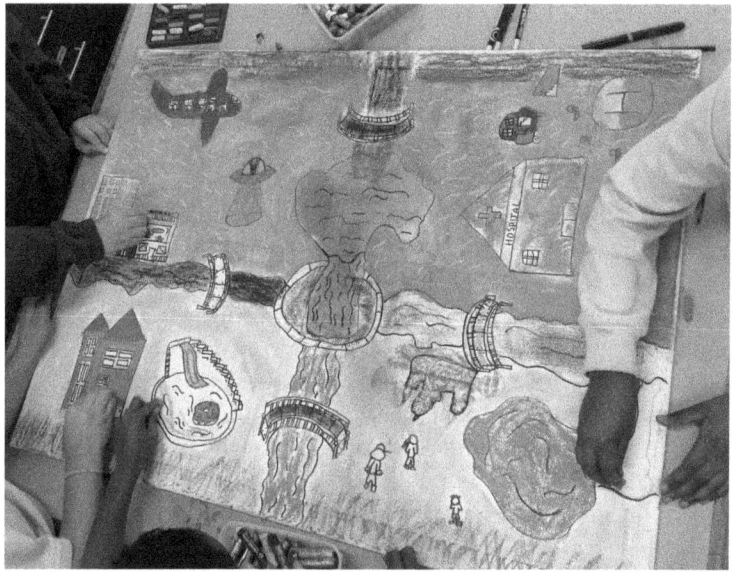

Figure 8.2 'Future City', in the centre of which is a tree of life, inner-north Melbourne, 2019

in sizeable tent communities under bridges in Manchester, and there have been ongoing protests attempting to negotiate the right to space for those who were sleeping rough (Rhoden-Paul, 2015). An old community radio studio was commandeered as a centre of the protest in Levenshulme and was covered in a huge cardboard sign, claiming the right to the city for the homeless (Maidment, 2020). The sign stated: 'HOMES FOR PEOPLE NOT FOR PROFIT'. The tent city in the centre of Manchester and the frenzy of media stories on the occupation of homeless people in the city (BBC, 2015a; BBC, 2015b; BBC, 2015c; Pidd, 2015) had clearly left an impression on the children's consciousness.

In two of the Manchester schools, a majority of the children were from refugee backgrounds. They were children who had had difficult journeys across countries, had been displaced, and in some instances, had arrived in England to less-than-desirable conditions. Media stories about refugee communities in Greece, Syria and Italy, alongside displaced people living in tents under Manchester bridges, brought up old memories of refugee centres or the experience of being without a home. These were things the children struggled to describe in words, but their art focusing on housing estates made clear the very real fear of being displaced once again. For many, their financial situation made this fear rational. Alongside the low-cost housing featured in artworks, children placed green spaces, zoos, carbon-neutral technologies, waterways: things that stopped climate change or were designed to try to stop climate change. Making art was a way of creating other worlds.

A few weeks later, when I was in south-east London, similar images of cities made up of high-rise apartments surrounding a park were generated by children who were concerned with housing availability and climate change. It was clear that, as far as these children are concerned, high-density living protects residents from possible homelessness and green spaces contribute to stopping climate change.

The image in Figure 8.3 speaks of a place belonging through the ways that the children have positioned their community on the edge of a river, which is analogous to their community's geographic

Figure 8.3 A city where 'everyone has a home', acrylic paint and felt-tip pen on canvas, south-east London, 2017

location on the banks of the Thames. As you can see, their future city features a church, a hospital, a mosque, a temple, housing estates, high-rises and a swing set, all built around a central green park. It is not dissimilar to the urban geography the children actually inhabit. The artwork provides a glimpse into the very things the children know they need in their lives, or are afraid of losing. Access to green and healthy environmental spaces, water, health services, religion, education and housing are central to their city. While Manchester and London have enduring issues with homelessness, so too do Melbourne and Sydney. Concerns about climate change and homelessness carried on in my Australian fieldwork, especially in the inner-urban Melbourne site where homelessness is clearly visible. The children involved in my project live almost entirely in highrise council housing estates. Some fieldwork notes from my work in the Melbourne school illustrate how the concern with homelessness is reflected in approaches to their future city planning.

Field notes, inner-north Melbourne

The children were alert and willing to contribute, but needed warming up and familiarising with the idea of a 'future city'. Various children spoke up and contributed ideas, including 'apartment buildings', 'people', 'nature' and other things. With some prompting, ideas around infrastructure and public buildings also emerged. Apartment living is important because it is affordable and it is where they live so it is what they know. (Fieldwork notes, Melbourne, 2019)

The children's concerns with homelessness, housing availability and climate change are significant. Children's voices on the issue of homelessness are not heard often enough (see Holland and Crowley, 2013).

Figure 8.4 was a practice drawing for what would later be quilt squares depicting what 'really matters' and stories of belonging. I googled the housing estate that the children live in and they used it as a reference point when making this picture. The image on my phone provided a resource that the children used to copy the level of floors in the building. The small house to the right is Frankie's imaginary house in a well-to-do suburb, an imagined disassociation from where he really lives. There is a lot of academic work on youth, families and homelessness (Flatau et al., 2010; McNamara, 2015; Minnery and Greenhalgh, 2007; Sharam and Hulse, 2014),

Figure 8.4 A housing estate where the children live, a soccer pitch, and Frankie's imaginary house, inner-north Melbourne, 2019

some of which focuses on children and homelessness, including academic work that values children's perspectives, (Kirkman et al., 2010; Moore, McArthur and Noble-Carr, 2008). Fear of homelessness and climate change speaks to children's immediate and broader contextual insecurities. Similar concerns around homelessness are expressed by children from Manchester, as shown in Figure 8.5. This image includes a high-rise housing estate featuring a Tesco supermarket.

The children in my ethnography are all attending either school, a mosque or a church when they participate in my workshops. They are not homeless, they have somewhere to live, but many are still scared of being or becoming homeless or of not having enough. Crowded apartments shared with many family members in old buildings can be stressful places for a child. Though their family lives may be loving, the experience of moving countries, leaving family members behind and then being given a small flat to occupy does not always create a secure environment for many

Other worlds / Neamhshaolta

Figure 8.5 High-rise housing with a Tesco on top, mixed media on canvas, Manchester, 2018

newly arrived refugee families. The children's concerns about this run through the visual and audio data and are present in the ways children imagine the possibility of a liveable future. The ones that don't live in council housing are often aware of the other students' situations and, in the cases of Manchester and London, are attuned to media narratives that highlight the class struggle to find suitable homes. So many children in my research imagined 'other worlds' – safer, more secure worlds – as a way of coping with the precarious nature of the everyday. Children journey across multiple countries to reach safety; grow up in a number of different places with multiple national identities; often feel ashamed of where they live and – like Frankie – might pretend they have a different house; or, like a girl in Manchester, draw poo over pictures of themselves. These are experiences that the children in my ethnography have shared with me through their art and through their drawings. One example that stands out is from Frankie, whom I introduced above. He is an eleven-year-old boy from Melbourne, who lives with his carer after

Figure 8.6 Frankie and his uncle in a canoe, mixed media on fabric, Melbourne, 2018

escaping the conflict in West Papua. His stories and images resonate with precarity and violence. He and his uncle fleeing in a canoe, for example, was one of the first images Frankie made.

The image of Frankie in the canoe with his uncle (Figure 8.6) shows the flag from his country, and they are holding a gun to protect themselves. Frankie said people were always trying to kill them. Frankie also had complicated relationships with adults. He often drew images of war and guns, and I imagine his impressions of adults from childhood involved a lot of violence and fighting, which is why, he said, they had to escape. Frankie often felt angry and easily misrepresented. The very first task that I asked the children in Frankie's class to undertake was to draw a self-portrait and turn it into a three-dimensional collage. Frankie drew an image of rubbish floating with guns in the ocean as his self-portrait. This piece of data can be read in multiple ways. One reading, which I have explored elsewhere (Hickey-Moody, Horn and Willcox, 2019), relates to Frankie's awareness of climate change and his rising

Other worlds / Neamhshaolta

Figure 8.7 Frankie's self-portrait, mixed media on paper, Melbourne, 2018

anxiety around it. I suggest that polluted waterways and rising sea levels are emblematic of our contemporary moment.

Another reading of this 'portrait' is that Frankie sees himself as rubbish. His journey across the ocean from West Papua to Australia was clearly a foundational experience for him, and I wonder if his depiction of himself as rubbish floating in the water could also be read in terms of his journey across the water, and his incredibly low self-esteem.

Frankie explained his self-portrait (Figure 8.7) as a picture about climate change featuring weapons in the ocean:

Frankie: That's the sea, and that's the grass.
Anna: Why is the pistol in the ocean, is it just swimming?
Frankie: Because some people chucked it in there and then they went out of the ocean.
Anna: So, they chuck the pistols in the rivers and the oceans.
Frankie: Yes.
Anna: And do you want to tell me about your picture? We like to learn by sharing stories about our pictures.

Frankie: Okay, this is a butterfly changing, this is a whirlpool, this is heaps of beer bottles, this is three knives, one pistol and a double-barrelled shotgun, these are plastic bags with bottles in them. And this is a bird getting stuck in the rubbish.

(Inner-north Melbourne interview, 2019)

Beer bottles, three knives, one pistol and a double-barrelled shotgun are not what I would expect to find in the Australian ocean. I have the sense that Frankie's identity ocean is a mixture of West Papua and Australia, and Frankie (as both butterfly and bird) is both caught up in, and weighed down by, the rubbish or residue of both places mixed together.

I came to better understand Frankie's bad feelings about himself in one of the exercises he undertook with his class. Working with two other boys, Frankie made a future city. The boys named the future city with their initials. The future city was fantastic, with a recycling plant that could fly and locate itself wherever recycling needed to happen, a large mosque, high-rise apartments, a hospital and a cemetery. A photograph of the collaborative city on canvas is included in Figure 8.8, taken when the work was two-thirds complete. Significantly, the landscape features the images of two of the boys who drew the city and an image of Frankie, which was drawn by his friends. This caused Frankie great distress. Upon seeing an image of himself on canvas, Frankie burst into tears and howled. He was completely inconsolable until the drawing representing him was covered over by another hastily drawn minaret, not actually attached to the mosque (Figure 8.8).

Frankie's visual depictions of his sadness and anxiety are also visible in this canvas, where he has drawn dead bodies falling out of an army helicopter. There are two helicopters – they are blue with a parachute underneath, and the dead bodies falling out are sketched in pencil. Frankie's friends' representation of him in the future city is entombed in (and covered over by) a minaret towering up from a high-rise housing estate. Later that year, Frankie had a fight with his art teacher and pushed her over. The teacher, who was amazingly dedicated and passionate, went on indefinite sick leave, and was clearly worried about working with Frankie, who could, at times, be volatile and difficult to control. In addition to being volatile, Frankie was very vulnerable and was clearly living

Figure 8.8 Two of the boys drew themselves into the future city, mixed media on canvas, Melbourne, 2019

with post-traumatic stress. This profound fragility and distress was more acute in Frankie than in many other research participants, but in many other children involved in the project, insecurity and fear were expressed through worries about homelessness and climate change. A focus on inventions that make life better, on cars that have feathered wings, on sustainable cities, flying recycling centres and rivers for streets, clearly demonstrate the appeal for children of making other worlds.

Conclusion

Possibilities of better worlds, and ideas of other worlds, other beings, higher powers, life after death, clearly sustain both the adults and children involved in my work. Parents' faith means that the possibility of an afterlife, or an all-encompassing power that has a reason for life events, are thoughts that can bring relief and help them cope with day-to-day life. The emotional landscapes of the children involved in the project were equally composed of fear and joy. Anxiety about climate change and homelessness constituted the well-founded fears to which children responded by creating other worlds in their art. They possess questions about climate change to which there are, as yet, no answers. How will our planet survive? Concern for others' needs, demonstrated by the demand that 'everyone has a home', also shows the empathetic and thoughtful capacities of children from the ages of six to twelve. Further, some children have grown up with such profound personal and political insecurity that they have internalised this to the extent that they feel that they *are* the problem, and have learnt to hate themselves, as evidenced by Frankie howling with tears and hiding under the table when his friends attempted to draw him alongside themselves on their collaborative canvas. In this chapter, I have tried to share the feeling that other worlds are possible, or perhaps already exist alongside the world we experience. This was an enduring sense that ran through my explorations of faith.

Conclusion / *Conclúid*

Faith sustains everyone in different ways through troubling times. Across diverse places, cultures and ages, children and adults are sustained by very different forms of faith. The implications of this for further research are that faith systems very much need to be seen as part of children's lives, as well as continuing to be acknowledged as shaping adults' worlds. Whether they are taught to believe in capitalism, Hinduism or climate change, children are born into belief systems that come to be part of who they are. I began this book by suggesting that we all have faith in something. This is because my qualitative empirical research has shown me that people are similar in the respect that we are all sustained by faith, faith that our children's lives will be better than ours; that life after death will be better than it is now; faith in the 'truth' of science and the Enlightenment; in the fact that humans will never know all there is to this world; in the hope that our partner will outlive us; in whatever it is we need to believe.

The ways we come to have faith are complex and are different for everyone. The consistent thing about how we come to have faith is that everyone's stories are different. Capitalism, Christianity and Islam are the three most powerful and therefore popular belief systems into which people in my research are born. Participation in these systems is largely a result of *where* people are born and raised. Religion and capitalism are entwined in complex ways, and these relationships shape children's imaginaries and community cultures. As I have argued, faith mixtures are material: they are smells, memories, symbols and icons, places, words and sounds. We are born into lived mixtures that have been made through biography, geography, race and class. While we can modify these, we cannot completely change them.

In the communities with whom I worked, there is a gap between media (or popular) representations of faith and the way faith works. Terrorism is not necessarily seen by communities or individuals as an expression of religion. Memorialisation is a community response to terrorism and has significantly changed the physical and virtual landscapes of my research sites in Manchester, London and Sydney. Community, heritage and a feeling of belonging are the main reasons why those who identify as religious do so (Iner, 2015). As I have shown, there are specific subcultures of faith that transcend religion: children have faith in climate change (Hickey-Moody, Knight and Florence, 2021; Malone, 2017; Murris, 2016), friendship and virtual worlds, and adults have faith in something that is more than flesh, even if sometimes, they are not sure what that is. Others are sustained by the connection to the past and their family that religion brings (Cockburn, 2013). Children of all religions and class backgrounds are brought together by a concern about the environment. These arguments run across this book.

I began in Chapter 1 by bringing to life the locations in which my research took place and explained the place-based mixtures of faith attachment that community members felt. Reconciliation is an uncompleted project, and a broad context of colonial racism is embedded in my research sites. I tried to convey a sense of place attachment and share my experiences of being in place. West Sydney still reminds me viscerally of being stuck to a train seat, falafel, hot bitumen, telephone wires, rows and rows of pick-up trucks parked outside mosques on Fridays. Manchester brings to mind blue and yellow 'magic' buses with Wi-Fi, colourful corner shops, red-brick buildings, mosque visits and the black-red-gold Shia shrine to the massacre of Karbala, featuring mock bloodstained child corpses, hot school rooms, an empty shopping trolley in the corner of the women's prayer room and an especially domineering teaching assistant. For me, London was Tesco sandwiches, the Docklands Light Railway wobbling along its tracks, grey buildings, the Thames and loneliness. London is so big, and one can be so alone at times in that city. The lost lending library: an amazing make-believe world invented inside a south-east Primary School that was designed to show children all the places that reading can take them. Adelaide

Conclusion / Conclúid

was a spectacular tapestry couch, dates and coffee served by mothers and friends on said tapestry couch, the outdoor chapel, empty streets and two worlds. Outside the liberal and open church and the friendly mosque community who gave me bread and vegetables, also I noticed the women with pearl earrings, gold shoes and turned-up collars in Norwood. For me, Melbourne was the council housing towers, rapping and football, cold morning drives out to the problem of 'helping disadvantaged kids' and family stories of resilience. Canberra was orange, biryani, a bird in a fallen building and fear of otherness.

Moving from trying to share my sense of the mixtures that make up place attachment to the discourses that construct and communicate faith systems, I discussed how popular media and social policy have demonised Islam through black-panic discourses (Aly and Walker, 2007; Brasted, 2001; Kwansah-Aidoo and Mapedzahama, 2018; Noble, 2008). Privilege, conflict and attachment situate me in the research.

In Chapter 2, I developed a new materialist philosophy of faith. Through mobilising affect theory and writings from the new materialisms, I demonstrated how faith operates as both a form of what Lauren Berlant calls 'cruel optimism' and, alternatively, as a means of creating what Spinoza calls joy. I showed that a change in the capacity to act (affect), such as that created through belief, is an experience that unites both secular and religious people. For example, belief in the superiority of secular culture over religious culture, and vice versa, are two affectively similar corporeal orientations that, to quote Braidotti, show how we are 'all too human' (2019: 1–5) and all 'in-this-together-but-not-one-and-the-same' (2019: 157). I outlined the three scales across which faith entanglements and resulting unconscious orientations articulate: macro, meso and micro. I argued that, on a macro level, global material economies and worldviews, geographies and networks of faith impact substantively upon an individual's capacities to act, as these assemblages are both political and world-making. On a meso level, the individual and community geographies of belonging that constitute people's everyday lives demonstrate the complex entanglements of matter and belief that make up lived faith worlds. At a micro level, as I have suggested, faith is both a form of what Spinoza (1677) would call joy and, in some circumstances, what Berlant (2011) calls 'cruel optimism'. We are all consciously or unconsciously enmeshed in various systems of faith relation, both formal and informal, religious and secular. This chapter puts forward a unified approach to thinking about the social and individual politics of orientation as expressions of different forms of faith.

In Chapter 3, I moved on to discuss methods for researching with children and understanding their lifeworlds, and researching the communities in which they reside in relation to the global and local issues that shape them. Multi-sited ethnography and socially engaged arts practice (Hage, 2005; Marcus, 1995, 1998, 2011) were the two methodologies that animated my research, and these were complemented by focus groups with parents and community members, and follow-up in-depth interviews with focus group participants. Chapter 3 explained the bespoke developments I made to methods for undertaking arts-based research with children. The idea of being 'with children in their worlds' was an organising principle for the way I encouraged children to make art (Coleman, 2016). The materials children use to make art become absolutely central to the meanings art has for children. Making creates mixtures of meaning-place-community-belonging that are material, emotional and intra-active. Places, smells, colours and textures are part of how children come to express themselves and to know. I explained multi-sited ethnography as a way of adopting a critical perspective on how images and meanings circulate globally across places. Community, belonging and historical connections are surfaces of attachment, mixtures of belonging and ideas that span all places.

In Chapter 4, I examined joy and affect as products of faith and as material ways of coping that are developed by having faith. Increased capacity to act, brought about by empathy for others, insight into different experiences and a desire to be the change the world needs to see are examples of the positive affects that are engendered by faith. Rituals, icons, objects and places become networked systems that support connections and capacity to collaborate and share perspectives. Coping with difference, making new systems of belonging and negotiating conflict are some of the positive affects created through everyday faith. Spinoza, and after him, Deleuze and Guattari, offer ways of understanding the tectonics of emotion as they flow through assemblages of place, objects and bodies. Examining these ideas, I look at the patterns, practices and feelings of opening up that articulate across surfaces of faith.

Examining outside belongings in Chapter 5, I foregrounded the voices of participants to examine intersections between race, class, gender and religion. I explored how my research participants' experiences taught me about shifting landscapes of inclusion, exclusion, belonging and unbelonging. These feelings made up spaces of everyday life for the people in my ethnography, and while this chapter explored the dynamics of a few individuals and their families, the themes highlighted of being in between lines of race, class, sexuality and religion resonated across a significant number of my research participants. One of the main points I made in this chapter pertained to the racialised limits of cultural studies scholarship on class. I argued that lines of inclusion and exclusion are created in literature that discusses class, which is often only applicable to communities who have lived in places for longer than one generation and often focus on white cultures. Drawing on Elspeth Probyn's notion of outside belongings and attachments to surfaces and places, I examined migration, global inequality, education markets, social class and religion. I explored how these forces and practices create interiors, exteriors and intersections that can leave people in between dominant lines of identification and belonging. These are complicated issues that are mobile and diverse: intersections of religion and class are different from intersections of migration, inequality, and education markets. However, they are brought together by the feeling of being left out that people experience when they are outside changing contours of culture. The process of engaging with, and coming to understand experiences of being in between lines of identification, or experiencing 'outside belongings', has also led me to interrogate my own experiences of outside belonging, in terms of class, ethnicity, sexuality and religion, alongside those of my research participants. This process connects many people's stories and experiences. Only some of the stories I have collected were able to be included in this chapter, which presents a theme that extends across the lives of many more research participants.

In Chapter 6, I followed unexpected connections that sustained adults and children. Class and race, particularly class and whiteness is a significant theme that connects experiences from council estates in my research. This sense of connection is complicated in the experiences of Black migrant families. Football, both as a material cultural practice of significance and a mediated, symbolic way of diversifying representations of whiteness is another theme I explore in this chapter. Children made artworks about the ethnically diverse football stars they love, which express the superdiverse worlds in which they live. They play football whenever possible: even in classrooms. Ice-cream and the popular combination of football and ice-cream is another site of global connection for the children with whom I worked. Family relationships, friendships and happy moments of solitude were seemingly best experienced and expressed through the consumption of ice-cream. Finally, digital games, both as a mode of social engagement and as a source of creative inspiration really inspired many who were involved in my research.

I explored the sets of negative affects that attach to faith practices in Chapter 7. Promises, objects and imagined exchange values can become complicated ways of stopping engagement with the here and now, in favour of imagined possibilities to come. I unpacked histories of colonisation carried on in new ways and contemporary performances of racism. I also examined contemporary expressions of racism as spaces of discomfort. While I work to stop racism and I opposed expressions of racism in my fieldwork, creating enduring change is complicated and I have not yet found a way to do so. I think about these complexities in the hope this may create future changes.

In Chapter 8, I examined the idea of other worlds. Faith is a way that adults sustain possibilities of a better life or a better future. For adults, other worlds after death are a reason to live well and are something to look forward to. Other worlds also inspire children. When asked about 'what really matters', the 343 children involved in art-making developed a shared voice that spanned place, culture and religion to articulate their fears of homelessness and climate change. Some, but by no means all, of the children in my study were quite vulnerable. All of the children were worried about climate change. Some were scared of homelessness. For children, these concerns came above organised religion, with climate change – and their faith in climate change – being the most enduring fear present in their minds. Many children's families spent special time together at the mosque or at church, and while for some children, in some instances, this seemed more significant than football, for many, football was the most important community in their life.

Privilege, conflict and attachment

The embodied position from which I speak, work and experience the world co-produces my research findings. I try to acknowledge this wherever possible, alongside the ways my heritage and lived experience shape my interests and orientations. One of the ways I do this is to begin all of my focus groups with adults in Australia by acknowledging the unceded Aboriginal land on which we meet and, in both UK and Australia, by acknowledging my own privilege, living as a white woman in dominantly Anglo-Saxon, diverse social and cultural contexts. As I have suggested, both Australia and England are dominated by negative discourses in relation to Islam, and its relationship to contemporary incidences of terrorism (as I acutely observed during my fieldwork when the Manchester and London terrorist attacks occurred in mid-2017). Privilege is also associated with my role as a widely respected university professor. In the context of my research, I assume the position of the asker of questions and the agent who wants to map engagement and listen. As well as a listening researcher, I am a speaking and caring person. I identify myself to research participants in terms of my history of conflict and attachment, especially with the Catholic Church, which provides me with some insight into their experiences. They also contribute to the emotional labour of care involved in this project, which is often a heavy weight to bear.

Where next?

In focus groups and individual interviews, 285 adults, who spoke 22 languages between them and belonged to a range of formal and informal faith systems, told me about their ways of worshipping, observing, ways of communicating. Often, we shared food and we always shared our experiences. In exploring subcultures of faith, I shared stories from people who believed that there is more than what 'we know' to life and death, but didn't know what that is. I also examined subcultures of Muslim faith: Muslim diversity and connections with secular cultures, the spectre of terrorism, empathy, religious and personal identities, and global flows of cosmopolitan Muslim culture.

The body of research that informs this book sets forward a new research agenda for those working with children and migrant communities to examine faith practices. This begins with the awareness that faith is bigger than religion (Ammerman, 2013; Dessing, Jeldtoft and Woodhead, 2016) and brings together the complicated ways that people are motivated and sustained by their faith practices. Future researchers need to investigate faith and belief systems in ways that respond to empirical experiences rather than theoretical framings. I am trying to make a contribution to cultural studies of everyday life, by highlighting the significance of quotidian meanings in religion, spirituality and community. Such everyday experiences are core to the fabric of our society.

References

Abbit, B. 2017. 'The 22 bees mural – A tribute to those killed at Manchester Arena', *Manchester Evening News*, 5 June, viewed 1 April 2019, www.manchestereveningnews.co.uk/news/greater-manchester-news/22-bees-mural-tribute-those-13137016.
Abu-Ras, W.M. and Suarez, Z.E. 2009. 'Muslim men and women's perception of discrimination, hate crimes, and PTSD symptoms post 9/11', *Traumatology*, vol. 15, no. 3, pp. 48–63.
Ahmed, S. and Matthes, J. 2017. 'Media representation of Muslims and Islam from 2000 to 2015: A meta-analysis', *International Communication Gazette*, vol. 79, no. 3, pp. 219–44, doi: 10.1177/1748048516656305.
Aly, W. 2007. *People like us: How arrogance is dividing Islam and the West*, Pan Macmillan, Sydney, Australia.
Aly, A. and Green, L. 2008. '"Moderate Islam": Defining the good citizen', *A Journal of Media & Culture*, vol. 11, no. 1, viewed 21 December 2022, http://journal.mediaculture.org.au/index.php/mcjournal/article/viewArticle/28.
Aly, A. and Walker, D. 2007. 'Veiled threats: Recurrent cultural anxieties in Australia', *Journal of Muslim Minority Affairs*, vol. 27, no. 2, pp. 203–14.
Amar, A.S. 2012. 'Integrating texts and material culture: Methodological approaches to the study of premodern religions', *Material Religion*, vol. 8, no. 4, pp. 528–9, doi: 10.2752/175183412X13522006994971.
Ammerman, N.T. 2013. 'Spiritual but not religious? Beyond binary choices in the study of religion', *Journal for the Scientific Study of Religion*, vol. 52, no. 2, pp. 258–78, doi: 10.1111/jssr.12024.
Ammerman, N.T. 2014. 'Finding religion in everyday life', *Sociology of Religion*, vol. 75, no. 2, pp. 189–207.
Ammerman, N.T. 2016. 'Lived religion as an emerging field: An assessment of its contours and frontiers', *Nordic Journal of Religion and Society*, vol. 1, no. 02, pp. 83–99, doi: 10.18261/issn.1890-7008-2016-02-01.

Anderson, B. 1983. *Imagined communities: Reflections on the origins and spread of nationalism*, Verso, London, UK.
Apperley, T. 2010. *Gaming rhythms: Play and counterplay from the situated to the global*, Institute of Network Cultures, Amsterdam, Netherlands.
Arab, P.T. 2019. 'Spinoza, arch-father of the material religion approach and new materialisms', *Material Religion*, vol. 15, no. 5, pp. 624–6, doi: 10.1080/17432200.2019.1666583.
Archer, J. and Lloyd, B. 2002. *Sex and gender*, 2nd edn, Cambridge University Press, Cambridge.
Archer, L., Hollingworth, S. and Halsall, A. 2007. '"University's not for me – I'm a Nike person": Urban, working-class young people's negotiations of "style", identity and educational engagement', *Sociology*, vol. 41, no. 2, pp. 219–37, doi: 10.1177/0038038507074798.
Askins, K. 2015. 'Being together: Everyday geographies and the quiet politics of belonging', *ACME: An International E-Journal for Critical Geographies*, vol. 14, no. 2, pp. 470–8.
Askins, K. 2016. 'Emotional citizenry: Everyday geographies of befriending, belonging and intercultural encounter', *Transactions of the Institute of British Geographers*, vol. 41, no. 4, pp. 515–27, doi: 10.1111/tran.12135.
Australian Bureau of Statistics. 2016. *2016 Census QuickStats: Marion*, ABS, Canberra, viewed 3 February 2020, https://quickstats.censusdata.abs.gov.au/census_services/getproduct/census/2016/quickstat/SSC10106?opendocument.
Awan, I. 2012. '"I am a Muslim not an extremist": How the Prevent Strategy has constructed a "suspect" community', *Politics & Policy*, vol. 40, no. 6, pp. 1158–85.
Bağlı, H. 2015. 'Material culture of religion: New approaches to functionality in Islamic objects', *The Design Journal*, vol. 18, no. 3, pp. 305–25, doi: 10.1080/14606925.2015.1059598.
Baker-Lewton, A., Sonn, C.C., Vincent, D.N. and Curnow, F. 2017. '"I haven't lost hope of reaching out…": Exposing racism in sport by elevating counternarratives', *International Journal of Inclusive Education*, vol. 21, no. 11, pp. 1097–12.
Barad, K. 2003. 'Posthumanist performativity: Toward an understanding of how matter comes to matter', *Signs*, vol. 28, no. 3, pp. 801–31, doi: 10.1086/345321.
Barker-Perez, E.J. Feinstein and Robbie, K. 2019. *RMIT Interfaith Childhoods impact review*, Think Impact, North Melbourne, Australia.
Baugut, P. and Neumann, K. 2019. 'Online news media and propaganda influence on radicalized individuals: Findings from interviews with Islamist prisoners and former Islamists', *New Media & Society*, vol. 22, no. 8, pp. 1437–61, doi: 10.1177/1461444819879423.

BBC. 2015a. 'Manchester homeless camps banned from city centre', *BBC News*, 30 July, viewed 22 May 2020, www.bbc.com/news/uk-england-manchester-33717978/.
BBC. 2015b. 'Manchester homeless protest camp moves to new site', *BBC News*, 19 May, viewed 22 May 2020, www.bbc.com/news/uk-england-manchester-32624915/.
BBC. 2015c. 'Homeless evicted from Manchester city centre camp', *BBC News*, 19 September, viewed 22 May 2022, www.bbc.com/news/uk-england-manchester-34290299.
Bell, D. 1998. *Ngarrindjeri Wurruwarrin: A world that is, was and will be*, Spinnifex Press, North Melbourne, Australia.
Berlant, L. 2011. *Cruel optimism*, Duke University Press, Durham, NC.
Bishop, C. 2005. 'The social turn: Collaboration and its discontents', *Artforum*, vol. 44, no. 6, viewed 12 September 2021, http://cam.usf.edu/cam/exhibitions/2008_8_torolab/readings/the_social_turn_cbishop.pdf.
Blaise, M. 2010. 'Kiss and tell: Gendered narratives and childhood sexuality', *Australasian Journal of Early Childhood*, vol. 35, no. 1, pp. 1–9, doi: 10.1177/183693911003500102.
Boivin, N. 2009. 'Grasping the elusive and unknowable: Material culture in ritual practice', *Material Religion*, vol. 5, no. 3, pp. 226–87, doi: 10.2752/175183409X12550007729860.
Bond Stockton, K. 2009. *The queer child, or growing sideways in the 21st century*, Duke University Press, Durham, NC and London, UK.
Braidotti, R. 1994. *Nomadic subjects. Embodiment and sexual difference in contemporary feminist theory*, Columbia University Press, New York.
Braidotti, R. 2008. 'In spite of the times: The postsecular turn in feminism', *Theory, Culture & Society*, vol. 25, no. 6, pp. 1–24, doi: 10.1177/0263276408095542.
Braidotti, R. 2018. 'Affirmative ethics, posthuman subjectivity, and intimate scholarship: A conversation with Rosi Braidotti', in K. Strom, T. Mills and A. Ovens (eds), *Decentering the researcher in intimate scholarship: Critical posthuman methodological perspectives in education*, Emerald Publishing, Bingley, UK, pp. 179–88.
Braidotti, R. 2019. *Posthuman knowledge*, Polity Press, Cambridge, UK.
Brandt, S.A. and Carmichael, C.L. 2020. 'Does online support matter? The relationship between online identity-related support, mattering, and well-being in sexual minority men', *Computers in Human Behavior*, vol. 111, pp. 1–11, doi: 10.1016/j.chb.2020.106429.
Brasted, H.V. 2001. 'Contested representations in historical perspective: Images of Islam and the Australian press 1950–2000', in A. Saeed and S. Akbarzadeh (eds), *Muslim communities in Australia*, University of New South Wales Press, Sydney, Australia, pp. 206–27.

Bräunlein, P.J. 2019. 'Studying material religion from a non-anthropocentric perspective? Some considerations on new materialisms', *Material Religion*, vol. 15, no. 5, pp. 622–3, doi: 10.1080/17432200.2019.1666582.
Brown, L. and Richards, B. 2016. 'Media representations of Islam in Britain: A sojourner perspective', *Journal of Muslim Minority Affairs*, vol. 36, no. 3, pp. 350–63, doi: 10.1080/13602004.2016.1216627.
Burawoy, M. 2000. 'Introduction', in M. Burawoy (ed.), *Global ethnography: Forces, connections, and imaginations in a postmodern world*, University of California Press, Berkeley, CA, pp. 1–41.
Burchardt, M. 2019. 'Assembling the profane materialities of urban religion', *Material Religion*, vol. 15, no. 5, pp. 627–8, doi: 10.1080/17432200.2019.1666584.
Carrington, B. 1998. '"Football's coming home", but whose home? And do we want it?: Nation, football and the politics of exclusion', in A. Brown (ed.), *Fanatics!: Power, identity and fandom in football*, Routledge, London, UK, pp. 21–143.
Chambers, C. and Watkins, S. 2012. 'Postcolonial feminism?', *Journal of Commonwealth Literature*, vol. 47, no. 3, pp. 297–301.
Clayton, J.P., Blackburn, A.M. and Carroll, T.D. 2006. *Religions, reasons and gods: Essays in cross-cultural philosophy of religion*, Cambridge University Press, New York, doi: 10.1017/CBO9780511488399.
Cleland, J. 2014. 'Racism, football fans, and online message boards: How social media has added a new dimension to racist discourse in English football', *Journal of Sport and Social Issues*, vol. 38, no. 5, pp. 415–31.
Clough, P.T. 2008. 'The affective turn: Political economy, biomedia and bodies', *Theory, Culture & Society*, vol. 25, no. 1, pp. 1–22, doi: 10.1177/0263276407085156.
Cockburn, T. 2013. *Rethinking children's citizenship*, Palgrave Macmillan, Basingstoke, UK.
Cohen, S. 1972. *Folk devils and moral panics*, Taylor & Francis, Abingdon, UK.
Coleman, R. 2016. 'Collaging workshops II: Play and uncertainty', *temporal repertoires*, blog post, 10 October, viewed 20 April 2020, www.temporalrepertoires.org/blog/collaging-workshops-ii-play-and-uncertainty.
Coleman, R. 2018. 'Theorizing the present: Digital media, pre-emergence and infra-structures of feeling', *Cultural Studies*, vol. 32, no. 4, pp. 600–22, doi: 10.1080/09502386.2017.1413121.
Coleman, R. 2020. *Glitterworlds: The future politics of a ubiquitous thing*, MIT Press, Cambridge, MA.
Coleman, R., Page, T. and Palmer, H. 2019. 'Feminist new materialist practice: The mattering of methods', *MAI Feminism and Visual Culture*,

Spring Issue, no. 3, viewed 12 September 2021, https://maifeminism.com/feminist-new-materialisms-the-mattering-of-methods-editors-note/.

Cort, J.E. 1996. 'Art, religion, and material culture: Some reflections on method', *Journal of the American Academy of Religion*, vol. 64, no. 3, pp. 613–32, doi: 10.1093/jaarel/LXIV.3.613.

Cusack, C.M. 2016. 'Fiction into religion: Imagination, other worlds, and play in the formation of community', *Religion*, vol. 46, no. 4, pp. 575–90, doi: 10.1080/0048721X.2016.1210390.

Dekker, R., Belabas, W. and Scholten, P. 2015. 'Interethnic contact online: Contextualising the implications of social media use by second-generation migrant youth', *Journal of Intercultural Studies*, vol. 36, no. 4, pp. 450–67, doi: 10.1080/07256868.2015.1049981.

Deleuze, G. 1988. *Spinoza, practical philosophy*, translated by Robert Hurley, City Lights Publishers, San Francisco, CA.

Deleuze, G. 1992a. *Expressionism in philosophy: Spinoza*, Zone Books, New York.

Deleuze, G. 1992b. 'Postscript on the societies of control', *October*, vol. 59, pp. 3–7.

Deleuze, G. and Guattari, F. 1988. *A thousand plateaus*, translated by Brian Massumi, vol. 2 of *Capitalism and schizophrenia*, Continuum, London, UK.

Deleuze, G. and Guattari, F. 1996. *What is philosophy?*, Verso Books, London.

Dessing, N.M., Jeldtoft, N. and Woodhead, L. 2016. *Everyday lived Islam in Europe*, Routledge, London, UK.

DiAngelo, R. 2018. *White fragility: Why it's so hard for white people to talk about racism*, Beacon Press, Boston, MA.

Duff, C. 1966. *Six days to shake an empire: Events and factors behind the Irish Rebellion of 1916. An account of that rebellion and its suppression and of the final struggle for self-government, with an epilogue on the dissolution of the British Empire into the British Commonwealth of Nations*, Dent, London, UK.

Duff, C. 2014. *Assemblages of health: Deleuze's empiricism and the ethology of life*, 1st edn, Springer, Dordrecht, Netherlands.

Eddo-Lodge, R. 2017. *Why I'm no longer talking to white people about race*, Bloomsbury Publishing, London, UK.

Feinberg, R.E. and Padrón Cueto, C. 2018. 'To understand Cuba's emerging class system, try the ice cream', *Quartz Magazine*, 29 July, viewed 22 May 2020, https://qz.com/1320584/ice-cream-in-cuba-reveals-the-growing-class-divide-between-rich-and-poor/.

Feldman, A. 2018. 'Re/entangling Irish and Nigerian diasporas: Colonial amnesias, decolonial aesthetics and archive-assemblage praxis', *Cultural Dynamics*, vol. 30, no. 3, pp. 173–98.

Ferro, A. 2006. 'Desired mobility or satisfied immobility? Migratory aspirations among knowledge workers' *Journal of Education and Work*, vol. 19, no. 2, pp. 171–200.

Fiske, J. 1989. 'Cultural studies and the culture of everyday life', in L. Grossberg, C. Nelson and P. Treichler (eds), *Cultural studies*, Routledge, New York, pp. 154–73.

Flatau, P., Spencer, M., Eardley, T., Edwards, R., Conroy, E. and Forbes, C. 2010. 'Intergenerational homelessness and lifetime experiences of homelessness in Australia: Evidence for the need for early interventions', *Parity*, vol. 23, no. 7, viewed 12 July 2012, www.ahuri.edu.au/sites/default/files/migration/documents/AHURI_Final_Report_No200_Lifetime-and-intergenerational-experiences-of-homelessness-in-Australia.pdf.

Floyd, E.C. and Promey, S.M. 2018. 'Collaborative scholarly communities and access in the study of material and visual cultures of religion', *Religion*, vol. 482, pp. 262–75, doi: 10.1080/0048721X.2018.1445603.

Foster, L.E. 1988. *Australian multiculturalism: A documentary history and critique*, vol. 37, Multilingual Matters, Bristol, UK.

Fowler, M., Roberts, A. and Rigney, L.-I. 2016. 'The "very stillness of things": object biographies of sailcloth and fishing net from the Point Pearce Aboriginal Mission (Burgiyana) colonial archive, South Australia', *World Archaeology*, vol. 48, no. 2, pp. 210–25, doi: 10.1080/00438243.2016.1195770.

Francisco-Menchavez, V. 2018. *The labor of care: Filipina migrants and transnational families in the digital age*, University of Illinois Press, Urbana, IL.

Frankenberg, R. 1993. *White women, race matters: The social construction of whiteness*, University of Minnesota Press, Minneapolis, MN.

Ganter, R. 2012. 'Remembering Muslim histories of Australia', *The La Trobe Journal*, vol. 89, pp. 48–62.

Gatens, M. and Lloyd, G. 1999. *Collective imaginings: Spinoza, past and present*, Routledge, New York.

Giroux, H. 2000. 'Public pedagogy as cultural politics: Stuart Hall and the crisis of culture', *Cultural Studies*, vol. 14, no. 2, pp. 341–60, doi: 10.1080/095023800334913.

Giroux, H.A. 2010. 'Rethinking education as the practice of freedom: Paulo Freire and the promise of critical pedagogy', *Policy Futures in Education*, vol. 8, no. 6, pp. 715–21, doi: 10.2304/pfie.2010.8.6.715.

Gray, B. 2004. *Women and the Irish diaspora*, Routledge, New York and London, UK.

Gruber, C. 2017. 'Back to nature: The votive in Islamic visual and material cultures', *Material Religion*, vol. 13, no. 1, doi: 10.1080/17432200.2017.1272737.

Grzymala-Kazlowska, A. 2018. 'Capturing the flexibility of adaptation and settlement: Anchoring in a mobile society', *Mobilities*, pp. 1–15, doi: 10.1080/17450101.2017.1421023.

Hage, G. 2003. *Searching for hope in a shrinking society*, Pluto Press, Sydney, Australia.

Hage, G. 2005. 'A not so multi-sited ethnography of a not so imagined community', *Anthropological Theory*, vol. 5, no. 4, pp. 463–75.

Halafoff, A., Shipley, H., Young, P.D., Singleton, A., Rasmussen, M.L. and Bouma, G. 2020. 'Complex, critical and caring: Young people's diverse religious, spiritual and non-religious worldviews in Australia and Canada', *Religions*, vol. 11, no. 4, pp. 1–12, doi: 10.3390/rel11040166.

Hanifie, S. 2019. 'Muslim Australians found to suffer the "most disturbing" experiences in public among all faiths', *ABC News*, 7 May, viewed 10 June 2020, abc.net.au/news/2019-05-07/muslim-australians-found-to-suffer-most-disturbing-experiences/11058582.

Hanisch, C. 2000. 'The personal is political', in B.A. Chow (ed.), *Radical feminism: A documentary reader*, New York University Press, New York, pp. 113–21.

Hanley, L. 2012. *Estates: An intimate history*, Granta Books, London, UK.

Harris, A. 2017. *Creativity, religion and youth cultures*, Taylor & Francis, New York.

Haslam, D.M., Tee, A. and Baker, S. 2017. 'The use of social media as a mechanism of social support in parents', *Journal of Child and Family Studies*, vol. 26, no. 7, pp. 2026–37.

Hazard, S. 2019. 'Two ways of thinking about new materialism', *Material Religion*, vol. 15, no. 5, pp. 629–31, doi: 10.1080/17432200.2019.1666585.

Heath-Kelly, C. 2013. 'Counter-terrorism and the counterfactual: Producing the "radicalisation" discourse and the UK PREVENT strategy', *The British Journal of Politics and International Relations*, vol. 15, no. 3, pp. 394–415.

Hersi, A. 2018. *Conceptualisation of integration: An Australian Muslim counter-narrative*, Springer, Sydney, Australia.

Hickey-Moody, A. 2009. *Unimaginable bodies: Intellectual disability, performance and becomings*, Sense, Rotterdam, Netherlands, doi: 10.1163/9789087908553_003.

Hickey-Moody, A. 2011. 'Corporeal and sonic diagrams for cinematic ethics in Rolf De Heer's Dance Me to My Song', in A. Hickey-Moody and V. Crowley (eds), *Disability matters: Pedagogy, media and affect*, Routledge, New York and London, UK, pp. 96–108.

Hickey-Moody, A. 2013a. 'Affect as method: Feelings, aesthetics and affective pedagogy', in R. Coleman and J. Ringrose (eds), *Deleuze and research methodologies*, Edinburgh University Press, Edinburgh, UK, pp. 79–95.

Hickey-Moody, A. 2013b. *Youth, arts and education: Reassembling subjectivity through affect*, Routledge, Abingdon, UK, doi: 10.4324/9780203855829.

Hickey-Moody, A. 2015. 'Open space: Slow life and ecologies of sensation', *Feminist Review*, vol. 111, no. 1, pp. 140–8, doi: 10.1057/fr.2015.40.

Hickey-Moody, A. 2018. 'Materialising the social', *Ruukku Studies in Artistic Research*, vol. 9, doi: 10.22501/ruu.371583.

Hickey-Moody, A. 2019. 'Three ways of knowing failure', *Mai: Feminism and Visual Culture*, 15 May, viewed 14 February 2020, https://maifeminism.com/three-ways-of-knowing-failure/.

Hickey-Moody, A. 2020. 'Faith', *Philosophy Today*, vol. 63, no. 4, pp. 927–41.

Hickey-Moody, A. and Willcox, M. 2019. 'Entanglements of difference as community togetherness: Faith, art and feminism', *Social Sciences*, vol. 8, no. 9, p. 264.

Hickey-Moody, A. and Willcox, M. 2020. 'Feminist affect and children's embodied trauma', *Matter: Journal of New Materialist Research*, vol. 1, no. 2, pp. 1–26.

Hickey-Moody, A. Horn, C. and Garg, D. 2023. *Art and media representations of superdiversity: Being different together*, Amsterdam University Press, Netherlands.

Hickey-Moody, A., Horn, C. and Willcox, M. 2019. 'STEAM education, art/science and quiet activism', in P. Burnard and L. Colucci-Gray (eds), *Why science and art creativities matter: (Re-)configuring STEAM for future-making generations*, Brill, Leiden, Netherlands, pp. 200–28.

Hickey-Moody, A., Horn, C. and Willcox, M. 2023 (in press). *Art, multiculturalism and media representations of superdiversity: Being different together*, Amsterdam University Press, Amsterdam, Netherlands.

Hickey-Moody, A. Horn, C. Willcox, M. and Florence, E. 2021. *Arts-based methods for research with children*, Palgrave Macmillan, Cham.

Hickey-Moody, A., Knight, L. and Florence, E. 2021. *Childhood, citizenship and the Anthropocene: Posthuman publics and civics*, Rowman & Littlefield, London, UK.

Hinton, P., Mehrabi, T. and Barla, J. 2015. 'New materialisms/new colonialisms', Proceedings of ISCH COST Action IS1307: New Materialism working group two: New Materialism on the Crossroads of the Natural and Human Sciences.

Holland, S. and Crowley, A. 2013. 'Looked-after children and their birth families: Using sociology to explore changing relationships, hidden histories and nomadic childhoods', *Child & Family Social Work*, vol. 18, no. 1, pp. 57–66, doi: 10.1111/cfs.12032.

Human Rights Law Centre. 2015. 'UN finds Australia's treatment of asylum seekers violates the Convention Against Torture', *Human Rights Law Centre*, 9 March, viewed 3 February 2020, www.hrlc.org.au/news/un-finds-australias-treatment-of-asylum-seekers-violates-the-convention-against-torture.

Hussain, A. 2014. 'Transgressing community: The case of Muslims in a twenty-first-century British city', *Ethnic and Racial Studies*, vol. 37, no. 4, pp. 621–35.

Hygen, B.W., Belsky, J., Stenseng, F., Skalicka, V., Kvande, M.N., Zahl-Thanem, T. and Wichstrøm, L. 2019. 'Time spent gaming and social competence in children: Reciprocal effects across childhood', *Child Development*, vol. 91, no. 3, pp. 1–15.

Ignatiev, N. 1995. *How the Irish became white*, Routledge, London, UK and New York.

Iner, D. 2015. 'A threefold sense of belonging: Practising home-grown Muslims' sense of belonging to religion, ethnicity and nation', in D. Iner and S. Yucel (eds), *Muslim identity formation in religiously diverse societies*, Cambridge Scholars Publishing, Newcastle upon Tyne, UK, pp. 155–78.

Jeffery, B. 2018. '"I probably would never move, but ideally like I'd love to move this week": Class and residential experience, beyond elective belonging', *Sociology*, vol. 52, no. 2, pp. 245–61.

Jeldtoft, N. 2011. 'Lived Islam: Religious identity with "non organized" Muslim minorities', *Ethnic and Racial Studies*, vol. 34, no. 7, pp. 1134–51, doi: 10.1080/01419870.2010.528441.

Jones, P. and Kenny, A. 2010. *Australia's Muslim cameleers: Pioneers of the inland, 1860s–1930s*, Wakefield Press, Mile End, Australia.

Kabir, N. 2006. 'Representation of Islam and Muslims in the Australian media, 2001–2005', *Journal of Muslim Minority Affairs*, vol. 26, no. 3, pp. 313–28, doi: 10.1080/13602000601141281.

Kabir, N. 2007. 'Muslims in Australia: The double edge of terrorism', *Journal of Ethnic and Migration Studies*, vol. 33, no. 8, pp. 1277–97, doi: 10.1080/13691830701614072.

Kaplan, U. 2017. 'From the tea to the coffee ceremony: Modernizing Buddhist material culture in contemporary Korea', *Material Religion*, vol. 13, no. 1, pp. 1–22, doi: 10.1080/17432200.2016.1271969.

Kastoryano, R. 2018. 'Multiculturalism and interculturalism: Redefining nationhood and solidarity', *Comparative Migration Studies*, vol. 6, no. 1, p. 17, doi: 10.1186/s40878-018-0082-6.

Kenway, J., Kraack, A. and Hickey-Moody, A. 2006. *Masculinity beyond the metropolis*, Springer, New York.

Kfir, I. 2019. *Strategy: 18 years and counting*, Australian Strategic Policy Institute, 10 April, viewed 21 May 2020, www.aspi.org.au/report/18-years-and-counting.

Khan, M. 2020. *It's not about the burqa*, Picador, London, UK.

Kim, S.J. 2019. 'Counter-storytelling: Preschool children as creative authors', *Kappa Delta Pi Record*, vol. 55, no. 2, pp. 72–7, doi: 10.1080/00228958.2019.1580985.

Kirkman, M., Keys, D., Bodzak, D. and Turner, A. 2010. '"Are we moving again this week?" Children's experiences of homelessness in Victoria, Australia', *Social Science & Medicine*, vol. 70, no. 7, pp. 994–1001, doi: 10.1016/j.socscimed.2009.12.004.

Kitching, K. 2020. *Childhood, religion and school injustice*, Cork University Press, Cork, Ireland.

Knight, L. 2019. 'Playing: Inefficiently mapping human and inhuman play in urban commonplaces', in B.D. Hodgins (ed.), *Feminist research for 21st century childhoods: Common worlds methods*, Bloomsbury, London, UK, pp. 139–48.

Kowert, R. 2014. *Video games and social competence*, Routledge, London, UK.

Kwansah-Aidoo, K. and Mapedzahama, V. 2018. 'Black bodies in/out of place?: Afrocentric perspectives and/on racialised belonging in Australia', *The Australasian Review of African Studies*, vol. 39, no. 2, pp. 95–121.

Lam, W.S.E. and Smirnov, N. 2017. 'Identity in mediated contexts of transnationalism and mobility', in S.L. Thorne and S. May (eds), *Language, Education and Technology*, Springer International Publishing, Cham, Switzerland, pp. 105–17, doi: 10.1007/978-3-319-02237-6_8.

Langton, M. 1996. 'The Hindmarsh Island Bridge affair: How Aboriginal women's religion became an administerable affair', *Australian Feminist Studies*, vol. 11, no. 24, pp. 211–17, doi: 10.1080/08164649.1996.9994819.

Langton, M. 2018. *Welcome to country: A travel guide to Indigenous Australia*, Hardie Grant Publishing, Melbourne, Australia.

Lankala, S. 2006. 'Mediated nationalisms and "Islamic Terror": The articulation of religious and postcolonial secular nationalisms in India', *Westminster Papers in Communication & Culture*, vol. 3, no. 2, pp. 86–102.

Leppänen, T. 2018. 'Race', *New Materialism*, 2 April, viewed 14 February 2020, https://newmaterialism.eu/almanac/r/race.html.

Levi, J.M. 1998. 'The bow and the blanket: Religion, identity and resistance in Rarámuri material culture', *Journal of Anthropological Research*, vol. 54, no. 3, pp. 299–324, doi: 10.1086/jar.54.3.3630650.

Levrau, F. and Loobuyck, P. 2018. 'Introduction: Mapping the multiculturalism-interculturalism debate', *Comparative Migration Studies*, vol. 6, no. 1, pp. 1–13, doi: 10.1186/s40878-018-0080-8.

Lewis, J. (ed.) 2012. *Terrorism and news narratives*, SAGE Publications, London, UK, doi: 10.4135/9781446288429.

Liebelt, B., Roberts, A., O'Loughlin, C. and Milera, D. 2016. '"We had to be off by sundown": Narungga contributions to farming industries on Yorke Peninsula (Guuranda), South Australia', *Aboriginal History*, vol. 40, pp. 89–117, viewed 21 December 2022, https://search.informit.org/doi/10.3316/ielapa.610470481558003.

Mahmod, J. 2019. 'New online communities – new identity making: The curious case of the Kurdish diaspora', *Journal of Ethnic and Cultural Studies*, vol. 6, no. 2, p. 34, doi: 10.29333/ejecs/245.

Maidment, A. 2020. 'Squatters living in Manchester radio station hit back as they're booted out … they say they had been doing it for the homeless', *Manchester Evening News*, 13 January, viewed 22 May 2020, www.manchestereveningnews.co.uk/news/greater-manchester-news/squatters-homeless-levenshulme-winter-shelter-17560728.

Malone, K. 2017. *Children in the Anthropocene*, Palgrave Macmillan, London, UK.

Mann, R.D. 2014. 'Material culture and the study of Hinduism and Buddhism', *Religion Compass*, vol. 8, pp. 264–73, doi: 10.1111/rec3.12116.

Marcus, G.E. 1995. 'Ethnography in/of the world system: The emergence of multi-sited ethnography', *Annual Review of Anthropology*, vol. 24, no. 1, pp. 95–117, doi: 10.1146/annurev.an.24.100195.000523.

Marcus, G.E. 1998. *Ethnography through thick and thin*, Princeton University Press, Princeton, NJ.

Marcus, G.E. 2011. 'Multi-sited ethnography', in S. Coleman and P. von Hellermann (eds), *Multi-sited ethnography: Problems and possibilities in the translocation of research methods*, CRC Press, Boca Raton, FL, pp. 16–32.

Marino, S. 2015. 'Making space, making place: Digital togetherness and the redefinition of migrant identities online', *Social Media + Society*, vol. 1, no. 2, doi: 10.1177/2056305115622479.

Marlatt, R. 2020. 'Capitalizing on the craze of Fortnite: Toward a conceptual framework for understanding how gamers construct communities of practice', *Journal of Education*, vol. 200, no. 1, pp. 3–11.

Marrati, P. 2006. 'Time and affects: Deleuze on gender and sexual difference', *Australian Feminist Studies*, vol. 21, no. 51, pp. 313–25.

Martin, M. 2019. 'Rwandan diaspora online: Social connections and identity narratives', *Crossings: Journal of Migration & Culture*, vol. 10, no. 2, pp. 223–41, doi: 10.1386/cjmc_00004_1.

Matthews-Jones, L. and Jones, T.W. 2015. 'Introduction: Materiality and religious history', in T.W. Jones and L. Matthews-Jones (eds), *Material Religion in Modern Britain: The Spirit of Things*, Palgrave Macmillan, New York, pp. 1–14, doi: 10.1057/9781137540638_1.

McDannell, C. 1995. *Material Christianity: Religion and popular culture in America*, Yale University Press, New Haven, CT.

McGuire, M. 2008. *Lived religion: Faith and practice in everyday life*, Oxford University Press, Oxford, UK.

McNamara, P. 2015. 'Young people at risk of lifelong poverty: Youth homelessness in Australia', in E. Fernandez, A. Zeira, T. Vecchiato and C. Canali (eds), *Theoretical and empirical insights into child and family poverty: Cross national perspectives*, Springer International Publishing, Cham, Switzerland, pp. 217–38, doi: 10.1007/978-3-319-17506-5_14.

Meaney, G. 2010. *Gender, Ireland and cultural change: Race, sex and nation*, Routledge, New York.

Mechling, J. 2000. 'Don't play with your food', *Children's Folklore Review*, vol. 23, no. 1, pp. 7–24.

Menon, N., Thapar-Björkert, S. and Tlostanova, M. 2021. 'Anti-colonial struggles, postcolonial subversions: An interview with Nivedita Menon', in R. Koobak, M. Tlostanova and S. Thapar-Björkert (eds), *Postcolonial and postsocialist dialogues: Intersections, opacities, challenges in feminist theorizing and practice*, Taylor & Francis, Milton, UK, pp. 109–20.

Meyer, B. 2003. 'Material mediations and religious practices of world-making', in K. Lundby (ed.), *Religion across media: From early antiquity to late modernity*, Peter Lang, New York, pp. 1–19.

Meyer, B. 2010. 'Aesthetics of persuasion: Global Christianity and Pentecostalism's sensational forms', *South Atlantic Quarterly*, vol. 109, no. 4, pp. 741–63, doi: 10.1215/00382876-2010-015.

Meyer, B. 2015. 'How pictures matter: Religious objects and the imagination in Ghana', In O. Fuglerud and L. Wainwright (eds), *Objects and imagination: Perspectives on materialization and meaning*, Berghahn Books, New York, pp. 160–83.

Meyer, B. 2019. '"Material approaches to religion" meet "new materialism": Resonances and dissonances', *Material Religion*, vol. 15, no. 5, pp. 620–1.

Mignolo, W.D. 2000. '(Post)occidentalism, (post)coloniality, and (post)subalternity', in F. Afzal-Khan and K. Seshadri-Crooks (eds), *The preoccupation of postcolonial studies*, Duke University Press, Durham, NC, pp. 86–118.

Mignolo, W.D. 2007. 'Delinking: The rhetoric of modernity, the logic of coloniality and the grammar of de-coloniality', *Cultural Studies*, vol. 21, no. 2–3, pp. 449–514.

Miller, R.A. 2017. '"My voice is definitely strongest in online communities": Students using social media for queer and disability identity-making', *Journal of College Student Development*, vol. 58, no. 4, pp. 509–25, doi: 10.1353/csd.2017.0040.

Minnery, J. and Greenhalgh, E. 2007. 'Approaches to homelessness policy in Europe, the United States, and Australia', *Journal of Social Issues*, vol. 63, no. 3, pp. 641–55, doi: 10.1111/j.1540-4560.2007.00528.x.

Modood, T. 2007. 'Multiculturalism', *The Blackwell encyclopedia of sociology*, John Wiley & Sons, Hoboken, NJ, pp. 1–4.

Moore, K., Mason, P. and Lewis, J.M.W. 2008. 'Images of Islam in the UK: The representation of British Muslims in the national print news media 2000–2008', Cardiff University, Cardiff, UK, viewed 21 December 2022, http://jppsg.ac.uk/jomec/resources/08channel4-dispatches.pdf.

Moore, R.C. 2017. *Childhood's domain: Play and place in child development*, Routledge, London, UK.

Moore, T., McArthur, M. and Noble-Carr, D. 2008. 'Stuff you'd never think of', *Family Matters*, vol. 78, no. 8.

Morgan, D. 2015. 'The look of sympathy: Religion, visual culture, and the social life of feeling', *Material Religion: The Journal of Objects, Art and Belief*, vol. 5, no. 2, pp. 132–55, doi: 10.2752/174322009X12448040551567.

Murris, K. 2016. *The posthuman child: Educational transformation through philosophy with picturebooks*, Routledge, London, UK.

Noble, G. 2005. 'The discomfort of strangers: Racism, incivility and ontological security in a relaxed and comfortable nation', *Journal of Intercultural Studies*, vol. 26, no. 1–2, pp. 107–20, doi:10.1080/07256860500074128.

Noble, G. 2008. 'The face of evil: Demonising the Arab other in contemporary Australia', *Cultural Studies Review*, vol. 14, no. 2, pp. 14–33.

Nowicka, M. 2020. '(Dis)connecting migration: Transnationalism and nationalism beyond connectivity', *Comparative Migration Studies*, vol. 8, no. 1, p. 20, doi: 10.1186/s40878-020-00175-4.

Ó Cuinneagáin, E. 2018. *Awakening decoloniality in Irish studies*, Doctoral thesis, Department of Languages, Linnaeus University, Sweden.

O'Donnell, A. 2016. 'Securitisation, counterterrorism and the silencing of dissent: The educational implications of prevent', *British Journal of Educational Studies*, vol. 64, no. 1, pp. 53–76.

O'Donnell, A. 2018. 'Contagious ideas: Vulnerability, epistemic injustice and counter-terrorism in education', *Educational Philosophy and Theory*, vol. 50, no. 10, pp. 981–97.

Oppy, G. 2014. *Reinventing philosophy of religion: An opinionated introduction*, Palgrave Macmillan, London, UK, doi: 10.1057/9781137434562.

Parr, A. 2010. 'On secular forgiveness', in R. Faber, H. Krips and D. Pettus (eds), *Event and decision: Ontology and politics in Badiou, Deleuze and Whitehead*, Cambridge Scholars Publishing, Cambridge, UK, pp. 318–31.

Pedersen, S. and Lupton, D. 2018. '"What are you feeling right now?" Communities of maternal feeling on Mumsnet', *Emotion, Space and Society*, vol. 26, pp. 57–63, doi: 10.1016/j.emospa.2016.05.001.

Peel, M. 2003. *The lowest rung: Voices of Australian poverty*, Cambridge University Press, Cambridge, UK.

Pidd, H. 2015. 'Manchester homeless people face jail over city centre tent camps', *Guardian*, 30 September, viewed 22 May 2020, www.theguardian.com/uk-news/2015/sep/30/manchester-homeless-people-face-jail-over-city-centre-tent-camps.

Prato, G.B. 2016. 'Introduction – Beyond multiculturalism: Anthropology at the intersections between the local, the national and the global', in G.B. Prato (ed.), *Beyond multiculturalism: Views from anthropology*, Routledge, London, UK, pp. 1–20.

Preece, J. 2020. 'Belonging in working-class neighbourhoods: dis-identification, territorialisation and biographies of people and place', *Urban Studies*, vol. 57, no. 4, pp. 827–43.

Probyn, E. 1996. *Outside belongings*, Routledge, New York.

Proshansky, H.M., Fabian, A.K. and Kaminoff, R. 1983. 'Place-identity: Physical world socialization of the self', *Journal of Environmental Psychology*, vol. 3, no. 1, pp. 57–83.

Qurashi, F. 2016. 'Prevent gives people permission to hate Muslims – It has no place in schools', *Guardian*, 4 April, viewed 10 June 2020, www.theguardian.com/commentisfree/2016/apr/04/prevent-hate-muslims-schools-terrorism-teachers-reject.

Rasmussen, M.L. 2006. *Becoming subjects: Sexualities and secondary schooling*, Routledge, London, UK.

Rasmussen, M.L. 2015. *Progressive sexuality education: The conceits of secularism*, Routledge, London, UK.

Rasmussen, M.L. 2016. 'Faith, progressive sexuality education, and queer secularism: Unsettling associations', in M. Allen and M.L. Rasmussen (eds), *The Palgrave handbook of sexuality education*, Palgrave Macmillan, New York, pp. 115–35.

Rasmussen, M.L. 2017. 'Critical exchange: Religion and schooling: What should their relationship be?', *Research in Education*, vol. 97, no. 1, pp. 4–15.

Reay, D. 2006. 'The Zombie stalking English schools: Social class and educational inequality', *British Journal of Educational Studies*, vol. 54, no. 3, pp. 288–307, doi: 10.1111/j.1467-8527.2006.00351.x.

Reay, D. and Lucey, H. 2000. 'Children, school choice and social differences', *Educational Studies*, vol. 26, no. 1, pp. 83–100.

Renold, E. 2005. *Girls, boys, and junior sexualities: Exploring children's gender and sexual relations in the primary school*, Routledge Falmer, London, UK.

Renold, E.J. and Ivinson, G. 2022. 'Posthuman co-production: Becoming response-able with what matters', *Qualitative Research Journal*, vol. 22, no. 1, pp. 108–28.

Rhoden-Paul, A. 2015. 'Homeless protesters face eviction from Manchester city centre', *Guardian*, 29 June, viewed 22 May 2020, www.theguardian.com/uk-news/the-northerner/2015/jun/29/homeless-protesters-face-eviction-from-manchester-city-centre.

Richardson, I., Hjorth, L. and Davies, H. 2022. *Understanding games and game cultures*, Sage, London, UK.

Russell, L. 2020. *Glitch feminism: A manifesto*, Verso, London, UK.

Said, E. 1979. *Orientalism*, Vintage Books, New York.

Samak, T. 2017. 'Moroccan diaspora in France: Community building on Yabiladi Portal', *E-Journal of New World Sciences Academy*, vol. 12, no. 1, pp. 1–8, doi: 10.12739/NWSA.2017.12.1.4C0213.

Savage, M. 2015. *Social class in the 21st century*, Penguin, London, UK.

Savage, M., Allen, C., Atkinson, R., Burrows, R., Mendez, M.-L. and Watt, P. 2010. 'The politics of elective belonging', *Housing, Theory and Society*, vol. 27, no. 2, pp. 115–61.

Sharam, A. and Hulse, K. 2014. 'Understanding the nexus between poverty and homelessness: Relational poverty analysis of families experiencing homelessness in Australia', *Housing, Theory and Society*, vol. 31, no. 3, pp. 294–309, doi: 10.1080/14036096.2014.882405.

Sian, K. 2017. 'Born radicals? Prevent, positivism, and "race-thinking"', *Palgrave Communications*, vol. 3, no. 1, pp. 1–8.

Simons, M. 2003. *Meeting of the waters: The Hindmarsh Island affair*, Hodder Headline, Sydney, Australia.

Skeggs, B. 2002. *Formations of class and gender: Becoming respectable*, SAGE Publications, London, UK.

Spinoza, B. 1996. *Ethics*, 6th edn, translated by Edwin Curley, Penguin Books, London, UK.

Spinoza, B. 2001. *Ethics*, Wordsworth Editions, Kent, UK.

Spinoza, B. 2021. *The Ethics*, Global Grey books, viewed 12 January 2021, www.globalgreyebooks.com/ethics-spinoza-ebook.html.

Spivak, G.C. 1983. 'Can the subaltern speak?', in R. Morris (ed.), *Can the subaltern speak?: Reflections on the history of an idea*, Columbia University Press, New York.

Spivak, G.C. 2010. 'Translating in a world of languages', *Profession*, pp. 35–43.

Tatz, C. 1995. 'Racism and sport in Australia', *Race & Class*, vol. 36, no. 4, pp. 43–54.
Thomson, P. 2002. *Schooling the rustbelt kids: Making the difference in changing times*, Allen & Unwin, Crows Nest, Australia.
Tindongan, C.W. 2011. 'Negotiating Muslim youth identity in a post-9/11 world', *High School Journal*, vol. 95, no. 1, pp. 72–87, doi: 10.1353/hsj.2011.0012.
UK Home Office. 2015. *Statutory guidance: Prevent duty guidance*, UK Home Office, 12 March, viewed 21 May 2020, www.gov.uk/government/publications/prevent-duty-guidance.
UK Office for National Statistics. 2011a. *Millwall Ward (as of 2011) Local Area Report*, Nomis Web, viewed 3 February 2020, www.nomisweb.co.uk/reports/localarea?compare=E05000583.
UK Office for National Statistics. 2011b. *UK 2011 Census*, Nomis Web, viewed 3 February 2020, www.nomisweb.co.uk.
van der Tuin, I. 2015. *Generational feminism: New materialist introduction to a generative approach*, Lexington Books, Lanham, MD.
van der Tuin, I. 2018. 'Diffraction', in R. Braidotti and M. Hlavajova (eds), *Posthuman glossary*, Bloomsbury Academic, London, UK, pp. 99–101.
Vergès, F. 2021. *A decolonial feminism*, Pluto Press, London, UK.
Vertovec, S. 2005a. 'Opinion: Super-diversity revealed', *BBC Online*, 20 September, viewed 21 May 2020, http://news.bbc.co.uk/2/hi/uk_news/4266102.stm.
Vertovec, S. 2005b, 'Born abroad', *Guardian*, 20 September, viewed 10 June 2020, http://news.bbc.co.uk/2/hi/uk_news/4266102.stm.
Vertovec, S. 2007. 'Super-diversity and its implications', *Ethnic and Racial Studies*, vol. 30, no. 6, pp. 1024–54, doi: 10.1080/01419870701599465.
Vertovec, S. and Wessendorf, S. 2010. *The multiculturalism backlash: European discourses, policies and practices*, Routledge, London, UK.
Walkerdine, V. 2017. 'Of dinosaurs and divas: Is class still relevant to feminist research?', *Subjectivity*, vol. 10, no. 1, pp. 1–12.
Walkerdine, V. and Lucey, H. 1989. *Democracy in the kitchen: Regulating mothers and socialising daughters*, Virago, London, UK.
Wang, X. 2018. 'Rethinking material religion in the East: Orientalism and religious material culture in contemporary west academia', *Religions*, vol. 9, no. 2, pp. 1–12, doi: 10.3390/rel9020062.
Williams, R. 1977. *Marxism and literature*, Oxford University Press, Oxford, UK.
Williams Veazey, L. 2018. 'Navigating the intersections of migration and motherhood in online communities: Digital community mothering and migrant maternal imaginaries', PhD thesis, Department of Sociology and Social Policy, Faculty of Arts and Social Sciences, The University of

Sydney, Sydney, Australia, viewed 21 December 2022, https://ses.library.usyd.edu.au/handle/2123/19697.

Williamson, R. 2016. 'Everyday space, mobile subjects and place-based belonging in suburban Sydney', *Journal of Ethnic and Migration Studies*, vol. 42, no. 14, pp. 2328–44, doi: 10.1080/1369183X.2016.1205803.

Willis, P. 1978. *Learning to labour: How working-class kids get working-class jobs*, Taylor & Francis, London, UK.

Woodhead, L. 2011. 'Five concepts of religion', *International Review of Sociology*,vol.21,no.1,pp.121–43,doi:10.1080/03906701.2011.544192.

Zeybek, O. 2020. 'Introducing the city to the children, youngsters and tourists via installation art: Manchester and Ankara', in M. Zencirkiran (ed.), *Trends in landscape, agriculture, forest and natural science*, Cambridge Scholars Publishing, Newcastle Upon Tyne, UK, pp. 63–73.

Index

9/11 terrorist attacks (2001) 147–8

Abbit, B. 149
ABC (Australian Broadcasting Corporation) publicity of arts-based workshops 14
Abdel-Magied, Y. 159
Aboriginal and Torres Strait Islander peoples
    colonisation and 66
    worldview of 141–3
    see also discrimination; racism
Abu-Ras, W.M. 148
act, capacity to *see* capacity to act
Adelaide, Australia 5, 10–12
    see also focus groups discussions
adults and community engagement 60
affect/*affectus*/*affectiones*
    as capacity to act 24, 40
    belief and 24
    definition 40–1
    embodiment and 30
    emotion and 41
    faith and 39–42
    geographic places and 95
    joy and 77–94
    materiality and 30
    method and 66
    power and 81, 84
    'social turn' and 67
    sounds and 95
ag déanamh (making) 49–76
Ahmed, S. 86–7
Aly, A. 86, 158, 189
Amar, A. 34
Ammerman, N.T. 54–6, 117, 194
Anderson, B. 123–6
Apperley, T. 133, 137
apps (computer software), belonging and use of 96–9
    see also online communities
Arab, P.T. 25
Archer, J. 137
Archer, L. 161, 163
art
    communicating complex blocs of sensation 67, 79–81
    relationship-building and 6
art media
    drawing, children's 68–9
    drawing, on iPads 72–3
    papier-mâché 6, 69–70
    tents 70–1
    textiles (patchwork quilts) 71–2
    see also children's artworks
arts-based research workshops 4–6, 66–73
    see also ethnography, multi-sited; fieldwork notes
artworks as communications of faith 49
artworks by children *see* children's artworks
Askins, K. 101
assemblages
    community impacts and 156, 163

faith and 41
food and 38
joy resulting from 119–40
macro level impacts and 189
places and 42
social class and 163–8
space/time impacts and 141–2
unconscious orientations
  towards faith and 24
see also attachments;
  immigration and faith
asylum seekers
  faith and 39–40
  see also refugees
áthas (joy) 77–94
Atherton Gardens, Fitzroy,
  Melbourne, Australia 13,
  122–3
  see also focus groups discussions
attachments
  adults' experiences of 5, 95
  Catholicism and 4
  faith and 41, 45–6, 49, 188
  surfaces and 100–18
attitudes
  of children 66–73
  of research participants 11–12
Auburn, west Sydney, Australia
  18n.1
  see also focus groups discussions
Australia and racism 141–5
Australian Broadcasting
  Corporation (ABC) publicity
  of arts-based workshops 14
Australian Research Council (ARC)
  grant funding achieved 4
Australian Strategic Policy Institute
  (ASPI) 146
Awan, I. 146, 157

Bağli, H. 35
Baker-Lewton, A. 126
Barad, K. 39
Barker-Perez, E.J. Feinstein 6
Barla, J. 65
Baugut, P. 86
BBC (British Broadcasting
  Corporation) 177

bee symbolism 148–51
Belabas, W. 96
belief 24, 55
Bell, D. 142
belonging 95–118
  communication of, through
    artworks 49
  experiences of 5, 59–61
  faith orientation and 85
  online communities and 96–9,
    133–40
  religious communities and 61–3
  sport and 121–9
  varieties of 54, 106–10
  see also communities/
    community; council housing
    estates; family
Berlant, L. 24, 44–7, 189
Bishop, C. 67
'black panics' 145–7
black/blackness see skin colour
Blackburn, A.M. 28–9
Blaise, M. 130
blocs of sensation 79–81
bodies 25, 28–9, 40–2, 78–9, 94,
  184
  new materialism and 66
  in philosophy 33
  see also embodiment
Boivin, N. 36
Bond Stockton, K. 56, 130
Bouma, G. 111
boys
  dancing 134, 138
  Fortnite's importance to 133–7
  see also embodiment
Braidotti, R. 15, 24–5, 28–30,
  32–3, 64, 189
Brandt, S.A. 97
Brasted, H.V. 158, 189
Bräunlein, P.J. 25, 33
British Broadcasting Corporation
  (BBC) 177
Brown, L. 86
Buddhists 54, 115
Burawoy, M. 50
Burchardt, M. 25
burqas 53, 145, 156, 159

Canberra, Australia 5, 14, 23n.12
  see also focus groups discussions
capacity to act
  faith and 25, 29–30
  joy and 85
Carmichael, C.L. 97
Carrington, B. 123
Carroll, T.D. 28–9
Catholic piety, Irish 2–3
Chambers, C. 65
Charlton, London, UK 10, 20n.5
  see also focus groups discussions
children
  arts-based research workshops with 66–73
  as research participants 4–5
  belonging to communities 60, 96–9
  climate change and 51–2, 56, 62, 174–6
  collaboration amongst 68
  future cities envisioned by 68–9, 130–1, 151, 174–9, 184–5
  games and 129–30, 133–7
  hopes of 68–9, 81, 171–86
  ice cream and 56, 128–33
  identity definition of 51
  imagination and memories of 7
  refugees 179–85
  soccer (football) and 121–9
  using arts as self-expression 6, 60, 62–4, 67–73, 134, 138
  video-making by 59–60
  'what really matters' to 68–9, 77–85
  worker bee's importance to 148–51
children's artworks 60–73, 179–85
  as research outcomes 5
  value in creation of 49, 77–85
  see also art media
childworlds expressed through art 62, 174–9, 184–5
Christianity and colonisation 31–2
Christianity and Islam 154–5
Christians and faith 39–40
churches
  attitudes of members towards research 11–12
  community/communities within 99–100
  see also belonging; communities/community; religion/religions
Clayton, J.P. 28–9
Cleland, J. 126–7
climate change and children 51–2, 56, 62, 174–6
clothing and headwear (Muslim)
  racism and 152–3
  see also Muslims
Clough, P.T. 40
Cockburn, T. 188
Cohen, S. 145
Coleman, R. 25, 49, 71, 190
colonisation
  in Australia, and racism 141–5
  Christianity and 31
  see also decolonisation; power
comhthéacs (contexts) 1–23
communication and art 49, 62, 67, 78–85, 170–86
communities/community
  adults and 60–1
  as assemblages of joy 119–40
  children's sense of 59–60
  church and mosque as sites of 61–3
  complexities of belonging to 100–5
  within council housing estates 120–3
  examples 100–5
  faith and 25, 55
  lived experiences of 57–9, 100–11
  participating in research 5
  religion and 55
  sport and 121–9
  see also belonging; ethnic groups
connection and internal systems 119–40
consciousness and feeling of affect 41
contexts, cultural and social 1–23
  belief and 33
  philosophy and 33
  religious faith and 28–9
Cort, J.E. 30, 33

council housing estates 120–3, 162
Crowley, A. 179
'cruel optimism'
  as 'slow death' 44–7
  definition 24
  faith and 39, 44–7, 189
  prayer and 46–7
cultural studies tradition and present research 16
culture
  diversity of practices 53
  faith and 16–17
  religion and 54
Curnow, F. 126
Cusack, C.M. 171

dancing and boys 134, 138
Davies, H. 137
decolonisation
  new materialism and 66
  postcolonialism and 64–6
  research strategies of 49
  see also colonisation; new materialism; research methodology
Dekker, B. 96
Deleuze, G. 27, 29, 31, 33, 40–4, 47, 78–82, 84–5, 140, 190
Dessing, N.M. 194
devotional aids
  Ramadan 90, 93
  rosary beads as 3
  statues as 2–3
  see also faith; materiality; piety, Irish Catholic
DiAngelo, R. 167
discrimination 92, 102, 105–11, 143
  Australia 156, 158
  ignorance and 85–94, 102
  UK *Counter-Terrorism and Security Act (2015)* 156
  see also intolerance; racism; violence
drawing
  on iPads, children's 72–3
  subjects of children's 68–9
  see also art media
Duff, C. 2, 41

economic and social class see social class
education and social class 163–8
embodiment 26–30, 34–5
  see also bodies
emotion, children's depiction of 68
empathy 85–94
engagement see belonging; communities/community
ethnic groups
  belonging and communities within 100–5
  see also multiculturalism
ethnography, 'classic', definition of 50–1
ethnography, multi-sited
  definition and purpose 51–2
  focus and methodology 56
  research findings, qualitative 5
  research overview 1–23
  see also arts-based research workshops
ethnography, multi-sited: research sites
  Auburn, west Sydney, Australia 7–8, 18n.1
  Canberra, Australia 7, 11, 22n.10
  Charlton, London, UK 10, 20n.5
  Fitzroy, Melbourne, Australia 13, 22n.10
  Hulme, Manchester, UK 18n.4
  Levenshulme, Manchester, UK 8–9, 18n.2
  London, UK 10
  Manchester, UK 8–10
  Marion, Adelaide, Australia 21n.8
  Melbourne, Australia 5, 12–13
  Millwall, London, UK 10, 21n.6
  Moss Side, Manchester, UK 9, 18n.3
  Noble Park, Melbourne, Australia 12–13, 22n.9
  Norwood, Adelaide, Australia 21n.7
  Sydney, Australia 5
  Weston, Canberra, Australia 14

see also focus groups
  discussions; focus groups
  questions
exchange value as 'cruel optimism'
  45–7
experience, lived
  arts-based methods as
    communication of 49
  as unifier between people 24

Fabian, A.K. 148
faith
  affect and 77–94
  as bodily affect 39–42
  as community engagement 25, 27
  as joy 24, 39, 41–4, 81, 85–94
  as map of life 41
  as sustenance 39
  as unifying force 17
  attachments 41, 45–6, 49, 188
  belief and 55
  belonging and 27, 85–94
  capacity to act and 29–30
  communication of, through artworks 49
  creative arts and 171
  'cruel optimism' and 39, 44–7
  definitions 15, 25, 36
  embodiment and 26–30
  materiality and 32–3, 45–6
  micro, meso, macro level impacts and 38–9
  new materialist studies of religion and 27–8
  orientations to 15–17
  power and 33, 48, 88, 185
  reason and 43–4
  religion and 25–6, 31, 55
  social class and 16–17
  structures of feeling and 16
  varieties of 53, 187
  violence and 31
  see also devotional aids
faith and lived experiences 5, 17, 26, 28, 35, 41, 85–94, 111, 187
families 96–8, 100, 122–3, 160–8, 175, 179, 181, 191–2
  non-binary 25–6, 106–10

family 9–10, 25, 35–9, 54–6, 82–4, 86, 89, 98–100, 112–13, 134
  children and 69–72, 78, 180
  feelings see emotion, children's depiction of
Feinberg, R.E. 131–2
Feldman, A. 65
Ferro, A. 161, 163
fieldwork notes 126, 137–8, 175–6, 179
fieldwork sites, overview of 5–15
Fiske, J. 49
Fitzroy, Melbourne, Australia 13, 22n.10
  see also focus groups discussions
Flatau, P. 179
Florence, E. 5, 174, 176, 188
Floyd, E.C. 48
focus groups discussions
  Adelaide, Australia 25–6, 38–9, 58, 60–2, 89–91, 95, 97–8, 106–13, 147
  Canberra, Australia 14, 57–8, 93, 104
  London, UK 58, 82–4, 104–5, 110, 113–14, 120–3, 127, 152–3, 155, 162, 165–6, 168
  Manchester, UK 40–2, 58–9, 61, 87–8, 91–4, 151–2, 155, 167–8
  Melbourne, Australia 39–40, 47, 57, 86–7, 91–3, 114, 116–17, 122–3, 172–3, 180–5
  Sydney, Australia 6–7, 54, 58, 61, 93, 101, 112, 132, 159, 172
  see also ethnography, multi-sited: research sites; fieldwork notes; research methodology
focus groups questions 73–5
football (soccer) 121–9
Fortnite (computer game) 129–30, 133–7
Foster, L.E. 169n.1
Fowler, M. 108
Francisco-Menchavez, V. 50
Frankenberg, R. 165
friendship amongst children 137–40

fundamentalism and Islam 85–94
future cities envisioned by children 68–9, 130–1, 151, 174–9, 184–5

Gallery P21, site of outreach work 15
games/gaming and children 133–7
Ganter, R. 158
Garg, D. 5, 49
Gatens, M. 33
gender 32, 52–3, 113
  belonging and 105–11
  children and 129–30, 135
  Muslims and 117
  orientations, unconscious, and 55
  prayer practices and 55–6
  sport and 125–6
  terrorist violence and 148–51
  see also sexuality
gentrification
  of Fitzroy, Melbourne 13
  of London 10
Giroux, H.A. 79
globally important issues
  climate change 82
  multi-sited ethnography and 50–1
  religion 31
  sport 121–9
  see also 'what really matters' to children
God/gods 15–16, 28–30, 33, 35, 40–1, 62, 84, 91, 111, 140, 172–3
  children and 55
  faith in 25, 172–3
  prayer and 47
Gray, B. 65
Green, L. 86
Greenhalgh, E. 179
Grosz, E. 34
groups *see* arts-based research workshops; belonging; churches; communities/community; ethnic groups; focus groups discussions; messaging (computer software apps); mosques, attitudes of members towards research; social media and community belonging
Gruber, C. 37
Gryzmala-Kazlowska, A. 101
Guadalupe, Our Lady of *see* Mary, Blessed Virgin
Guattari, F. 29, 31, 40, 79–82, 84–5, 140, 190

Hage, G. 50–1, 156, 190
Halafoff, A. 111
Halsall, A. 161, 163
Hanifie, S. 144
Hanisch, C. 129
Hanley, L. 120
Hanson, Pauline (senator, Australia) 146, 156
Harris, A. 49
Hazard, S. 25
Heath-Kelly, C. 146, 157
Hekmoun, J. 159
Hickey-Moody, A. 5, 8, 27, 40–1, 49–50, 59, 66–7, 70, 122, 130, 145–6, 148, 174–5, 182, 188
  Catholicism and 1–4
  personal story 1–3, 11–12, 141–2, 144, 157–8, 160–1
hijabs 14, 16, 86, 127–8
Hindmarsh Island Bridge Act (1997) 143
Hindmarsh Island Royal Commission (1995) 142–3
Hinduism, statistics of 31
Hindus and religious practices 54
Hinton, P. 65
Hjorth, L. 137
Holland, S. 179
Hollingworth, S. 161, 163
homelessness, refugee children's concerns about 171–81
hope, faith and 44, 47, 55, 94, 174
Horn, C. 5, 8, 49, 174–5, 182
housing
  children's future cities and 176–81
  council estates and 120–3

Hulme, Manchester, UK 18n.4
  see also focus groups discussions
Hulse, K. 179
Human Rights Law Centre (Australia) 146
Hussain, A. 102–3
Hygen, B. 136–7

ice cream, significance of 56, 128–33, 192
identifications as religious, varieties of 16–17
identity definition
  belonging to communities and 97–8
  children's 66–73
  multi-sited ethnography and 51
  see also gender; sexuality
Ignatiev, N. 65
image affections/ideas, being different from affects 78–9
images/imagery/imagination
  animation displaying 132
  artworks displaying 128–9, 131, 135
  children's imaginary worlds 171–86
  communicating complex information 49
  importance of, to children 7, 63–4
immigrants
  community/communities 60–1
  to Manchester area 8–10
  to west Sydney area 7–8
  see also asylum seekers; refugees
immigration and faith 38
  see also assemblages
impacts on unconscious orientations 24
imperialism *see* colonisation
indigenous Australians *see* Aboriginal and Torres Strait Islander peoples
Iner, D. 105, 188
Interfaith Childhoods project 67
interviews after focus groups discussions 74–5

intolerance 4, 40, 85–94
  see also discrimination; faith; racism; violence
Irish people and Catholic Church 2
Islam/Islamophobia
  community responsibility and 61
  fundamentalism and 85–94
  ignorance and 115–17
  statistics 31
  see also Muslims
Ivinson, G. 78

Jeffery, B. 106, 164
Jeldtoft, N. 117, 194
Jones, P. 158
Jones, W.T. 30–2
joy
  children and 78–85, 137–40
  connections and 119–40
  faith and 24, 41–4, 77–94
  power and 40–3

Kabir, N. 116, 147
Kaminoff, R. 148
Kaplan, U. 37
Kastoryano, R. 97
Kenny, A. 158
Kenway, J. 50
Kfir, I. 146
Khan, M. 159
Kim, S.J. 130
Kirkman, M. 180
Kitching, K. 4, 16, 63
Knight, L. 129, 174, 176, 188
Kowert, R. 137
Kraack, A. 50
Kwansah-Aidoo, K. 189

Lam, W.S.E. 96
Langton, M. 141–2
languages/linguistic diversity
  within communities 52–3, 163–8
  within multi-sited ethnography 49
Lankala, S. 148
Leppänen, T. 65
Levenshulme, Manchester, UK 8–9, 18 n.2
  see also focus groups discussions

Levi, J. 34
Levrau, F. 169n.1
Lewis, J.M.W. 86
Liebelt, B. 108
lived experience *see* experience, lived
Lloyd, B. 137
Lloyd, G. 33
London, UK 10
  see also focus groups discussions
Loobuyck, P. 169n.1
love, centrality of 78
Lucey, H. 161, 163
Lupton, D. 97

McArthur, M. 180
McDannell, C. 32–3
McGuire, M. 111
McNamara, P. 179
macro level impacts 24, 37–8
Mahmod, J. 96
Mahmood, S. 16
Maidment, A. 177
Malone, K. 188
Manchester, UK 8–10
  worker bee symbol of 148–51
  see also focus groups discussions
Manchester Arena terrorist attacks 87, 148–50
Manchester Central Mosque 11
Manchester Metropolitan University (MMU) 8
Mann, R.D. 32
Mapedzahama, V. 189
mapping, multi-sited ethnography and 51
maps, children's drawings of 71–2
Marcus, G.E. 50–1, 57, 63, 190
marginalisation 108, 119–40
Marino, S. 96
Marion, Adelaide, Australia 21n.8
  see also focus groups discussions
Marlatt, R. 133, 135–6
Marrati, P. 40
Martin, M. 96
Mary, Blessed Virgin
  devotion to Our Lady of Guadalupe 3
  statues of 2–3
Maryam (biblical figure) 4, 148–51
Mason, P. 86
mass media
  misrepresentations of Muslims, effects of 85–94, 147–51
  power of 88
materialism, new *see* new materialism
materiality
  affect and 30
  class and whiteness 164–8
  cultural meanings of objects 51–2
  embodiment and 34–5
  faith and 28, 32–4, 45–6, 51–2
  patterns of feeling and 32–3
  in religion 28
  see also devotional aids; new materialism
Matthes, J. 86–7
Matthews-Jones, L. 30–2
Meaney, G. 65
Mechling, J. 130–1
media *see* mass media; social media
  and community belonging
Mehrabi, T. 65
Melbourne, Australia 5, 12–13
  see also focus groups discussions
memory/memorialising
  communication of, through artworks 49
  importance 7
Menon, N. 49
meso level impacts
  faith and 38
  on unconscious orientations 24
messaging (computer software apps) 96–9
methodology of research *see* research methodology
Meyer, B. 25, 27–8
micro level impacts
  faith and 38–9
  on unconscious orientations 24
Mignolo, W.D. 64–5, 155

migration *see* asylum seekers; immigrants; immigration and faith; refugees
Milera, D. 108
Millwall, London, UK 10, 20n.6
  see also focus groups discussions
Minnery, J. 179
Modood, T. 169n.1
Moore, K. 86, 129
Moore, T. 180
Morgan, D. 34
mosques, attitudes of members towards research 11–12
  see also belonging; communities/community; Muslims
Moss Side, Manchester, UK 9, 18n.3
  see also focus groups discussions
muintearas (belonging) 95–118
multiculturalism
  in Australia 7–8, 11–14, 22n.9, 22n.10
  definition 169n.1
  statistics 18n.1
  'superdiversity' of 169n.2
  in UK 8–10
  see also asylum seekers; ethnic groups; focus groups discussions
multi-sited ethnography *see* ethnography, multi-sited
Murris, K. 188
Muslims
  in Australia 158
  clothing, headwear 53, 55, 145, 152, 154, 156
  faith and 39–40
  fundamentalism and 85–94
  gender and 55–6
  lived experiences of 102–3
  racism against 141–70
  religious practices amongst 16, 54
  in society 85–94
  see also communities/community; Islam/Islamophobia; mosques, attitudes of members towards research; multiculturalism; Ramadan

naisc (connection) 119–40
neamhábaltacht (incapacity) 141–70
Neumann, K. 86
new materialism 24–7, 34, 36, 48, 64–5, 114, 189
  decolonising research strategies within 66
  see also affect/*affectus*/*affectiones*; materiality
new materialist philosophy of faith
  affect theory and 24–48
  development of 24–5
Noble, G. 156, 158, 189
Noble Park, Melbourne, Australia 12–13, 22n.9
  see also focus groups discussions
Noble-Carr, D. 180
Norwood, Adelaide, SA 21n.7
  see also focus groups discussions
Nowicka, M. 96

Ó Cuinneagáin, E. 65
objects *see* materiality
O'Donnell, A. 147
O'Loughlin, C. 108
online communities 96–9, 133–40
Oppy, G. 26–7
'optimism, cruel' *see* 'cruel optimism'
orientations, unconscious
  different forms of faith and 24
  gender and 105–11
  materiality and 32–3
Our Lady, Blessed Virgin Mary *see* Mary, Blessed Virgin
outreach work in galleries 15

P21 Gallery, London, outreach work site 15
Padrón Cueto, C. 131–2
Page, T. 49
Palmer, H. 49
Parr, A. 40
participants in the research *see* research participants
participation *see* belonging; communities/community

Pedersen, S. 97
Peel, M. 163, 165
percept/perception and art 80–1
philosophy of faith, materialist *see* new materialism
philosophy of religion
　cross-cultural studies and 28–9
　faith and 25–7
Pidd, H. 177
piety, Irish Catholic 2–3
place, importance of 17, 188–9
pleasure and 'cruel optimism' 24
postcolonialism and decolonialism 64–6
'post-secular' world and faith 29–30
power
　as affect/*affectus*/*affectiones* 81, 84
　as capacity to act 43–4, 78, 85
　colonial 64, 77, 141, 145, 155
　faith and 33, 48, 88
　joy and 40–3
　mass media and 88
　religion and 61
　see also colonisation; terrorism
Prato, G.B. 169n 1
prayer
　as exchange value 46–7
　'cruel optimism' and 46–7
　gender and 55–6
　practices 2–3, 16, 54–5, 93–4
　see also devotional aids; mosques, attitudes of members towards research
Preece, J. 161
Prevent Agenda (UK) 146, 156–7
Probyn, E. 100, 105, 117, 160, 190
Procreate (digital application) and children 72–3
Promey, S.M. 48
Proshansky, H.M. 148

Qurashi, F. 157

Racial Discrimination Act (1975) 143
racism 116, 126, 142–7, 152–6, 159, 188, 192
　as consequence of change 157–8
　in Australia 105–11, 141–5, 155–6
　within communities 52
　discrimination and 85–94, 105–11
　due to media misrepresentation 86–8, 92
　Muslims as victims of 86–9, 104–5
Ramadan 90, 93
Rasmussen, M.L. 56, 62, 111, 117, 130
reason and faith 43–4
Reay, D. 163, 165
refugees 47, 132, 155, 177, 179–85
　belonging 159–63
　'black panics' and 147
　child 179–85
　faith amongst 38
　insecurities of 177–85
　Melbourne housing for 122–3
　Muslim 116–17
　see also asylum seekers; belonging; children; communities/community; faith; migration
religion/religions
　as site of belonging to community 61–3
　cultural practices and 16–17, 53–5
　diversity and varieties of 16–17, 53–4
　faith and 25–6, 31, 55
　globalisation and 31–2
　orientations to, amongst research participants 15–17
　philosophy and 26–7
　sexuality and 56
　similarities between believers 40
　violence and 4, 16–17, 26, 40
　visual and material cultures of 29–31
　see also churches; intolerance; mosques, attitudes of members towards research; terrorism
religious objects *see* devotional aids; materiality

Renold, E. 78, 130
research methodology 5, 49
 working with children and 63–4
 see also decolonisation, research strategies of; focus groups questions
research participants 15–17
research sites *see* ethnography, multi-sited: research sites
Rhoden-Paul, A. 177
Richards, B. 86
Richardson, I. 137
Rigney, L.-I. 108
ritual performances, faith and 36–7
 see also devotional aids; materiality
Robbie, K. 6
Roberts, A. 108
rosary beads and Catholic piety 3
Russell, L. 124

sacred space, interviewee's description of 6–7
Said, E. 158
saints, importance of 7
Samak, T. 96
Savage, M. 165, 168
Scholten, P. 96
sensation, blocs of 79–81
sensory experiences and faith 31
September 11 terrorist attacks (2001) 147–8
sexuality
 belonging and 106–10
 children and 56
 religion and 56
 see also gender; identity definition
Sharam, A. 179
Shipley, H. 111
Sian, K. 146, 157
signs and symbols
 in religion 35–6
 worker bee as 148–51
 see also devotional aids
Simons, M. 141–2
Singleton, A. 111
Skeggs, B. 162–3
skin colour 163–8
 see also 'black panics'; discrimination; racism; White Australia Policy (1901)
'slow death' and 'cruel optimism' 44–7
Smirvov, N. 96
soccer (football)
 children and 121–9
 creating community 121–9
social class
 aspiration to, via education 163–8
 council housing estate residents and 120–3
 expressions of 52
 faith and 16–17
 language and 163–8
social media and community belonging 96–9
 see also messaging (computer software apps)
'social turn' and collaborative art-making 67
Sonn, C.C. 126
space, sacred, interviewee's description of 6–7
Spinoza, B. 24, 27, 39–44, 47, 77–8, 84–5, 88, 92, 94, 119, 189–90
spirituality, significance of 62
Spivak, G.C. 65
sport
 global importance of football (soccer) 121–9
 national sentiments and 124–6
 significance of, to children 126–9
St Gabriel's Church, Dublin, Ireland 2, 4
statues *see* devotional aids; materiality; piety, Irish Catholic
structures of feeling, and faith 16
Suarez, Z.E. 148
'superdiversity' and multiculturalism 169n.2
surface attachments and belonging 100–18

Sydney, Australia 5
  see also focus groups discussions
symbols *see* signs and symbols

taqiyahs 55
Tatz, C. 126
tents
  arts-based research workshops 68–9, 163–8
  Fortnite (computer game) elements as decoration of 133–4
terrorism
  9/11 attack 148
  Arena bombing, Manchester, UK 87, 148–50
  child's thoughts on 151
  religion and 148–51
  see also Islam/Islamophobia; violence
Thapar-Björkert, S. 49
Thomson, P. 163, 165
Tindongan, C.W. 148
Tlostanova, M. 49
Turner, Victor 36–7

UK *Counter-Terrorism and Security Act (2015)* 156–7
UK Home Office, *Statutory guidance: Prevent duty guide (2015)* 146
unconscious orientations *see* orientations, unconscious
University of Sydney, Faculty of Arts and Social Sciences 5

van der Tuin, I. 25, 27, 34
Vergès, F. 65
Vertovec, S. 6, 169n.2
video-making, children's 59–60, 70
Vincent, D.N. 126
violence
  Islamic extremists and 87
  religion/religions and 4, 16–17, 26, 40
  see also intolerance; terrorism
Virgin Mary *see* Mary, Blessed Virgin

virtues encouraged by faith practices 90–4

Walker, D. 86, 189
Walkerdine, V. 123, 161
Wang, X. 36
Watkins, S. 65
Wessendorf, S. 6
Weston, Canberra, Australia 14
  see also focus groups discussions
'what really matters' to children 4–7, 68–9, 82–4, 128–39
  climate change 51–2, 56, 62, 174–6
  communicated through artworks 49, 131–2, 135, 139
  football (soccer) 121–9
  Fortnite (computer game) 133–7
  friendship 137–40
  future cities envisioned 68, 130–1, 151, 174–9, 184–5
  homelessness and housing 176–91
  ice cream 56, 128–33
  terrorism 151
  worker bee 148–51
White Australia Policy (1901) 156
white/whiteness *see* skin colour
Whitworth Gallery, Manchester, site of outreach work 15
Willcox, M. 5, 8, 59, 122, 174, 176, 182
Williams, Raymond 4
Williams Veasey, L. 97
Williamson, R. 101
Willis, P. 161, 163, 165
women
  indigenous Australian, sacred places of 142–3
  targets of terrorist violence 148–51
  see also focus groups discussions
Woodhead, L. 111, 113, 194
worker bee symbolism 148–51

Zeybek, O. 148

EU authorised representative for GPSR:
Easy Access System Europe, Mustamäe tee 50,
10621 Tallinn, Estonia
gpsr.requests@easproject.com

www.ingramcontent.com/pod-product-compliance
Ingram Content Group UK Ltd.
Pitfield, Milton Keynes, MK11 3LW, UK
UKHW021823140426

5217IPUK00004B/67